WHEN RUNNING WAS YOUNG AND SO WERE WE

JACK D. WELCH

foreword by Don Kardong

First published in 2014 by D & B Publishing

British Library Cataloguing-in-Publication Data
A catalogue record for this book is available from the British Library.

ISBN: 978 1 90945 716 4

All sales enquiries should be directed to D&B Publishing:
e-mail: info@dandbpublishing.com; website: www.dandbpublishing.com

Some of the material in this book is based on articles published in
Track & Field News, *Running*, *Running Magazine*, *Running Times*
and *American Runner*.

For Peggy

Cover photo is Alberto Salazar (no. 1) and the author.
Most photos are courtesy of Jeff Johnson. Others courtesy of the author.
Steve Spence from Steve Spence. Dick Beardsley from Dick Beardsley.

Cover design by Horatio Monteverde.
Printed and bound by Versa Press in the US.

A surprising book! Surprised to learn more about runners I competed against. Surprised to learn more about races I was in. No surprise - this is a book for runners by a runner who can really write.

Alberto Salazar

Reading When Running Was Young And So Were We *brought back not just good memories of that Golden Age of road racing, and the stunning excitement of what felt like a new sport beginning here in the USA, but also the friendship of so many of the runners highlighted here, and the great spirit of comraderie that existed then. Perhaps those days were the launchpad for the Running Boom. I still love to run, and always will, thanks in part to writers like Jack D. Welch who worked so hard to reveal all aspects of running!*

Bill Rodgers,
Four-time winner of NY City Marathon, four-time winner Boston Marathon

Jack D. Welch writes like a sports reporter, a news journalist, an author, and all is written with his unparalleled quick wit.

As well, he has a unique perspective as a competitive runner. Jack is the perfect author to accompany today's runner through a retrospective visit to the Golden Age of running with his keen observations on the day's elite runners, and their physical and mental attributes from start to finish line.

Jacqueline Hansen
1973 Boston Marathon winner, twice marathon World Record holder

When U.S. distance running was younger than it is now, and smaller, it was also faster. The mid-1970s and the decade beyond was a golden age for road racers. Never before (or, alas, since) have so many Americans run so well: almost annual victories at the Boston and New York City Marathons by Bill Rodgers and then Alberto Salazar... world records for Salazar and Joan Benoit... Benoit's Olympic gold medal. Jack Welch saw it all, and from many angles: runner, magazine publisher, shoe-company executive and writer. You couldn't ask for a better tour guide of those golden years than the author of this book.

Joe Henderson, Former longtime editor of *Runner's World*

['Remembering Pre'] is one of the best, most powerful pieces of writing I have ever read. Your short declarative sentences hit like hammers. You wrote as Pre ran. I can imagine no other writer who could have told his story as well. Runners everywhere probably wish you had written more. I certainly do."

Jeff Johnson, Nike's first employee

If you were running in the '80's and '90's this book should bring back pleasant memories of days gone by. For the rest, it is a good starting place to learn about the roots of American distance running.

Benji Durden, 1980 Olympian

Contents

Acknowledgments 6

Foreword by Don Kardong 7

About this Book 11

1 Personal Best 13

2 Some of the Men 33

3 Some of the Women 90

4 In their Own Words 125

5 Training and the Coaches 150

6 At the Races 188

7 More than a Business 230

8 Politics and Money 274

9 The Greatest 293

Acknowledgments

Thanks must go to Dr. Dave Castle, Kevin Harper, Tom Raynor, Joe Henderson, Dr. E.C. Frederick, Jeff Johnson and Walt Chadwick. I also want to thank Garry Hill, Sieg Lindstrom, Jon Hendershott and Scott Douglas. And every volunteer who ever worked a race.

Thousands of miles were not run alone. Those who pushed me will always be remembered: Pat, Wayne, Walt, Ned, Scott, Werner, Vern, John, Lee, Eric, Bill, Michael T., Ed, Roger, Mike and Jose.

Foreword

Don Kardong

This book is a collection of stories about the people and events of a time when massive road races were springing up everywhere, as running moved from being the secret passion of a few to the preoccupation of millions. This was a movement unprecedented in the history of the world, and Jack Welch was sitting, and running, right in the middle of this maelstrom, pen in hand. Pen, figuratively speaking.

The first contact I ever had with Jack was when he wrote a nasty letter to the running store I co-owned. I don't remember Jack's exact words, but it was something to the effect of, "How are your customers ever going to buy my magazine when you have it buried under a bunch of other magazines?"

This was a curious comment for a number of reasons. For one, since our store was hundreds of miles distant from where Jack lived, it made it seem like the guy had dispatched spies to the handful of running stores then in existence to monitor the placement of the magazine he co-owned, *Running*. For another, it suggested the only thing that was keeping his magazine from hitting the big-time was bad rack placement.

Running had no color in its pages, and may well have been stapled together in Jack's dining room. Its tagline was, "The Thinking Runner's Magazine," and I seem to remember at some point Jack's column also made the point that "The magazine that cares more about your running than Bill Rodgers'." He and his magazine partner, Ned Frederick, had obviously tak-

ously taken a remarkably different path from the editorial route other running publications of the day had taken, one that prided itself on a serious scientific approach to improving running performance.

So, let me just say this. As much as I admired the magazine's focus on high-level content, I can assure you that with optimum placement, a good month at our store might have resulted in the sale of three *Running* magazines. Be that as it may, I moved the magazines to a more prominent spot on the rack.

I wondered a lot then about this guy who could have fit all his magazine's subscribers into a mid-sized ballroom, but who was nevertheless fighting for every sale. This was an interesting character. And, since we considered ourselves thinking runners, we running store workers read his magazine religiously every month, before putting it back in a prominent spot on the magazine rack for someone else to buy. Sorry about that, Jack.

Running may not have cared about Bill Rodgers' running, but when Jack ran a personal best marathon of 2:46:07, we found out he cared a lot about his own. "Two-Forty-Six-Oh-Seven" is a classic story of personal satisfaction at achieving something difficult. We read it at the store and laughed out loud, because it summed up so perfectly what it feels like for any runner of any ability to set a personal best. Euphoria, that is.

Jack's unique approach to reporting on running lived on when Nike purchased his magazine and ratcheted up its sex appeal. The new, colorized version of *Running* only lasted a few years, but it was also a very different kind of running magazine, one that hired famous writers like Hunter S. Thompson and Ken Kesey to hang around the running world and opine on what they observed. The story Kesey wrote took up one whole issue.

As luck would have it, I was invited write for this new, more marketable *Running* magazine, too. That explains how I finally met Jack in person, and how I later ended up watching the end of the 1981 Boston Marathon with Jack, now one of the three editors of the publication (yes, there were three people in charge, don't ask me why). We watched the end of that Boston marathon from a fire escape overlooking the final stages of the race. After watching George Sheehan and Jim Fixx finish, Jack began announcing the winners of various divisions that he invented on the spot.

"There's the first finisher in black high-tops!" Jack yelled. "There's the first sweater finisher! There's the first finisher in fluorescent shoes! There's the first hoodlum! The first illegal alien! The first Halloween finisher!

Did I mention that beer may have been involved?

Later, we yelled for people whose names were on their shirts—Paul, Tricia, Barbara, Super Sue, Carol, Harold, Pat, Martha, Rocky and the Havliceks (Muriel and Ed).

And finally, we yelled for whatever was on the runners' T-shirts: No Nukes! Small is Beautiful! Save the Whales! Oregon! Free the Shah! Spam!

Maybe you had to be there. Anyway, when someone on the fire escape asked us, "What magazine did you guys say you were from?" we decided we weren't doing the publication any favor, and we moved on.

I don't want you to get the idea this book is about Jack. In fact, Jack's stories celebrate a time when running was booming and Americans figured prominently. People like Alberto Salazar, Joan Benoit Samuelson, Mary Decker Slaney, and Steve Prefontaine, to name a few. And a bunch of other outstanding runners, whose names have begun to fade from the collective consciousness of the sport. Jack's interviews with these stand the test of time, largely because the individuals interviewed are also, in a way, timeless, at least in terms of their influence on the sport. Jack's admiration for them is palpable. Clearly, as I learned over the years, Jack cares a lot about the sport and the running of elite athletes like Bill Rodgers. That comes through in spades as he interviews the top runners and major figures of the sport in what many consider its golden years. He cared deeply about the sport. It's just that he cared in a way that was distinctly his own.

Part of the fun of this collection is that the character who is Jack Welch also shines through. Who else, after all, in the middle of a very intense and illuminating discussion about athletic fame with Joan Benoit Samuelson, suddenly asks the Olympic champion, "So what's so special about lobstering?" Or who gets Nike founder Phil Knight laughing about the man's competitive ability when he jabs, "You lost a lot of races. Watched a lot of behinds, Phil."

Maybe you've never heard of Jack Welch. Most likely, you're just planning to read this book because you're interested in learning more about the individuals who built the current sport of running or elevated it through their magnificent performances. That, after all, is the reason Jack wrote these articles in the first place.

But as you'll find out, the interviewer is always right there between the lines, if not on top of them. So give the interviewer some respect too. After all, he's got spies everywhere.

Don Kardong, February 2014
Olympic marathoner (1976), running journalist,
Race Director of the Lilac Bloomsday Run in Spokane, Washington.

About this Book

I have been able to enjoy an amazing life. An amazing era in that life was the time when running was young and so were we. And in that era, a Golden Age, if you will, one of the more amazing aspects was some of the men and women I got to meet and watch compete. Many other friendships grew among coaches and business people, who also loved the simple act of putting one foot in front of the other foot faster than another guy.

I think I was at Big Sky – off-season, of course – where the jocular Abe Lemons told us how easy it was to coach track. "How hard can it be?" Abe asked. "You just tell 'em to stay to the left and get back as soon as you can."

Running is not simple. And the people in this book are really among the pioneers who helped to move the sport forward. Many, many are missing from these pages. But I got to meet a bunch and write about a few. I just wanted to take this opportunity to salute these folks many years later as I watch my five grand-children run this way and that. So young, so full of life and fire, burning so brightly...

And I wanted to say to all of you, "Thanks." – JDW

On the road in the early 70's

Chapter One
Personal Best

Of all the many races in which I competed, turns out I only wrote about three. (Not a big market for stories about the escapades of "the world's slowest professional runner.") I wrote about my worst marathon (3:30:35), my best marathon, and a race I only ran in my imagination.

The imaginary race can be seen perhaps as an amalgamation of all the races I ever ran. At my best, I wasn't as good as the best runners, but I was faster than most of the rest. I recall one event in Phoenix where I was running ahead of a rather large field. Spectators, who I had to guess, hadn't been spectating long, cheered me loudly as I strode past them. I admit it, I waved like I deserved the applause.

I know they hadn't been there long, because if they had been, they'd have seen the lead pack - so far ahead - pass by a few minutes earlier.

Another time, I was at a small race, so small you could look over the milling crowd and basically determine your finishing position before the gun even sounded. I was thinking maybe low single digits myself, when a long, many-windowed van came to a sudden stop in a cloud of dust. A coterie of lithe young kids leaped out. Oh, crap, it's the Tuba City cross-county team. Suddenly, I am thinking mid-teens, if I have a good day. Well, I had a good day, a few guys got away and I am running alone, just knowing any minute now a bunch of speedy Native-American children are going to come scampering past, they have no mercy and frankly their talent is scary. I can hear their footsteps and so I accelerate and when I hit a turn, I surge, trying to get away, trying until I can't really try any more all I can do to hold this pace, which is too fast. I can hear their footsteps, so finally I work up the courage to turn around and see how many of them there are. And there is no one there.

In the Spirit of Pheidippides
May 1978

Chuck Smead, Jack D. Welch, Don Kardong (l.-r.) atop the victory podium in Olympic Stadium

We file off the air-conditioned bus into the oppressive heat of the Greek afternoon. These are the Plains of Marathon and there is no escape from the sun.

There is some manner of locker-room-cum-outhouse structure that becomes our refuge. Dark and dank, it is also crowded with runners seeking the cool shade which the stone edifice provides.

What a motley assemblage. Marathoners from a dozen countries eye each other in disbelief. They speak in a number of tongues and, without understanding more than one, the listener is aware many of them ask the same questions: "What are we doing here? Why are we doing this?"

Olympian Don Kardong shares a bench with two Greek joggers. One guy's thigh must weigh as much as Don's entire body. They eye each other quizzically.

Another Greek looks at Kardong's specially designed Nike racing shoes; Don examines the Greek's high-top basketball sneakers. Both men are incredulous. The Greek has glued – really – approximately one inch of foam rubber (kitchen sponge?) to the soles of his tennies. The mind boggles. Suppose this guy runs 2:15 in those suckers? Jim Fixx and Ned Frederick seem to be contemplating exclusive distribution rights for the U.S.A.

Too soon we must go back into the heat. No one warms up, it seems redundant. Some entrants are already beginning to show signs of heat exhaustion. Other runners have begun to shuffle and limp even before the starting gun sounds. The course is that tough.

Curiously, as we gather at the starting line, no one wants to stand in front of the field. It's almost as if the runners somehow hope to postpone the misery.

They can't.

The gun sounds and we flee for our lives. Unknown F. Harry Stowe is the early leader, but he is soon overtaken by Kardong and Chuck Smead. A mysterious Ethiopian follows. He appears too large to be world-class, but marathoners have learned to expect much from these Lions of the Desert. There is a rumor that he is even coached by an Albanian. It just doesn't seem fair.

I tuck in behind two Greeks as we start off into a headwind. Two other Americans – John Ayforgette and Spencer Chapman – accompany us. The pace is good, too good. Although we haven't yet run a mile, we have – speaking for myself – already signed our own death certificates. We are cruising along at 6:10 pace, jockeying with the Greeks and each other.

We are crazy. The official temperature is 81 degrees F. F'in hot. But they must have that thermometer under a rock in the shade. My body is already smoldering and I begin to wonder if a human being can spontaneously combust. I hear cows do it all the time.

We dispose of the Greeks, Spencer drops back, and John and I are alone behind the studs. At the first aid station, we both holler out for water. We gulp and dump the remainder over our heads.

"AAAAAAAAAAAAAAA!!!" I hear a scream. Due to the language barrier, John has been handed a large paper cup filled with heavily sugared lemonade. He can't take sugar in a race – instant cramp. He is also very sticky.

Now I am alone. Of course, in a marathon, you are always alone. Even in the largest events, the runner is alone... alone with his body and mind, alone with the distance.

Alone with the pain and the glory. I know I'm running too fast. Before the 10-kilometer mark, I have already experienced two or three of the early warning sign of heat exhaustion. My goose flesh has goose flesh.

Just 20 miles to go.

Every little town provides a boost. The peasants are out *en masse* (which is French for the Greek word meaning "in a group"). Those who are not on their feet at roadside wave from their windows or from the open air taverns. The spectators appear to be enjoying themselves more than I am.

Many of the women seem attractive but then I left home a week ago. I should not be noticing. I should be concentrating on the race, but it's too late and I know it. At 15 kilometers, my race is over. My lack of conditioning, the oppressive heat, an imprudent early pace, a nagging injury and those grinding hills have reconfirmed one of my strongest beliefs – you can't fake a marathon.

And it's a shame. I am running in sixth place. The fourth and fifth position runners are just ahead, staggering in their search for shade. Hell, they look worse than even I do. The Ethiopian, who had the audacity to challenge Chuck and Don, has paid the price. This Saharan strider has demonstrated one's national heritage has little to do with the ability to run fast marathons. So large and powerful in Marathon, he seems much smaller now on the road to Athens.

Who am I to talk? Or whisper hoarsely? I can't even swallow. I could have "easily" placed third in my first international marathon, if I was only prescient. If only I had known no one would run fast today. Oh, if only...

If only I didn't feel so bad. At 20 kilometers, without consciously deciding to, I screech to a halt at an aid station. (It was a muted screech... more like a "skreessh.") They are not offering what I need. What I need is a transfusion, but the Greeks' idea of refreshment is lemon quarters. One suck on that fruit and my entire body will turn itself inside out. Whoosh!!

Feeling dizzy, I start to lean across an ice box. A SEGAS (Greece's version of the AAU) official grabs me.

"No, no, no! No rest! Run, run!," he shouts, as he takes me by the shoulders and shoves me down the road.

He reminds me of my dad.

And I'm out on my feet. I don't really hurt – I don't think I do – but I can barely move. The heat has drained my body, my muscles, my mind.

Less than 14 miles to go. Only 14 miles. Just 14,000 strides... if I could stride.

I pretend I can. No one is fooled, least of all myself. So, I shuffle along.

At 25 km, I hear my first split. I don't understand it, I just hear it. The timekeeper's thick accent and the cobwebs in my head obliterate any comprehension. Doesn't matter. I practically crawled the last two miles and I shall crawl some more.

The progression of runners who pass me begins to resemble Macy's Easter parade. They all have a kind word for me, and why shouldn't they? My very appearance demands sympathy.

I'm not really cognizant of my surroundings. I know it's hot and hilly and I hurt. I know that. The countryside has become a metropolis. I am running at a funereal pace, walking really as much as jogging. I begin to fantasize. Will my life flash in front of me like some deathly farewell?

I wish I had done more.

One huge hill looms in front of me. I am sure if I can get to the top of that one huge hill, I can finish. It is literally all downhill from there. I slow to a walk.

Soon I hear footsteps. Two guys walking faster than I am walking. Then Dr. Joan Ullyot, running at the same pace at which she began. There is something Medusan about her. I look into her eyes and turn to stone. The other two men see her and break into a jog, chasing up the hill after her... can't let a woman beat them.

I can. I can let a woman beat me. No problem. Not that I am "letting" Joan beat me; she's doing it by herself, by her strength and wisdom. Me, by my stupidity and hubris.

The pain would be incredible if I didn't believe it. But I do. I think of

George Sheehan's maximal stress test and I, too, wonder: "When can I see the baby?" I start to laugh and then I cry.

So helpless in the middle of an Athenian highway with horns beeping and people clapping at intersections and taverns, and I hurt so much. Dismayed. Somehow ashamed. More sorry for myself than anything else. I wanted so much to run well. Burnt away from the heat, ground down by the pain, my facade has dropped away. Crashed. I am exposed. The Greeks see my skeleton, my insides. They see me.

Dizzy again, I ease my way up to a refreshment station. (I long ago figured out there was little aid to be had.) There's a large bucket of dirty water, sponges floating around. I stick my head down into the bucket, and I am alive again, though barely. Five miles to the finish line and I will walk the entire distance if I have to.

I'd sorta like to walk the rest of the way. But, how can I walk when people are cheering and applauding? So, I try to run and I can run for perhaps twenty yards before the pain becomes unbearable.

"Hey, American! I take you to the Stadium – no charge," yells a cabbie.

No, thank you. It's too late now. I can't quit. The pain has subsided and I try to run again. Forty yards this time. Forty yards closer to that damn medal. I'd have to feel better to die.

I can sense every muscle, every joint, every nerve. My body is working like some poorly conjured Rube Goldberg construction... slowly... piece... by... piece.

But I am going to finish. There is absolutely no doubt about that. I have won the battle, and the realization seems to lift my spirits, if not my legs.

Suddenly, I'm "slapping five" with giggling Greek children. I even stop at an intersection to shake the traffic cop's hand.

"*Efharisto*, my friend," I exclaimed, exhausting my knowledge of the spoken Greek language. The cop's reply is lost in the lack of translation, though the look on his face seemed to transcend cultural barriers – "Let go of my hand."

Just as quickly as it arose, my elation dissipates. Two hundred yards to go and I am walking. How pathetic.

I start to jog and, for the first time in ten miles, I am actually running. My stride is probably six inches long and I am not moving fast. But you could describe the movement as running. You could if you were kind.

I can see the finish line now, 100 yards down the cinder track. It was supposed to be such a thrill, such a marvelous experience, entering this site of the first modern Olympics. As close as I'll ever get to being an Olympic athlete.

But it's just another finish line. The race may have been special, but the finish line is now just the end of my struggle. If I get there, I can stop.

Sobbing, what's left of me crosses the line. I blubber apologies for my poor performance, as a beautiful woman drapes that precious medal around my neck and someone else wraps a blanket around my torso. I can hardly stand and I can't stop whimpering. Steve Ayforgette (no relation) hands me a beer and the pieces – ever so slowly – start coming back to-gether.

I learned something running in the footsteps of a legend. I learned I do not *ever* want to go through anything like that again. I had meant to rec-reate Pheidippides' run, not his demise.

As race winner Chuck Smead offered, "Now I know why Pheidippides died."

Probably drank too much lemonade.

Two-Forty-Six-Oh-Seven
September 1979

The author sets a PR (September 9, 1979)

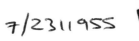

2:46:07. Two-forty-six-oh-seven. Two hours, forty-six minutes and seven seconds.

I ran the Nike/OTC Marathon in 2:46:07, and I am incredulous. I imagine those who have been victimized by my recent grumbling also have some difficulty believing it.

As you might remember, I have discussed – despondently – the injured, overweight, undertrained, wracked-with-pain body that burdened my soul. I was depressed, and I thought I had good reason. I hadn't run for a week; I hadn't run a real good race in 2½ years. I was a mess.

Well, thank you for the cards and letters, but you can stop now. Save the postage. I am reborn, revivified.

For a few short hours I became a runner again. I don't really know how I did it. I was in 2:54 shape at best, aiming at 2:49:59 only because Messrs. Cloney and Semple demand it. I did – honest – dream about running 2:48:44, but that was just a dream.

We went past 5 kilometers in 19:17. We were already 3½ minutes behind the leaders and some 30 seconds ahead of our goal pace. (Okay, if Jeff Wells and Tony Sandoval want it that badly, let them have the win – we're going to Boston.) We slowed.

We also maintained the pace. I think. I don't know for sure because I was born in the we-don't-do-metric USA, before New Math. By the time I divided 5 kilometers into 19:17 minutes, we were at 10k in 38:48. That's 3.88 minutes per kilometer... there are 42.195 kilometers in a marathon. You can imagine my dilemma. I began to sense symptoms of mathematical prostration. Could Steinmetz run this pace and do complicated equations? Could Einstein even?

At 26 kilometers I came upon a friend doing the only smart thing to do at a marathon – he was watching. I burst into song, *a cappella*, of course: "You take the high road and I'll take the low road."

I began to accelerate. If one can sing, one can run faster. (Isn't that a line from a Mike Spino book?)

I was passing people now. My friend and sometime training partner John Frey – imagine Mr. Magoo, running 2:50 – said hello. Most of the rest just grunted. I was careful to express encouragement to the few people I truly enjoyed leaving behind. They knew, and I knew they knew. They knew, too, I was a runner again. Even I was beginning to believe.

Around 30k, I put the pedal to the metal. (If Bill Rodgers is a Ferrari, then I'm a '72 Pontiac sedan. With a six-cylinder engine.)

I pushed. I hammered. I fought. I struggled, fought some more – a typical marathon.

At 40 kilometers, I began to hit The Wall. But I refused. I was running a personal best... I didn't have time to slow down.

The digital clock above the finish line read 2:46:07. My wife had that "son-of-a-gun-you've-done-it-again" expression. And the pain lightened, falling away like a snake's old skin. Release washed over me as the dike of my concentration broke. I began to sob. I could stop running.

But I can't stop now. I have reaffirmed my runnerness. I may not be the best, but I am better than I ever was. Finally.

That is enough.

For now at least. For now I am content. My legs still hurt. I still avoid hills, hard surfaces, speedwork, and talented training partners. But I am running. No longer do local runners ask, "Didn't you used to be a fairly good runner?" When queried about my marathon PR, I can now answer with different numbers.

Numbers, times. They don't really mean much. Tony Sandoval (2:10:20 PR) and Dick Quax (2:11:13 PR) told me a couple days after the race that my personal best was every bit as valuable, as meaningful, as their own records. Perhaps as amazing, too. They saw little difference.

The numbers are different, but... it's the feeling. Flying down towards that finish, seeing nothing, missing nothing. It's THE FEELING, a sensation so intense, so consuming, so unlike any other that it defies my limited command of the English language.

The feeling that comes when your body, your mind, your very soul... the feeling of attempting more than you can possibly do, and then actually doing it.

The difference perhaps between living and being alive.

I hope you understand. 2:46:07. Damn.

Duel Meet
December 1978

The author...sometimes a front runner, never a kicker

Our destiny is to run to the edge of the world and beyond, off into the darkness. – Thomas Aquinas

The Front Runner...

You yawn.

You always yawn before a race. Every race, but you yawn a little longer and a little yawnier before this race, today's race.

Can't help but notice the breeze. The trees bold with autumn, bold with the colors of change.

You jog to loosen up, break a sweat. You feel especially good or maybe kinda putrid, but you can't really tell for sure. You do some pick-ups, short sprints building slowly in speed. Try not to run into anybody. Controlled accelerations. Like pulling away from a stoplight.

Whoaaaa. You feel springy, light on your feet, up on your toes, so light it's a secret you can't wait to share. You tell no one.

You make absolutely certain your shoes are tied tight. You make absolutely certain twice. You look serious when someone calls your name. You have no idea who the hell is calling, yet you wave in that direction anyway. You think you may have to pee again, but there's no time, and you understand it's just your nerves.

Inspect the knots in your laces.

You strip off your sweats and check again to make sure your number is still pinned on. Wonder what you overlooked.

You are always relieved to see you remembered your shorts.

You shake hands all around, sincerely, and notice the starter looks like a huge penguin. You mumble greetings. Hear nothing.

Not even the gun. You do not have time to think. You react and suddenly you are elbows and jostling and bump and then right in the middle of it. Go!!

Settle down. You tell yourself that – settle down – but it's hard. You are running so fast just to keep up.

They say each race has a life of its own. They say you can live an entire life in a single race.

The first lap, you are a child, full of energy and hope. Ready for anything, open to anything. You have much to look forward to. You know all you have to do is keep moving and stay out of trouble and your time will come. Just as surely as the morning sun. When you are a child, you are growing bigger and stronger and smarter and faster all the time. The first lap is play.

Second lap, you are still strong but beginning to experience doubts. Tiny doubts. You shake them off. More decisions come your way and they come faster and some you understand right away and others seem more complex but it is early. The second lap is a time for study.

The third time around, you know the middle ages can be the darkest time. The pace quickens and the flesh is weak, here little news about your body is ever good news. You have to dig deep within yourself and you are more often concerned what you will find. You learn to hang tough. And the value of hard work.

The last lap, all she wrote. All that has gone before matters not, but what you've got at the end is all that counts. And how you will be remembered is the only question left unanswered. The finish line becomes a matter of life and death. Your final time an epitaph. Clock stops.

So, in the early running, you look around you and recognize some familiar faces. The other runners are like playmates, together you are out to have a good time. You are a big fan of your own sport and you secretly doubt your own ability to compete with the best. Too late to worry.

You are not a worrier. You cover every move, as pale pretenders trail away like trash fluttering off the bed of a pickup truck. As meaningless as litter. You learned long ago, playing in the streets, not to get cornered. A voice tells you to get free.

You stay focused. Hold back.

You want to bolt too soon, everybody knows you are impatient. It is your nature, they say. You see yourself the opportunist and, when an opening appears as if a miraculous mirage, you do not question, and fill the empty space boldly, assuredly. Let them worry about you.

Relax, you tell yourself. Suddenly, your leg stings. Feel the blood trickle down your calf from a nasty spike wound. You are a warrior. You could get tired but you decide to get mad instead. Get even. The other runners no longer allies. You must flee from them, get away. Get away.

Get free. Must get free.

First sign of weakness, you go and you go hard and you keep going until you think you can't, your body screams to slow down, lungs screaming, oxygen gone, you can't maintain the surge but you do and then you keep going because right here you can win the race, steal away.

Put it in your pocket like a shoplifter.

You never know what you can do until you try. Let then try to catch you, see what good it does them.

You are away. Wind stiffer than you thought. Everybody can see you now, exposed. Everybody out to get you.

You are not the kind of guy who takes a lead for granted. Truth is, you cannot remember a lead like this before, not so early. Well, might've been one lead this big once, you can't remember.

This is not a big lead anyway, a gap maybe. Other people might think it's a big lead, may look like a big lead to some but it doesn't feel big to you. Feels like a stride, a couple strides at most. Feels good though. Very good. Sneaky good like illicit sex. Good enough to hold on to, clutch close to your chest.

Too good to be true.

The chase is a rush, you are high on flight.

You are not a worrier. Stay free, they might be getting closer.

You begin to get worried, start to imagine, so real, there's someone behind you. He's gaining, you can hear his stealthy footsteps getting closer. Sneaky. A faint whisper first. Like bones clicking far off. Getting louder.

You can actually hear imaginary footsteps. Stay free.

You wonder, maybe a prodigious kicker was sitting back there all the time, just waiting to pounce. Bullies. Damn predators.

Closer. Don't look back. Can't look back. Don't. Can't. Their kind always takes heart, if they see you glance around, telegraph a sign of fear. You wonder if you can be scared of the sound of another man's footsteps and you know the answer.

But you are a warrior, so you go faster. You know why they are chasing you. You know you are going faster, you can feel yourself going faster. It hurts. Footsteps. Can you hear them? Whose are they? Does it matter? Maybe there are two chasers, working together. Maybe a whole pack. Ganging up on you. Waiting to devour you like wolves after a deer.

You are alone. You look for shadows. Maybe the slightest peek on the next turn, out of the corner of your eyes. Those bastards.

All the beers you didn't drink. All those early bedtimes. Must not be in vain.

You own this lead – it's yours. They want it; don't let them have it. They want to finish ahead of you. Must not let them. You are going as fast as you can, you can't go any faster, you must go faster.

Must go faster.

Not much longer. Dread drives you like an outboard motor up your butt. You remember all the mornings you wanted to sleep in, just roll over and doze off, but you couldn't. Cold mornings, wet mornings, dark mornings.

Go faster. If they catch you now, you might let them get past, so you must not be caught. You would probably give up.

The damn finish line, never where you hope. Always more distant. Dark, wet, cold mornings. No, you wouldn't give up. Not you.

You figure the best way to keep the other guy from winning is to win the race yourself. You don't give up.

You never give up.

They will have to catch you first.

The Kicker...

You are late.

You are often late, so you are always in a rush. You like your rest.

You oversleep, doze right through the clanging of the alarm. Grab a couple of fistfuls of breakfast cereal as you pass through the kitchen, put a banana in your pocket, blow by your family, blow a kiss and a wave over your shoulder and bolt out the house. The door always slamming with a bang behind you.

You miss the bus.

Wait.

You don't like racing against the clock. Ask your grandparents who is going to win that race. Your mom once quipped you'd be late for your own funeral and you thought that sounded like a good idea. Always trying to play catch up. You like the challenge.

Fast enough to catch the bus.

Timing is key. The problem you learned long ago: tardiness is not so much about when you arrive, but about how soon you get started. Begin early enough, the endings most always take care of themselves.

You often wait too late.

So, you catch a ride with friends. A friend is anybody who will give you a ride. Missed the bus one time when you were little and ran all the way to school. There was a test you couldn't afford to fail.

Liked running. Liked the way it felt, the way you could feel your body flow. You are fast.

Having trouble getting your foot out of your warm-ups.

Liked running to school. Sometimes you ran home. Sometimes you beat the bus. And everybody on it. Learned all the shortcuts to school. But sometimes you found yourself taking the long way home.

You make the decision what route to take, when to leave and how fast to get there. Your running is all about freedom. Made you an individual, it did. Special. You are not on anybody else's schedule, you can leave when you want. No parking problems when you travel by foot. Your legs can take you wherever you want to go.

You ignore Walk/Don't Walk signs.

You have plenty of time. Wait.

When you are in a race, there is no past, there is no future. You are not as confident as you pretend to be. You have no doubts.

Having trouble getting psyched up for this.

You could have been a nifty wide receiver with your speed. But you hated to get hit. Really, what's the point? A race is like football without the tackling. A boxing match is more like it. A holds-barred free-for-all at first, usually a duel at the end. Punching each other with the pace, punching and counter-punching. *Mano a mano.* Until just one of you is left standing. Wait.

You are a counter-puncher. Have to be patient. Turn the other cheek. Takes discipline, takes a brave man not to strike back. Not until he's ready. You *will* strike. You will.

No time for stretching.

When you start the race, you don't always get into it straight away. You are just along for the ride. To tell the truth, you don't even think about competing much until the time's right. Until absolutely necessary.

Tie a rope with your mind around the waist of the pacesetter and pull tight. Focus your eyes on the middle of his shoulder blades and lock on.

His ass is yours. Lose me if you can, you tell him. And you never forget to always remember not to lose sight of the guy you are chasing. Wait.

One time you were actually back in the locker room, taking a dump, when the gun went off. Almost won that race. Would've, too, but you slipped coming around a wet corner.

You react. Cover every move, a blanket on any aspirations of escape. Keep that rope taut. Sometimes you can lead the race from behind. Just keep the pressure on.

Not even paying any special attention, but missing nothing, just something you sense, but you know other runners are dropping off the back of the pack like sparks flying from a camp fire. You can change gears at will. Wait.

You just run. Sweat a primal sheen. Your body sends signals, complicated reports from your cardiovascular system, your organs distant planets throughout your torso. Joints the outliers. Monitor the signals, listen to your body and all you hear is...nothing hurts yet. Wait.

Floating. Feel like a fresh foal. Recall the advice of that beautiful young boxer Mohammad Ali: float like a butterfly, sting like a bee. Imagine yourself as different creatures. Fly like an eagle, spring like a bear. Disassociation maybe.

Some think you are a Lamprey eel. Attached to the shark. Sucking scraps.

A parasite perhaps. That's okay... you are not here to make friends.

Holding back. You are a cheetah poised to pounce. Wait.

Check that rope. Make sure it's still stiff tight. He can run but he can't hide. You are the predator, he is the prey. Part of the food chain. Wait. A race is a game of tag between the armed and the unarmed, the way you look at it, and you are the hunter.

Sometimes you feel like you are a villain, the cowboy in the black hat. It's a gunfight for sure, but some people call you a bushwhacker. Bushwacker is a funny word, you think. Like there's a right and a wrong way to race. An honest way to finish first or a more cowardly method.

Doesn't matter. You like the idea of trying to take something away from somebody who is trying to take something away from you.

Plan the race, race the plan. It's no secret what you are going to do. You *are* your kick. For some reason – blame your parents – you refuse to move any faster than absolutely necessary. Saving energy. What's the hurry? Wait.

You actually hate waiting. But nothing else makes as much sense. Only one man in the world can stay ahead of all the rest of us. And you fairly sure he's not in this race. He's the only real front runner. Everybody else is merely the guy in the lead for now. They never give a prize to who's ahead in the middle. Seems to you a front runner must believe he is clearly superior to his competitors. Or he believes himself somehow inferior. You don't care.

Sure, a race is run over the entire distance, not simply the final furlong. Whatever a furlong is. You are willing to run as fast as anybody else. As fast as it takes. He is free to run so fast you can't keep up. Good luck. How fast would that be?, you wonder. You don't want to know. The proof is in the sprinting. Fast is as fast does. Wait.

Times are meaningless. No true measure of greatness. High school boys today clock better times than Little Mary Decker Slaney, but they are not greater runners. Guys you never heard of pushing the late-great-never-to-be-forgotten Steve Prefontaine down the all-time rankings. Like kicking sand in Mt. Rushmore's faces.

On the edge of oxygen debt, you remember something an old hippy told you once. Or maybe it was something Don Kardong said. He said, time is not linear in a front to back sense. Rather time is a depth measured from top to bottom. Today is not ahead of yesterday, but below tomorrow. The now is just a pebble dropped into the fathoms of the infinite forever. Life is the ripples which wreak havoc in ever widening circles. We don't get older, we get deeper. Which explains that sinking feeling you have.

Something like that.

Holding on. You don't chase statistics. You race people, not clocks, and this guy is strong. Real strong.

Sneak a peek. Looks strong, too. Clipping off the miles like a metronome. Tick. Tick. Tick.

He knows he must get away. But you still have him in your sights, there's a little red dot on his back. Run right through the pain. Ignore it. You blame *him*. He could slow down and make the pain go away. Starting to piss you off. Bet he doesn't know yet he can't possibly break loose. Idiot.

Hope you have something left. Wait. All you can do to keep up. You don't particularly enjoy pain. Simply makes sense, pain should be endured as briefly as possible. Why ask for it? Pain is not the point.

Time, like money, is how you keep score when there is no other way to pick a winner. Speed, the great equalizer, is the only currency on the track. Victory is priceless. Wait.

When it hurts, you know you will have to make it hurt more. That extra gear of yours is in a very dark place far away. And when you have to dig deep down inside yourself, you hope to find what you want, what you need. Don't want to think about it. Wait. Just the two of you now. The pain. Bastard surged again. Stop that! Hold on. Don't let him break the rope. Hold on. Wait.

Wonder if it's worth it. Why not just let him go? You have all the trophies you'll ever need. No. One thing you cannot do, not now, is lose your concentration. Focus. Wait.

Stay close. Damn, he's tough. Almost time. Wait. Almost time to make your move.

Now.

Chapter Two

Some of the Men

Van Cortlandt Park. Frank Shorter in Yale singlet.

I never wrote an article about Frank Shorter, although I have his autograph. (Got it for my mother. No, really.) I did a piece on Bill Rodgers, an interview which does not appear in this collection. Benji Durden and Don Kardong, two of my all-time favorites, not here. The athletes whose exploits are related here were newsmakers at a time when somebody was willing to pay a certain writer actual cash money. That simple.

Look Who Just Ran 2:09!

June 1981

What a breakthrough looks like.

"For two weeks after the race, I kept pinching myself to make sure I wasn't dreaming." The race was the Grandma's Marathon and Dick Beardsley wasn't dreaming. He had indeed won that event in 2:09:37, the second fastest time ever by an American. Only the 2:09:27 AR by Bill Rodgers is faster, and that could also be within reach of the 25-year-old Beardsley.

Grandma's was simply one of those "perfect waves" surfers used to talk about when people used to listen. Beardsley caught one.

"When the race started, it was about 50 degrees, calm. Overcast, occasionally misting. Marvelous marathoning weather," Beardsley recounts. "Garry Bjorklund and I broke away immediately [of course, a 4:50 opening mile helped, too]. We ran 4:54s every mile; really clipping them off.

"We hit 10 miles in 49:05 and I was feeling really relaxed. Garry, said, 'Dickie, it's your race. I'll try to help but you have to go for it.' I thought that was interesting, since he was really making the pace."

Beardsley was full of run through 24 miles, when he was hit by cramps in his lower diaphragm, induced by the cold water he had just consumed. Hardly able to breathe, Dick eased through a 5:20 mile. "After that, I began to feel good again." He must have felt even better when he saw his time at the finish.

His ascension to marathoning stardom was not entirely unexpected. Indeed, coach Billy Squires predicted 2:09:49 for the Grandma's race. That was Beardsley's tenth marathon ever and he set his tenth personal record. "I definitely won't be ashamed when that streak ends," he says.

His career began with a 2:33:45 in October of 1977. "The last three miles, I never hurt so badly in my life," he told Bruce Brothers of the *Minneapolis Tribune*. Dick served notice of his potential by briefly leading last fall's New York Marathon before finishing 9th in 2:13:56.

In 1981, Beardsley has been truly prodigious: 2:12:50 (Houston, January 10); 2:12:41 (Beppu, Japan, February 1); 2:11:48 (tied for 1st at London, March 29). Then Grandma's. Stockholm is in mid-August and don't be surprised to see him in New York in October. Why such self-abuse?

"I wanted to make a name for myself," Beardsley explained. "I have to admit I'm half-crazy to run so many marathons. But my body recovers quickly." He admits his 5-11/128 frame has no history of injury problems

– at the same time knocking on wood. As Squires says, "Dick recovers like Bill Rodgers. After ten days, they're ready for a good race. After three weeks, they're ready for a great race."

Beardsley will cut back drastically on future marathons. ("No more than three or four a year.") For one thing, he is hoping to get into some good 10,000s on the track. With a 28:37 road 10-kilometer best, he may have some hard running ahead of him. But with training of 120-140 miles weekly at 5:40 per mile average, he may be able to crush some track races.

As for the future, Beardsley says, "I might never run another 2:09. But I feel I've got a faster marathon in me."

The Man Who Pushed Salazar
April 1982

When Mrs. Beardsley's boy Dick ran the second fastest time in U.S. history last June, winning the Grandma's Marathon in 2:09:37, he was shocked.

"For two weeks after the race," Beardsley said, "I kept pinching myself to make sure I wasn't dreaming." The 5-11/128 Minnesotan must be black and blue after chasing Alberto Salazar to a Boston record 2:08:51.

While the World Record holder was lunching intravenously in the parking garage of the prudential Center, Beardsley was glassy-eyed as a result of his 2:08:53. He had said last year, "I might never run another 2:09, but I feel I've got a faster marathon in me."

Well, it's out of him now. Previously second-fastest behind Alberto The Great, Dick remains in the same position on the all–time U.S. list. Not bad for a guy who ran his first marathon in October, 1977, in 2:33:45. "The last three miles I never hurt so badly in my life," he remembers.

Obviously, the pain diminishes when you spend less time actually on the road. Regarding Boston, Beardsley said, "I felt as good as I ever had after a marathon."

Dick is justifiably proud of his 11th personal record. He has established a pattern of improvement and sees no reason to stop now. "I think I can run better," Beardsley opined. "Maybe we'll find out at Fukuoka next."

Before Fukuoka though, there'll be Grandma's again, just down the road a piece from his 100-year-old log cabin home. "I usually recuperate rapidly after a marathon," explains Beardsley, "but I don't know how well I'll do in June. I do think my 2:08 at Boston really legitimizes my 2:09 at Grandma's... for that matter, it legitimizes that event itself. Duluth is fast."

So, too, is Dick Beardsley, and his speed does not arise from awesome natural ability but from hard work. "I went to Atlanta two months before Boston," Beardsley offers. "Why? I needed a place I could train in a T-shirt and shorts. People up here were wearing snowmobile suits!"

Dick trained with Dean Matthews, the duo working together for a goal only one could achieve.

"We had some 140-mile weeks but they were just part of a build-up phase," he reveals. "After that, I cut back to 120 miles weekly and did some good quality work." Little was left to chance. From Atlanta, Beardsley flew to Boston to get acclimated, and to train on famously in-famous Heartbreak Hill. New England's weather, however, was less than accommodating, but, like any marathoner, Beardsley is tenacious.

Wearing a specially-designed pair of training shoes, Dick worked Heartbreak early before the snow piled up. There was enough traction to get in a good hill workout, but no way was Beardsley to battle the abominable snow mass. Back to Atlanta.

Beardsley is not necessarily a creature of habit, but there is one essential training exercise which occurs 12 days before every marathon – a 20-mile run... the hard way. Dick begins the workout with a two-mile warm-up, then the third mile goes past in 4:35. For 7 miles he cruises at 5:30 pace. During the next three miles, he throws in repeated one-minute surges. Deep breath, then three miles at 4:35 with six-minute "coasts" (5:20 pace) through 18 miles.

Back at the track he concludes his labors with two miles in 9:30. It is a decent effort. "I did that in 1:52 or so, nothing special," Beardsley recalls. "I've done that workout as quick as 1:45."

Twelve days later, that kind of time would've put him just a mile ahead of Grete Waitz, but Dick Beardsley wasn't running a workout twelve days later. This was the Boston Marathon – in the last year of its commercial virginity – and the man alongside was The Man.

"We shot out at the gun," Beardsley reminisces, "it seemed like a 100-yard dash. We hit the first mile mark in 4:33 or something but it didn't seem that fast 'cause it's downhill and the adrenaline's really pumping. I didn't feel too good the first five miles. We hit that at 23:58 and I finally got into a rhythm. There was a large lead pack... so big I didn't even get listed in the top ten."

"At 16 miles, [Bill] Rodgers threw in a burst on his favorite downhill section," continues Beardsley, the excitement of the competition obvious in his voice. "We stayed with him and at 17 miles, I figured, well, heck... I surged a little and Billy fell off by 15 meters."

Beardsley was still worried about Rodgers: "It's his course. Besides, I have more respect for Bill Rodgers than any other runner I know."

The four-time champion was beaten and, on the first hill, a surprising Ed Mendoza dropped when Dick worked the first major climb. "I felt great, really good going through the hills. My plan was to push every downhill section after Heartbreak."

Excuse me, but even the best laid plans do not often beat Alberto Salazar.

"I honestly thought I had him," Beardsley said, "because I thought he would make his move sooner. The biggest factor was my right hamstring knotted up badly at the Eliot Lounge. My stride fell to pieces and Alberto just swooped on by."

As he spoke, Beardsley seemed to return to Hereford Street. "Oddly, I stepped in a chuckhole and that strange movement seemed to make the charley-horse better. Any publicity about horses or motorcycles getting in my way... well, I did lose my concentration and rhythm, but I *still* thought I could get Alberto when I caught up to him again just before the finish line straightaway. He was just too tough."

Beardsley is not exactly a marshmallow himself. He'll run faster, he thinks. And he is eager – well, maybe not eager, but certainly willing – to run against Mr. Salazar again .

"If Alberto is human, if he's not made of iron parts or some miracle alloy," Dick offers, "then it is my feeling that he is beatable. I don't mean to take anything away from the man, but on a good day I feel I can beat him." Beardsley will have to take victory away from Salazar, because it certainly will not be surrendered.

"Alberto gave me a compliment at the awards ceremony," Beardsley said, lowering his voice as if to confide something important to a friend. "Alberto said he 'had never been pushed harder by anybody than he had by Dick Beardsley,' and that meant more to me than any medal or honor I've ever received or ever hope to receive."

Alberto Salazar, now that he is again eating with a knife and fork, is probably grateful to have experienced such a titanic competitive struggle. The World Record holder is not in this sport simply for the exercise. The man is here to test himself and to be tested. Dick Beardsley, a gentle man and an unlikely sports hero, provided that test.

"I was awarded second place," he points out, "but I don't feel like I lost."

Jon Sinclair's Identity Crisis
August 1982

Jon Sinclair and Michael Musyoki at the Maple Leaf Half-Marathon

Jon Sinclair. *Jon* Sinclair. Jon *Sinclair.* Sinclair, Jon. No matter how you say it, the name doesn't exactly jump in your face and demand attention. Even the "h" has deserted. What do you expect? This is clearly a case of Beaver Cleaver meets Rodney Dangerfield.

Looking like Huckleberry Finn's younger brother, Sinclair has been known best – if known at all – for running really well to finish in second place. All of that is changing now. Jon Sinclair is a winner.

Independence Day set Sinclair free, as the Peachtree 10k, with its cast of thousands, was the site of Jon's biggest win. His 28:17 was an equal 4th-fastest ever by an American, earned him $5000 and served eloquently to notify the world the former Colorado Stater is now a major force on the road circuit.

Sinclair's performances no longer beg for attention, they demand it. The 25-year-old Sinclair himself is less willing to seek notoriety. "I know I don't look like America's idea of a great athlete," admit the 5-7/127 pavement pounder.

"I get carded everywhere I go. I have to practically carry my birth certificate if I want a glass of wine with dinner" he admits. "When my wife and I go out on the town, we look like we're on our way to the senior prom." We should all be so youthful and speedy.

"Hey, I'm not a big star," he disclaims. "I'm just a guy who can move his feet quicker than most people." Ain't that the truth.

Sinclair's epic duel with Mike Musyoki at the Cascade RunOff a week before Peachtree might have been another bridesmaid placing, but it was also a 15-kilometer personal record of 43:14. Jon pocketed $6000 there, which is eleven grand in eight days for a guy who can still appreciate the value of a dollar.

In a world of under-the-table appearance fees, an unknown, regardless of his ability, doesn't exactly spend all his leisure time managing investments. And above-the-table paychecks haven't yet proved that lucrative. "I finally got some of my money back from [the national federation]," Sinclair says. "Of course, they also sent a bill saying I owed them more."

Sinclair first achieved a modicum of national attention when he won the USA Cross Country Championships in 1980. The victory – wouldn't you know it? – was somewhat tainted because it occurred at altitude over mushy terrain. The diminutive Sinclair, who lives at altitude in Fort

Collins, Colorado, won in a slow time. Everyone left Pocatello and prompt-ly forgot about the event.

"I didn't expect a lot from my victory," he confirms, "but I said before the race I thought I could win. I say to this day that I could have won it at sea level, anywhere. I was fit and everything clicked."

Everything seems to be clicking currently, because even when Jon fails to finish first, he still finishes strongly. One reason for his consistency is coach Damien Koch, a former Oregon distance runner.

"He's really been a big help," Sinclair explains. "A big reason for my re-cent success is that Damien's given me direction. I have always done in-tervals, for example, but always aimlessly. There was never any plan, no real purpose. Now we know what we did last week and what we need to do next."

One thing Sinclair needed was rest, and he took it in August. Oh, he still lifted weights, particularly to ameliorate a chronic problem with chon-dromalacia. And he daily swam up to a half-mile. And he still ran, averag-ing 90 miles weekly. "If I go over 100, it's only accidental," he points out. "I do make most of it as intense as possible."

But he did rest, particularly from the competitive rewards that accom-pany any race for first place. "I had a good enough spring to last me for a while," he notes, almost with a sigh. "I nearly went into hyper-warp back then, so I thought I'd better take a break." Such respite allows him to re-kindle the bright flame of greatness which glows in an athlete of his cali-ber. The rest allows him to go for the win at the upcoming Maple Leaf Half-Marathon and Virginia 10-Miler. Both are scheduled. And the New York City Marathon?

"Uh, well," he begins, measuring each word carefully, as if Salazar, Dix-on and Beardsley might overhear. "I don't want to run unless I am fit enough to win. My 2:13:29 [to win Bank One in 1981, in his serious de-but at the distance] was run on no training, so I'm sure I can run faster. I would plan on going under 2:10," he continues, still allowing dozing mara-thoners to lie undisturbed. "I think I can run with anybody. No one intimi-dates me."

He means it, fully realizing the truly top guys don't lose a great deal of sleep worrying about him either. But that's the way it has always been for Jon Sinclair, and it doesn't bother him anymore. He knows he is a superior athlete, he knows his peers recognize his ability. That is enough.

And if he does run New York and places, say, third in 2:09:19, in front of a million spectators and a national television audience... his parrot will still screech in his ear and his wife will still ask him to take out the trash.

When Opie leaves Mayberry and meets reality.

My Dinner With Greg Meyer
April 1983

Paul Cummings, Greg Meyer and Benji Durden battle at the 1983 Boston Marathon

"Boston can make a person, that's true," said Greg Meyer over dinner a day or two before being made. "But you are only as good as the people you beat. If the field weakens, it will be a shallow victory. The top runners will recognize that. And if it comes down to running for thousands of dollars somewhere or running for nothing here, you know what they'll do."

That paragraph, that quotation, goes a long way toward explaining or understanding Greg Meyer. Thoughtful, outspoken, a lover of children, chocolate eclairs and off-color jokes, the bearded, balding 27-year-old

winner of the 1983 BAA Marathon is nothing if not direct. If you don't understand Greg Meyer, it must be because you are not listening or he has chosen not to share himself.

JDW: What does the Boston win mean to you?

GM: Well, I tell you, I got kinda upset after winning the marathon, with everyone telling me how much Boston was worth financially. What it does for me athletically is much more important. It opens so many doors to better races and bigger competition.

JDW: What about the race itself?

GM: I was surprised Benji [Durden] ran so hard, so early. I thought he'd wait until 17 or 18, then go for it. Actually, I was surprised at how bad I felt the first half of the race.

JDW: You're credited with 2:09:01. Couldn't you have found a couple extra seconds somewhere?

GM: I know I was on World Record pace for 20 miles. But a record didn't matter. I was there for the win and that's all. I know I can run faster. The last mile was on automatic pilot; I did 5:26 or something like that. I had been holding up well, but I was looking around quite a bit to see if anyone was closing. Then some guy on the press truck hollered, "Man, there's nobody coming!" and I just shut down.

I was more than happy to be alone in the last few miles. I still have vivid memories of crawling on my face the last four miles in '81.

JDW: Why run Boston at all? Alberto [Salazar] didn't seem to think it was necessary.

GM: Al had already won it. I didn't feel people took me seriously as a marathoner last year, despite the third-fastest time in the country. I won Chicago in 2:10 and it was a deeper field than New York's, but it didn't seem to get the credit it should've. I figured people couldn't discount Boston. Except for Al and [Dick] Beardsley, it was a dry run for the Olympic Trials.

JDW: But you surrendered your berth at the World Championships.

GM: Looking at '84, I did not want to run only marathons. I thought that would hinder my development. Besides, I'm still looking for credibility on the track. I'd rather go to the Pan-Ams at 10 kilometers. People don't look at the roadie as important as the trackster. That's not fair.

Herb Lindsay, Jon Sinclair, me, we all had to build our reputations on the roads. Five years ago, it was a rare athlete who could come out of college and make a living at running. Roads were where the money was, so that's where we went. Now I want to show what I can do on the track.

JDW: *Did your 27:53 10k at the Colonial Relays tell you something? Something only hinted to the rest of us?*

GM: When I ran that time, I almost skipped Boston. It all seemed so easy and it was a solo. I only wanted a 28:40 or 28:30, but once I pushed the pace a little, I found myself alone. I figured why not keep the pressure on. After that 27:53, I felt confident that it would be real hard for three people to beat me out at 10k.

JDW: *27:53 is nice work, but it's hardly a guarantee.*

GM: It was really easy, but you're right. What's important is that it came at the end of my hardest preparation for Boston. After winning the Cherry Blossom 10-Miler unpressed in 46:13, I put in my biggest mileage week. After finishing 120 miles, I stepped on the track, I stepped on the track and ran 27:53.

JDW: *You've got quite a range of talent, having run a sub-4:00 mile and now a 2:09:01 marathon. Where do you see yourself on the Olympic team?*

GM: The event I would like to be in is the marathon. I think I can run in the low 2:08s, which I feel should be able to win a place on the team. And I feel I have a better chance at a medal in the marathon. There's more opportunity to use that talent you mentioned. The U.S. team should be very strong at the marathon, much more capable of success at the Games than in the 10k. We're simply more world class at the longer distance.

JDW: *What got you here?*

GM: You mean world-class? Well, I don't think Boston was my breakthrough. The key, if there's one in my training, is my hard 20-milers. They're good efforts. But the real key has to be the consistency of my training in the last three or four years. Guys like Salazar and [Craig] Virgin have always thought of themselves as world-class since they were kids. I never thought of myself that way. It's only recently that I've become focused, that I've begun to think of myself on a higher plane. I feel I have much more room for improvement.

JDW: *So, you expect some great things from yourself this summer?*

GM: Well, I did. I'm injured. It was at Boston actually. During the indoor season I developed tendinitis – could be an inflamed bursa – atop the Achilles. After the marathon, about two weeks after, I went for my first long run. Fifteen miles easy. The next day I could hardly walk. I did the usual stuff... ice, aspirin, etc.

JDW: How is your Achilles?

GM: Well, now the big problem is a metatarsal on my right foot. When I try to run it's like someone put a spike in it. I guess I hurt it compensating for my Achilles. I am having a cortisone shot in the Achilles but I don't know about the toe. And after the injection, I can't train for ten days or so.

This conversation – not unlike the film "My Dinner With Andre" – was interrupted continually as Meyer disappeared to refill his plate. The man eats like a shotputter with a tapeworm.

JDW: Anything going on in the sport you don't like?

GM: Well, I don't think it's intelligent to have the track trials so close to the marathon [trials]. A number of people will try to double back and we're just inviting them to get injured.

And the Olympics themselves. When's the men's race? Something like 5:30 in the afternoon. Summer in Los Angeles. What are those people thinking of? I ran a race there a few years back and I couldn't take a deep breath for six hours afterwards. And that was a steeplechase! Sure, people could breathe, but running 26 miles in 2:08 is an altogether different matter.

JDW: What else?

GM: Uh, I wouldn't mind seeing drug testing on the roads. A random check, every now and then... so the guys who don't want to take them [drugs] don't have to just to compete. If it was just a case of who could perform better, then I wouldn't be bothered. But when you put prize money into it, then you begin to interfere with someone's ability to earn a livelihood.

JDW: Bill Rodgers?

GM: He's a runner. I think he'll be back. He'll run 2:09 again.

JDW: Okay. So, who do you like in L.A. in '84?

GM: I don't have a problem with the heat. Alberto might. Seko has never run a warm weather marathon. De Castella doesn't seem to be bothered by anything.

I've run a 1:50 half-mile – although not recently – so I've got decent speed. I change into a sprint faster, change my gears quicker, than most marathoners.

A lot can happen in a year but I expect to be in the thick of it.

One assumes that last statement was not a pun about the Los Angeles smog.

Meyer enjoys life obviously, a little more now that the Boston Marathon victory is behind him and a baby is due July 15. (Greg, of course, thinks it will be early.)

The man seems to have a firm grip on life right now, almost as if it were a knife and fork.

Greg Meyer picks up the bill for half the table, including the mooching journalist, then clutches his wife's hand, and walks off without looking back.

Top Roadie Nenow Likes The Track
January 1985

At 5-8½, 130 pounds, Mark Nenow is smaller than Doug Flutie. At 27, Ne-now might have had a better season than the college football superstar.

Nenow (pronounced "Nee-no") doesn't have a million-dollar contract but then there aren't any 300 lb. men trying to push him through to the bottom of the earth either.

But Mr. Nenow put his own kind of pressure on the earth and the men who raced on roads during 1984 and no American road racer compiled a record superior to his. Nenow is the top-ranked road runner of 1984.

Like Flutie, Nenow received only one offer of an athletic grant after he graduated in 1976 from Anoka High, in a Minneapolis suburb. He headed for Kentucky to begin just his second year of running.

"I didn't have many options," Nenow explains. "I didn't start running until my senior year of high school, so I didn't have any track times to impress the recruiters."

He ran 4:17 and 9:20 in his first year and won the state cross-country title. His late start in running came because he had been a wrestler for the previous four years.

"God, I hated wrestling," he confesses. "It's a grueling sport and I just wanted to be involved in sports. So it was a real kick to shift to another activity and be successful."

Nenow's collegiate career was only moderately successful. "My first couple of years were nasty," he says. "In the SEC 10k my frosh year, I must have been lapped at least three times."

His best collegiate season was 1980 – his junior year – when he ran 28:32.7 and placed 7th in the NCAA 10,000. "I always felt my college career was so sketchy because I was still learning about running," he explains. "I didn't have the same high school background everybody else had."

Nenow picked up his accounting degree in 1980 and an MBA in 1982. He then became a graduate student of running.

"Getting out of college was the best thing that ever happened to me," he confides. "I run alone; I don't have a coach or an advisor. I just started doing my own thing."

His training emphasizes mileage, perhaps 15M daily. He covers ten miles at 2 or 3 in the afternoon, then another five miles at 10 or 11 *p.m.* "I never time myself, but the runs might be pretty quick," he points out. "I don't get caught up with training PRs and I don't do much track work. I feel I get sharp really quick with just a race or two."

At times, it seems Nenow competes only in a race or two. "In '83 I ran four road races; that's all I wanted. People assume you have a lot of down time if you don't race, but I just feel more comfortable not racing as much."

In '84, Nenow raced more — even if as a last-minute entry at Crescent City, where the wind helped propel him to the road 10k World Record. Yet that performance doesn't mean as much to Nenow as you might think.

"I know this is supposed to be a road article," he apologizes, "but I *really* love the track. I'd rather set a U.S. track record than a road WR. The bottom line in road racing is to win, but on the track, I don't care where I place as long as I run a great time."

Nenow led the U.S. in '84 at both 5000m and 10,000m around the oval (13:18.54/27:40.56). "I was only 5th in that Oslo 5000, but I felt as excited about that as about any race I've ever run. My old PR was 13:33. That's fun!"

But '84 wasn't all fun. He placed only 15th at Falmouth: "I ran terribly. I was sick with a fever, but when I stink it up, I don't mind saying so." And he was just 11th in the Olympic Trials 10,000. "I don't know what happened, but I know *I didn't* peak at Crescent City. I planned to run a good heat at the Trials and then go fast in the final. Guess I was wrong."

This year, Nenow says he wants to run well in road races like Continental Homes and Crescent City, but also in the TAC 10,000. "I want to run the World Cup. I'd also like to run in races in Europe that have fast guys in them," he says.

Then what? "Then I'll come home and train for a marathon in the fall. People say I should be able to run a good marathon. I guess I'll find out."

We all will. But Nenow prefers the oval, remember. Some roadie! Too bad they don't run the marathon on the track.

A Conversation With Mark Nenow
October 1986

Mark Nenow does not like to be called a loner. He belongs to the Todds Road Stumblers, a group of over 1,200 members. "A pretty big outfit, pretty organized," Nenow says from his Lexington, Kentucky home. "We've even got a little clubhouse out in the country."

But at age 28, Mark Nenow is clearly a man apart. He's an individualist. A man who doesn't like to talk about his running. Nenow somehow manages to be closemouthed and outspoken at the same time. His fame is a garment, in no way really him; just something he wears as a gift for efforts and success that came to him slowly, reluctantly, after years of hard work. He is often alone, but he is not a loner.

"In individual sports, in running, there's no one to blame but yourself," he explains. "Likewise, when you're successful, the gratification is all yours, 'cause you went it alone. The bottom line... when the guns go off, it's really just you out there."

No, Nenow is not a loner. He is *special. Check your watch. Look at it again in 27 minutes and 20 seconds. Mark Nenow can run ten kilometers in that time. Think about it.*

JDW: Last month you said, and I quote: "Obviously, an American Record on the track is within my grasp at 10,000 meters. Whether I'll ever hold it or not is a whole other question. But that would really be great for me if I could be an American Record holder on the track." Well, you've got your AR. How does it feel?

MN: It feels like I've finally accomplished something. I feel like I've really done it. I've earned a credential at last that makes me happy.

JDW: You've owned a 10k road World Record for some time now.

MN: A World Record on the road just doesn't compare to the American Record on the track. I was always proud of that road WR. I still am. Don't get me wrong. But, you know how you are introduced, "This is so-and-so. He's done this." Well, they usually only mention one thing you've done.

They normally name just a single credential.

Well, when people have mentioned my accomplishments, they'd almost always refer to the 10k road WR. I'd often cringe. I'd wish there was something more. Now, there is.

JDW: What makes the track so special for you?

MN: The track separates the men from the boys. It's universally comparable. How do you compare Crescent City to Continental Homes? You can't, not really. A 10k on the track is the same in Brussels or Oslo or Mt. Sac. The track... there's a sense that it is the pinnacle of my sport. It's running at its best.

JDW: And now, you are one of the best. Here's a Barbara Wawa question: Are you a star? Do you put people in the seats?

MN: [Chuckles] I certainly don't think of myself as a 'star.' I don't think other people do, either. I do think I am respected. I've been at or near the top of the 10k lists for the last few years. Meet directors, especially in Europe, realize that I'll run a fast race for them.

JDW: Let's talk about Brussels.

MN: Let's! Gosh, it was great! [Pauses.] It was a strange race. The rabbit, or rabbits, just weren't doing the job. They weren't doing much pacemaking. I think I had to do more work than the rabbits in the first half of the race. I had to spend the first 12 laps being more concerned about the pace than just trying to run hard. I probably led three laps myself.

JDW: Sounds pretty tough.

MN: It wasn't really easy. I started to realize that if I wanted to run fast I was going to have to do it by myself. I gave up on the others after actually telling the rabbit – at least three times – to go faster. Once I took off, I felt a lot better.

JDW: Do you remember your splits?

MN: We went out in 13:47, and came back in 13:33. I wanted 13:40. I'm convinced, if I'd sat back, they'd have brought me through in 13:55.

JDW: That won't get the job done.

MN: No, it won't. If they want a fast time... if meet directors want a World Record or even an American Record, they've got to set up a fast pace. You just can't go out in 13:50 and expect to get back in 13:10. But, where do you get a rabbit who can run 13:30 even on his bad day? That sounds like you need a runner who can do 13:10. And you're not going to get somebody to do that. Someone like that will want to run a real race, maybe the 5k.

JDW: Was the race set up specifically for you?

MN: No, I don't think so. It wasn't a packed field. [John] Treacy was there, a couple others. But it wasn't deep. The real key was that I had just planned to run well at Brussels.

JDW: Now, that's an insight. I didn't know Mark Nenow planned.

MN: C'mon, Jack. I plan. My races, at least.

JDW: So, let's talk about your training. It's 10 p.m. and you're just going out for your second run of the day. Pretty unusual plan. Why so late?

MN: I always run at night. 11 p.m. or so. Our college coach used to tell us to run extra miles at night occasionally. I got used to it. I enjoy it. I'm a night person.

JDW: How far do you run in the dark?

MN: There are street lights. I run about 6-7M.

JDW: When do you run your morning workouts?

MN: Well, um, 2 or 3 in the afternoon.

JDW: Right. [Pause] What kind of mileage are you doing?

MN: The same as always. About 100 miles a week. In the fall I usually do less. Try to give it a rest.

JDW: Mark, we better talk about this a little more, or we're gonna have half the joggers in the U.S. and most of the high school kids running off cliffs in the middle of the night, getting chased by cops or muggers or both.

What's your secret? Are you still staying off the track? I can't believe you can run 27:20 off 100 miles of nocturnal jogging.

MN: I had been off the track until I came home on break from the European circuit. And I did run 27:28 at Oslo off my usual training.

JDW: And then?

MN: I met an English coach over there. A guy named Alan Storey. He suggested I add some light track work to my usual program. So that's what I did for five weeks before Brussels.

JDW: I thought you didn't think much of coaches.

MN: I admit I haven't been a big fan of coaching, at least not for my-self. Only coaching I ever had was in college, and my college career was sketchy at best. The moment I left college, as soon as I was on my own, I excelled.

I believe you need to work one-on-one with a coach. He has to really know you. You have to be together. I've just not been willing to relocate to get coaching. I'm really comfortable in Lexington.

JDW: What did Storey have you doing?

MN: Intervals. The classic stuff. Nothing fancy. 4:40-ish. He was real careful. He wanted to alter my training, but he didn't want me to push it. He didn't want me to come up lame.

JDW: And that's your secret?

MN: I ran 27:28 on "nothing." When you toss on top of that some sprint drills, some repeat miles, maybe that is the difference. But I was really strong. Rome wasn't built in a day. Four weeks of track doesn't automatically get you 27:20.

JDW: "Nothing" doesn't get you 27:28. How were you training? How fast is your mileage?

MN: I don't really know. I really don't know the pace. I run how I feel. I just scatterbrain run around town. I never plot my week out. If I feel good on, say, Tuesday, then I run hard. If I'm feeling sluggish, I take it easy. I listen to my body.

I run alone always. There's a couple of reasons for that. First of all, there's no one around here to train with. And, secondly, I don't like to run faster than I want to run, and I don't like to run slower than I want.

JDW: I can remember at least once seeing you run slower than you wanted to. How about your 11th-place finish in the '84 Olympic Trials? You ever look back at that?

MN: Look back at that? And laugh, you mean?

JDW: In a word, how do you feel about that race?

MN: The word isn't sadness. In a word, I was embarrassed. I wasn't down. I wasn't mad. I was just embarrassed.

JDW: How do you feel now?

MN: You try to learn from your mistakes. I'm sure I'll benefit in the long run from that '84 experience.

JDW: No pun intended, right? What did you learn?

MN: I went into the '84 Trials without having run a single race in months. I thought I could make the team, I thought I could race well without having had any competition. I must have been a bit of a fool.

And I think I felt a lot of pressure from my friends, my family, my town, the local press. I got a lot more attention than usual. Everybody's hopes were up. I think a lot of people were counting on me. That all began to get to me.

I'll be able to deal with the pressure better next time. I realize now the world doesn't revolve around someone making the Olympic team.

JDW: You once told me you would run a marathon in the fall of '85. What happened?

MN: Jack, I lied. That's what I did – I lied. The marathon is like a big, smiling face with a hand stretched out to you. It seems friendly. There's so much glamour, so much hype, [chuckles] so much money. But... I have this feeling the marathon is the devil of disguise. There's an element of destruction in the marathon.

I don't want to mention any names, but you see guys running marathons... and, well, they're just never the same again. The marathon scares me.

JDW: I could mention some names.

MN: Don't. Actually, until recently, I've been thinking about the marathon. A month ago I thought I might do one this fall. I was about 50–50 on it. But, after, Brussels, I'm content to set it aside again. Brussels reminded me what I'm in track for.

JDW: And what's that?

MN: To go faster. To be the best I can be.

Mark Curp: Top Roadie of 1985
February 1986

Life is sometimes nothing more — perhaps nothing less — than a jigsaw puzzle. You just put the pieces together without much of a guarantee about the result. Consider these pieces.

The City of Brotherly Love. A major league event. A collection of world-class competitors seeking a big payday. A flat, fast course. Temperatures in the low 50s with little wind. A *strong* early pace that never abated. And Mark Curp.

Those pieces all came together at the Philadelphia Distance Run last September as Curp passed ten miles in 46:31 to beat Mike Musyoki and Nick Rose with a clocking of 1:00:55 for the half-marathon.

"It was just one of those days," Curp recounts. "One of those days when all the ingredients were there."

After the race one thing was missing; gone was Steve Jones's month-old WR of 1:01:14. Curp, the quintessential Midwestern farm boy, was suddenly a world record holder, a force on any given day, and now he is the 1985 Men's Road Racer of the Year.

In 1985, Curp, representing the New Balance Track Club, lost more races than he won, but he was beaten by only a handful of Americans. He displayed good range, racing over a variety of distances. He placed highly at many of the circuit's more prestigious events. In a year where no Americans stood out, the 5'9" Curp stood tallest. His performance at Philly was the prime reason.

"I didn't expect it to go that fast. I was running scared the last half mile, because I've been outkicked before in other races. But I was able to get up on my toes the last quarter mile.

"I will say one more thing about Philadelphia," continues Curp, so polite he wouldn't even say "Philly." "I actually dropped off the pace for a brief period right before 10k. I fought back, and that's something I'm proud of... I felt my best during the last three miles. Fortunately, that's a very good time to feel good."

Curp felt good about Philly in part because he hoped it presaged success in his first marathon. "I wanted a sub-1:02 to help me towards my marathon debut," Curp explained at the time. "With this result, I'm definitely positive."

Curp is still thinking about it. Last October, he arrived at Chicago, hopefully recovered from a cold which had plagued him for days. Fifteen miles at sub-5:00 pace proved his illness remained. The result was a DNF and a disappointed, if wiser, Mark Curp.

"Chicago gave me a sense of appreciation for the distance," he explains. "I thought I was over my cold, but it was obscured by medicine. I wouldn't approach the marathon differently in the future, but now I know for a fact that you can't race one well at less than 100%. It takes 110% to run the marathon the way it's meant to be run."

Curp has always given 100%, even 110%. He doesn't possess the pure talent to do otherwise. As a senior (1977) at Polo High School in Polo, Missouri — a town whose population has grown to 583 — Curp was only 5-2, 105 pounds. Nonetheless, he played wingback for the Panthers. He also ran track, recording a 4:35 mile and 9:58.2 for 2M.

When it was time to go to college, Curp didn't have many scholarship offers. "Only a couple of schools were interested in me," he recalls. One school that was interested was Central Missouri State. Curp repaid CMSU's confidence by becoming an All-American in both track and cross-country. When he graduated with two agri-business degrees, his times had improved to 4:13, 8:52, 14:02 and 28:14.62.

While progress was considerable, so too was the room for improvement. And that has come with maturation. Now 27, Curp is 7" taller than he was in high school and some 30 pounds heavier. He's also a family man, married to Linda for three years and father of Jonathon, born May 22, 1985.

Curp's training is nothing special. There are no secrets. During a race week, Mark will cover 10-12 miles in the morning on Monday, Wednesday and Friday, with a shorter run in the afternoon. On Tuesdays, Curp runs 11 miles, mostly in the 5:08-5:20 range. He'll do fartlek on Thursdays, holding, for example, 4:30 pace for three minutes, followed by a one-minute jog, then a five-minute run at 4:50 pace.

"I tend to do my hard runs in the morning as most of my races seem to be early in the day," notes the self-coached Curp. "I do all my speedwork on the roads unless I am preparing for a track race. Basically, I try to be flexible.

"I try to be flexible about my training *and* my racing. I think it is very important simply to listen to your body, especially if you race a lot."

Curp's philosophy seems to have worked. He's improved his mile time to 4:07 ("that's unofficial – just a time trial on the track"); he has also run 2M in 8:47, 5k on the track in 13:40.65, and a track 10k of 28:01.02. He's logged a 15k in 43:02 and, of course, there's that 1:00:55.

There is still room for improvement, and some of his goals are obvious. "Well, I definitely want to go under 28:00 for 10k and run in the 42s for 15k," Curp concedes. "My main goal is to do my best and to compete as long as possible, as long as I'm still competitive. I'll always run, even if I live to be 100.

"I don't ever plan on concentrating on the marathon," he says with feeling. "I am quite confident I can run it well; I just don't want to do it more than once a year. I think it takes a lot out of your body, and I'd like to race for a long time. I think if I concentrated on the marathon, I'd shorten my career."

His career seems much like the man. There's a steadiness, a calm, a strength that moderates the ebb and flow of adversity and triumph. There's a reason.

"God has blessed me with talent," Curp believes. "I'm a Christian. If God blesses me with a gold medal, that's great. If He doesn't, that's great, too. I wouldn't have accomplished what I have without Him. I never forget that."

No, Mark Curp won't forget. He really won't. Mark Curp has faith God knows how the puzzle works out.

John Gregorek Tracks Road Wins
April 1987

Gregorek tracking another steeple win

John Gregorek's a big guy, one who often seems to be lurking at the back of the lead pack, waiting to kick, waiting to blow by more diminutive competitors. At 6-1/160, he casts a large shadow on the road racing circuit. It's a shadow he himself sometimes seems to run in.

Past success as an Olympic steepler and as a 3:51 miler hangs on John Gregorek, road runner, like some oversized warmup suit. He just seems a bit out of place, as if he should be on a track somewhere – leaping over a water barrier perhaps. Who is John Gregorek and what's a nice guy like him doing on the roads?

"All this road running is geared toward the track," admits the 8:18:45

steepler. "Road races are just a test of my shape."

He seems to be passing the examinations. His 27:56 at the American Continental Homes 10k earned him second, just 5 seconds behind Arturo Barrios. Six weeks later, Gregorek won England's 10k road championships in 28:14, 2 seconds *ahead* of *Senor* Barrios. If he continues at this rate, John will certainly rank higher than last year's No.7 among U.S. roadies.

Just turned 27, Gregorek is looking to the roads for answers. Running just hasn't been the same for him since his efforts at the '84 Games, where he was a non-qualifying 11th in his heat.

"I haven't run the steeple since L.A.", says the Georgetown grad, now residing in Barrington, Rhode Island, a boating town 15 miles from Providence. "I didn't run the finals. That was very frustrating. It left a bitter taste in my mouth."

Gregorek's success on the roads – and the passing of time – has given him a fresher look at his sport. He explains, "A year ago I couldn't see running in '88. Now I feel like I could go another ten years. I feel good about my running."

He also knows how the change was made. "I'm finally learning to listen to myself. After years of looking for the magic system, the magic coach, the magic training partner... the secret potion," he reveals. "I'm finding my own answers. If running by myself is what it takes, then that's what I'm going to do. Basically, I've just been digging in, putting my head down."

Gregorek's labors are directed towards the Olympics, but they're focused on improvement, simply that. He overemphasized that quadrennial extravaganza once before; he won't do it again.

"My goal right now is top three at Nationals. Then get into the finals at World Champs," Gregorek says. "I need to get that experience."

John's only problem at the moment seems to be deciding in which event to gain that big meet exposure. He's a steepler, sure, but he's done that already.

"I still haven't decided. It's 50-50 between the steeple and 5k," he admits. "I would like to run the 5, but if I don't feel comfortable with my abilities at that, I'll go to the steeple."

Face it. The 5k presents a greater challenge. Gregorek's PR is a 13:29.3 run indoors in 1985 and that's probably not good enough. Gregorek knows it, too.

"I'm feeling a little more confident now after running a 13:43 for the final 5k at Continental Homes," Gregorek notes. "Running against Buckner, Barrios, Treacy, Bickford... well, I've proven I can run with guys like them."

Ed Eyestone: Best U.S. Roadie of 1990
January 1991

Ed Eyestone loves the feeling of victory

In Bountiful, Utah, the phone rang. Ed Eyestone stopped putting away the Christmas lights long enough to take the call. After convincing Erica, age 2½, she'd be better off practicing the kazoo with her mother in the kitchen, he took the news calmly.

"Road Racer Of The Year, huh? That's nice." He didn't seem to know what else to say. "Thank you. Ummm, I felt like it was a decent year for me. I'm happy with my progress."

He should be. He had no real reason to be surprised after a stellar season that saw a consistent series of quality performances, topped by a breakthrough 2:10:59 for 5th in the Chicago Marathon. You could hear the self-satisfaction in his voice: "I lowered my PR by a minute and a half."

He did indeed. Of course, as annual listings testify, the U.S.'s best still has a long way to run before being numbered among the world's true elite. In '90, 21 marathoners from 16 different nations ran faster than Eyestone, and it has been eight years since an American was ranked in the Top 10, the worst streak ever.

"I really don't think things are as dire as people would have us believe," Eyestone cautions. "It's just a matter of time before we'll see the factors that put an American in the Top 10. I still maintain it's gonna happen."

According to Eyestone, those factors will involve a finely conditioned athlete in the right race with the right weather. "I can't speak for everybody," he says, speaking for himself, "but I feel what I'm doing – which is the best I can – will be good enough." It's just a matter of being in the right place at the right time.

"Frankly, I get a little miffed with all the different theories as to why U.S. runners aren't as highly ranked as they may have been in the past," Eyestone offers. "The top Americans have about the same PRs as, say, Frank Shorter. We haven't declined, there's just a lot more competition."

Eyestone brushes aside criticism that the world's best marathoners spend more time avoiding one another than they do competing. "Frankly, avoiding other runners never enters my mind," the Boy Scout leader claims. "In my opinion, you're limited to two good performances a year, which means the top people simply can't meet as often as we'd like.

"Road racing, sure, it's the way I've fed the family for the last five years, but I don't look at which runners are going to show up. I look at how a race fits into my overall schedule."

Eyestone's 1990 forays onto the U.S. road circuit were essentially benchmark efforts designed to test his progress. They're lab experiments, really, aimed at making him a global force over 26M, 385y. "I feel like now I'm really more of a marathoner."

You can see the difference in his training. For the last year and a half, Eyestone has been working out thrice weekly with neighbor Paul Pilkington, no slouch himself with a 2:11:13 PR.

"For the first time since I left college," says the 29-year-old BYU alum, "training is fun again. Running with a peer, with someone at my own level, it's really helped."

So has the additional mileage. As a 10k specialist, Eyestone typically covered 80-90 miles weekly. As a marathoner, he might do as much as 120.

Competing in the '88 Olympic marathon, just his third go at the distance, "I ran it as a 10k runner. I was still doing basically the same mileage, except for a long run every two weeks. Now it's a 25-miler once a week."

For a berth on the Barcelona Olympic team in '92, Eyestone is definitely planning for the long run. "I feel like now I'm really more of a marathoner," he confirms. The transition is more than mental. "I'd say I've lost 10-15 seconds over 10k. The pace seems a lot faster than it used to. Needless to say," he says, "the marathon distance has become more comfortable."

While Eyestone has not made the transition from 25 laps on the track to 26+ miles on the road look easy, he has made it look doable. He has proven again, just as Mr. Shorter did a generation ago, an American track racer can compete successfully in the marathon.

Not yet a medal. Not yet the times of Alberto Salazar. Not yet even a Top 10 ranking. But one senses, after 1990, that Eyestone may be well on his way. He may even be next.

"I feel with the ability I've been given," he says, his voice filling with determination, "the marathon is more suitable to achieving my very best."

Which is the best he can do.

Steve Spence, World Beater
September 1991

Spence knew how to get ready for the day he needed to be ready

Track and field became so mesmerizing these past few months, I didn't give much thought to road racing. First time that's happened since, well, before Frank Shorter's Munich effort.

Then one morning, I walked into a friend's living room and noticed she had a television. I don't own a TV myself. I immediately turned hers on. Felt like I'd won the Florida lottery as the beer commercial ended and the World Championship Marathon popped onto the screen.

There was Steve Spence. Looking strong, with a style like a cocked trigger.

"Go, Steve!" I hollered. "Show 'em what you got."

He showed them good. Real good. Man ran a smart race.

The Steve Spence who stood on that victory stand, a World Championship bronze medal around his neck, is the same Steve Spence who's a dues-paying representative of professional road racing.

And the winner of the first WC [World Championship] medal of any kind by an American male marathoner.

Is he living proof U.S. athletes can compete on the lucrative pro circuit and still represent their country well internationally? Or, is his third place finish in Tokyo a singular random event?

I called Spence. I asked him how he'd pulled it off.

"I knew 10 months before the race I was going to run in the Worlds," the 29-year-old pointed out. "That proved very beneficial compared to the normal situation in this country. Like the '92 Olympics. We'll find out 4 months before the Games if we're on the team, then we're expected to be ready again in Barcelona. I had 10 months to prepare for Tokyo.

"I moved to Maine for the summer, running as much as 145 miles weekly," Spence said. He returned in August to his Chambersburg, Pennsylvania, home for heat training. "Two weeks before the race, I did a 2-hour-and-50-minute run. The first two hours were easy, 6:10s, followed by five miles at 5:15 pace, then a cool down. I felt prepared going in."

Asked about his strategy for the race, Spence continued to stress his preparation. His training was his strategy.

"I gave up speed because I knew the race wouldn't be fast," he stated. "I prepared for a hot and humid race. I trained for endurance."

Spence toed the starting line, determined to ride an evenly paced effort to a 2:15 finish and a place among the top 10. "I really wanted to be in the top five," Steve admitted. "But I didn't want to set my goals too high."

Spence ran the race he wanted. He was in 25th place when he passed the halfway point in 1:07:15. "I didn't think I'd ever even see the lead pack," confessed Spence. "At 37 kilometers, I caught them." He didn't keep them.

"My first thought was 'I am running so much faster than these guys; I'll just go right by,' he recalled. "Turned out half the pack was waiting for something to happen, the other half was hanging on."

In a sense, Spence broke open the race. It was here eventual gold medalist Hiromi Taniguchi surged to a lead he'd never surrender. And it was here Steve Spence earned a place in U.S. marathon history.

"I think for where I am now, I ran the best I could run in those conditions (mid-'80s, 75% humidity)," Steve recalled. "I remember feeling like I had accomplished something definitely significant."

Spence definitely breathed some fresh air into his country's distance running fraternity. The first medal in a coon's age and a pro road racer wins it. Does this end speculation the lucrative road circuit has worked to the disadvantage of many American runners?

Spence laughs at the thought. "I can't really call the U.S. road racing circuit lucrative," Spence said. "It's *not* lucrative. It's definitely the opposite. If the roads *were* lucrative, we wouldn't have to race so much to survive."

Spence points directly toward a $20,000 "training stipend" from the Columbus Marathon as a contributing factor to his success in Tokyo. He didn't have to rely on the roads for his daily bread.

Besides, the road circuit was never a problem for Spence. "I rarely have a bad race. I've been fairly selective. I wasn't over-raced in the past," Spence offered. "It just took me a while to learn how to run a marathon."

Watch for Steve Spence to learn how to run the next one faster.

The Chris Fox Files
October 1995

Hagerstown, Maryland, U.S.A. October, 1995

A fox – a feral dog... renowned throughout the ages for his intelligence.
Imagine you are Chris Fox.

You woke up one day, just a kid, wishing you could play basketball, but you didn't have the physical tools. Not for that game.

You loved basketball. Played basketball everyday, even when you ran one hundred miles a week. But you were four-feet-eleven, sixty-five pounds in the tenth grade. So, you lived running, because you were excited to finally excel at something and because you found a coach who was really into the sport.

You feel much the same way over twenty years later.

You were successful early. Wore the U.S.A. jersey more than once, still a kid. You made the national team in cross-country and helped capture the world championship in Dusseldorf, West Germany. When's the last time that happened? Ran 8:57 for two miles in high school. You competed for the United States vs. the Soviet Union. 14:21 for five kilometers. Learned the metric system sooner than most of your friends.

In the mid-Seventies, you and your buddies were just a fledging cross-country team. At your school, nobody ran, it was more like you were rebels. You all wore your hair a lot longer than the rest of the kids. You were rebels because you worked hard and proved fairly successful. Cultivated contrast against the teenage stereotype.

You've been running one hundred mile weeks since you were fifteen years old. The biggest thing you notice between high school and now, running is easier and more fun today. Seemed very hard for you back then. Even though you were pretty good, it was hard. Hard physically.

Wasn't such a game, more of a game today.

Running late.

You turned thirty-seven this month and racing faster than ever. This summer's personal best of 27:53 legitimizes you as a world class athlete. Fifteenth-fastest ten-kilometer runner in U.S. history. Only three guys have gone under twenty-eight minutes in this decade. And you are the oldest American in history to run so fast. Years older.

You don't count the years.

You don't count mileage, but you guess you were running about eighty miles a week, the middle of track season. The training is not complicated. You ran a big time track workout once a week, which might mean repeat miles fairly fast. Sub-4:15. Maybe some quick quarters after that, sub-sixty. Nothing very complicated. And then coming back the other hard day with fartlek, speed play, which is very controlled, say, two-minute runs off a minute rest. Or ninety-second runs with a minute's rest. Track workouts total three miles of hard stuff at the height of the racing season.

Actually, this past spring, you started something a little different, concentrating on a thousand meters. A thousand meters is a good distance for you from a training standpoint, because you can still get good quality speedwork, coming through the eight hundred meters in 2:07, then changing gears the last two hundred meters. That seems to work really well. Gives you that balance between long enough interval and quick enough.

This is the training you've been doing for the last eight years. Just an evolution of the same program. Same coach. Consistency in many things pays many dividends.

Known Coach Shank, Greg, since you were a thirteen-year-old kid. Staying with the same coach has been a big help. Surrounded by people who really believe in you. Not just your coach, but four or five good friends who really believe in your running. You have a good support crew and they keep it all very positive. Aces and eight years.

Something else. Three or four people in the coaching world, guys who know, told you to your face that you have all the tools, you just have to get them together.

And it finally has come together over the last year and a half. Shown glimpses here and there, since you ran 13:21 a decade ago, you could run at the level you are finally running at. But never on a consistent basis.

Not like now.

Can't pinpoint precisely the reasons for the breakthrough, this winning streak of great races you've been running. Consistency can be its own reason.

Your form is so much better than it used to be, you're square all the time. You seldom ever run on the roads. Those paths, dirt paths where you're at right now as matter of fact, you run on them at least ninety percent of the time the last eight years. Run on dirt paths, whether it's on the mountain or along the river. Love it out here. If you're doing a ten-mile run, sure, you might run a mile to get to the trails. But that's about the extent of your road time. Think soft surfaces prevent injury.

There was a time or two you wanted to quit. There was a time when you felt, "I just can't translate my hard work and talent into success in competition." You knew in your heart you were faster than other guys with better marks.

You worked it out. A gradual process. Give you credit for that, you worked it out. Been pushing hard for a long time. You could have quit but you never did.

Like your attitude today: I'm going to take a chance.

Imagine you are Chris Fox.

You have been one of the truly lucky guys in this sport, you know it. You have never been abused. Your high school coach didn't abuse you. Never ran you in dual meets. Rarely forced you to run too many intervals. Sure, you did the long slow miles back then but everybody else was into LSD. Auburn, no problems worth remembering. You didn't get abused at Eugene with the legendary Athletics West crowd. Because you were at Eugene, you weren't running on the roads, those guys didn't run on the roads. Ran on paths, too. They had a short season, then they went to Europe.

You certainly haven't been abused by Shank. Greg is a guy, well, he won't take a dime, he won't take a dime from you for his help. You see guys gets ruined by agents and everything else. And Greg Shank has never taken a penny. You came to town, and said, "would you help me?" Greg never hesitated. Greg always kept you focused on achieving your long term goals, not going for the quick buck.

Now that you think of it, Greg kinda abused your butt bad with some of those early long runs.

You were very, very short on mileage when the two of you started working together. Took you a long time to evolve into what Shank calls a long distance runner. You were a 3:59 miler, a five-kilometer specialist. That's really where you wanted to be. You didn't like doing anything past that.

Remember the first time Greg took you out for an hour and forty-five minutes. You had a lot of trouble. Literally fell apart the last couple of miles. Pieces of you all over the road. Took a lot of years to handle that kind of mileage. You can now. You can handle it. Last year, you were running 190 miles in ten days. Then backing off, dropping down to 170, then back up. Today you can do that type of thing with little stress, just the right kind of stress.

Moved up to the marathon, but you've always been very, very careful. Never put marathons back to back. Selected just one for your year. You've been lucky, but you've also been in a situation where you've been allowed to develop slowly. That 2:13 PR should be 2:09 at least.

Training, much easier for you than it was three or four years ago. You're programmed, you don't have to think about what's happening, you just do it.

Remember one day last summer, total heat wave, in a workout you would've had trouble with before... Wouldn't have wanted to do it, based on the conditions, which were awful, but there was a time crunch and you didn't question it at all. You were awesome. That's what Shank says. Actually seemed to relish in the fact you had to run in those kind of conditions.

You did a workout in terrible weather, ninety-two degrees and ninety percent humidity. Not only ran the workout great, you were very aggressive during the entire session. Three years ago, you would have put your head down and said, "'Let's do it some other day."

You feel young. Workout-wise, they've only gotten better over the last eight years. Just continued to evolve. No setbacks. You never get injured. Maybe it's because you're six-feet-one but just one hundred and thirty pounds. Body like a stiletto. Your light and lanky frame has proved a godsend. Unlike bulkier runners, your body has not suffered from the pounding punishment of two decades' competition. Last laugh is yours.

You like to think your career has been an evolutionary process that's working out fine. Never felt like you were slowing down. And you love running. As long as you're getting better, it's a lot of fun.

Half a dozen years ago, you had the reputation of a great workout guy and a guy who would have great races, then some not so great races, or maybe some races where you didn't compete well at all.

Everybody says you're a nice guy, one of the nicest guys in the sport. Shank always told you, some of these guys you're competing with, they aren't so nice. You had to become confident, a little cocky even, and you developed that attitude.

Fear held you back for a lot of years, admit it. But you are not afraid anymore. Fear doesn't play a role today. Now you are pretty aggressive. You stick your ass right out in front and get into the middle of the fray.

You're not sure what you were afraid of. You don't know. You don't know. Maybe you were afraid to really put it on the line. Whatever that means. You're not sure. As much as anything, you stopped having those fears when you got a little success. You don't know, You can't really tell me. You have always loved to compete, so that wasn't a problem. Maybe it was just fear of failing.

Lately, you've been leading. Pushing the pace every chance you get. Takes a brave man to battle fear for years.

You are not afraid anymore.

Imagine you are Chris Fox. You woke up one morning this spring in the best shape of your life.

Won the National twelve-kilometer road championship at Bay-To-Breakers in May, staying with a couple of world-record-type Kenyans much longer than anyone, including you and the Kenyans, would have believed. Had the balls to charge, take the lead up the big hill. Impressed yourself a little.

Once you found out what kind of shape you were really in, all you had to do was qualify and get to the national track championships. Felt pretty confident once you got there, you could make the team. A little track success never hurt a good marathoner.

The original plan was hit Bay-To-Breakers hard, then start getting ready to make the Olympic marathon team in February. Run a few road races. Success on the track doesn't really impact your marathon plans.

The way you look at it, the ten-kilometer just makes you a better marathoner. Strengthens what you already feel about the marathon. The track is only positive and doesn't keep you from wanting to run the marathon. That's your race in '96.

You can always come back and run the track Trials, since you have an Olympic qualifier. At more than one distance even. You have a real good shot at making the oval team, but your energy and your focus is on the marathon.

Haven't really begun preparing for the marathon itself. Track races are speed preparation, some might say. You can feel yourself getting stronger and faster. You'll begin to ease down this month. Get into your marathon training starting about the first of November. You'll roadrace infrequently from October to December, and then that will be it. You probably will not race in December, maybe run one in January, but it's not necessary, you don't think.

You do need to compete to pay your bills. You are, after all, a professional athlete. You've made a bit of money this year, and with the support from Brooks... Sometimes you forfeit immediate gratification for the long term and there is some big long-term money at the Olympic Trials this year. One hundred thousand dollars to the winner. Sometimes you have to sacrifice. You've never lived the Carl Lewis lifestyle, but you haven't missed any meals either. Grew up in a pretty simple lifestyle. Given a choice between 27:29 and driving a Ferrari, you'd take that 27:29.

Bay-To-Breakers to the Olympic marathon is still the plan. That is still the goal with some selected road races in between. Shank is of the opinion too much road racing is not good. One of the reasons you have been able to maintain your competitive running at this late stage is because you haven't run a lot of road races.

Track is stressful, mentally stressful more than physically stressful. An athlete must learn how to concentrate, and that is one thing you have lacked in the marathon. Concentration is an issue because when you are out there for two hours and ten minutes, you have to make sure you monitor what's happening to you and what's going on around you. Some people need to be taught concentration and the track teaches that.

Concentration may be the difference between some of these really good guys and some of the guys who are truly great.

Look at Alberto Salazar, when he first stepped on the line in New York, he was so young, but he had just come off a fast ten-thousand meters effort. That had to help his powers of concentration. Not that he wasn't the kind of guy who could always concentrate.

Point is, your fastest times at other distances don't equate to what you have run to date in the marathon. You can go much faster.

Imagine you are Chris Fox. You say you run best when you are angry. Anger concentrated can prove the focus of a distance runner. The races themselves are more cleansing than anything. Your biggest battles are always about getting there. Maybe that explains the long journey that is your career.

You petitioned for entry into the '95 National track championships. Officials demanded a qualifying time. Your buddies created a meet.

Called it the William "Buzz" Sawyer Invitational. Seven events and sanctioned. Of course, the highlight of the evening, you churning out sub-seventy second laps by yourself. Three other guys in the race but they were getting lapped left and right.

William "Buzz" Sawyer, in case anybody is interested, was a sub-nine-minute two-miler back when there was only a handful of guys doing track. Used to run the indoor circuit back in the Fifties. Sawyer is the founder of the Cumberland Valley Athletic Club.

Of which you are the most famous member.

You placed second at the Nationals. Still can't keep up with Todd Williams. Made the World Championship team. But they demanded another qualifying time.

You have never run that fast. But you know you can.

You had to find a great race to run a great time. The London Grand Prix seemed the proper place but Ian Stewart won't let you into the field. Said you are too slow. You haven't liked him since he outkicked Prefontaine for the bronze medal in Munich. Stewart said he had thirty-three people who could break twenty-eight minutes and you weren't one of them.

You fought it. Made all the phone calls you could. You called Steve Cram's people, Steve Jones made some calls for you. A lot of people went to bat for you. Stewart would just not let you in.

So, you ended up going to Montreal. Angry.

You were a little disappointed because you didn't come expecting a good race. But Rodolfo Gomez' group from Mexico showed up, he probably brought ten people, including two pacesetters.

Pleasant surprise, a beautiful night. Probably sixty degrees and zero wind. Like the Penn Relays at night, there were only about two hundred people there, but they were into it. Turned out to be a nice race. The pacesetters were a little slow at first, so you went to the lead in the first mile. Then the pacesetters got on it. You stayed on them, pushing them and talking to them and got them through five kilometers in 13:56. What must those Latin bunnies have been thinking with this gringo hollering at them. Faster, faster. Beep, beep.

Then Silva Guerrero moved up with you and another Mexican, Jorge Marquez, and you broke the rest of the field. Kept nailing 66s and 67s the rest of the way. You got in a little trouble just past five miles. You backed off and gave those guys about five seconds.

Then you kicked in. Last mile was about 4:21, the last quarter was only like a sixty-two, but it was good enough. You ran 27:53 for third place. 13:56. 13:56. Even splits.

You were racing. You like to race. Trying to win the damn thing. No denying you were aware of the times, because you had to run 28:08 to qualify for the World Championships.

You enjoy racing people. You don't enjoy running against the clock.

During this little hot streak you have going, you spend the entire race thinking solely about how the hell you can win the thing. You were a little more aware of splits this time than normal, of course. You just wanted to make sure the pace stayed hot, that's why you went to the lead four or five times. Just to keep it honest. You went into the race REALLY wanting to break twenty-eight.

Felt like you could go 27:40 next time. I mean, you had to work Montreal. You had to help the rabbits and you had to help after the rabbits. You'd like to get in a race where you don't have to do a thing, and see what happens. Of course, if there are Kenyans running 27:30's, there comes a point where you are just holding on. We'll see. Who knows?

You like to think you can be in the race.

Imagine you are Chris Fox. You were never in the race.

You got into the wrong heat at the World Championships. The first heat, Todd Williams ran 14:20 for the first 5k, before qualifying in 28:13.

Talking numbers off the top of your head, but real close. Which is what you had expected in both heats.

But in your heat, you got caught up in a little African war, between a couple of different tribes, and they just went at it. They reached the half in 13:40 something and then it only got quicker. All you could do is watch. You had run four 10ks on the track just to get there and face it, this was difficult. Before you started the race, Shank told you all you had to do was finish twelfth. If it was under 28:15, you're okay. Which is what you expected. They just went out hard and you were right there for six thousand meters.

Never saw two heats so different. Heat Two, your heat, won in 27:29, was the deepest final in the event's history. The twelfth finisher clocked 27:54 and he didn't make the final. You were next. This event is changing right in front of your eyes.

If you had gotten through the first round, you could've been in the top ten, just about like Todd. Todd looked like he was on the way down and you, face it, were right on the edge yourself. Just got in the wrong heat. Hell, took you a half dozen hard races just to get here.

It was a good learning experience, something that was a little rich for a marathoner. You mentally handled it well, physically no problem.

Already put it behind you.

You wanted to run one more road race, so you went to Falmouth two weeks later and beat Todd over 7.1 miles. Not making the WC finals made you a little fresher. Found yourself again adrift in a sea of Kenyans. Still you went to the lead a couple times. So you felt good about Falmouth, even though you were already showing signs of fatigue going in. First American finisher, only U.S. runner in top seventeen, placed tenth in 32:27, only seventeen seconds off the pace.

"I'm not satisfied with just being the first American," you told the press. Said you weren't as hungry as you should have been. Still pushing yourself.

Eight of the nine guys ahead of you were Kenyans. You are going to have to find a way around these guys.

Can't tell us any secrets or they wouldn't be secrets. For sure, your diet is going to be better than it's been in the past. Got some interesting things you want to try from a distance standpoint. Expect to run thirty miles certainly a couple of times, which you haven't done in the past.

You're an old dog and you need some new tricks.

After Falmouth, you took ten days off. Put on three or four pounds, ballooned. Started seventy miles a week, one run a day, one day off a week. Had it in your mind you wanted to race a couple more times, but Greg talked to you about that and eventually you came around to his way of thinking. You're hungry to train right now. Coach trying to hold you back. Shank making sure you take a day off. Don't want to get stale, go too hard too early.

You're looking at fourteen or sixteen weeks of serious, concentrated dedication. When you make that commitment, November 1, October 29, whatever that Sunday is, everything from thereon is geared around the '96 U.S. marathon Trials in Charlotte. February. When you start getting yourself ready for the biggest race of your life, it's just balls out after that. All it is, is Charlotte, Charlotte, Charlotte, everything you do.

It'll be all Charlotte.

The philosophy is you don't want to go in merely capable of making the team. You want to go into the Trials thinking this is for all the marbles here. You went to Charlotte last year for the Nationals, You were short, you knew you were short, you were supposed to be short. But you're not going to be short this time. You're gonna go right to the very edge.

Imagine you are Chris Fox. You are going to shoot for the moon, because this is probably your last Olympic shot. Realize this is the antithesis of everything your career stands for but you are going to turn up the volume for the marathon.

Try a few different things. Although maybe you don't have to go to the extremes you originally thought you did, because you are not going to extremes now and you are getting results. So, you'll stick to the same program and the same coach, but increase your mileage ten to fifteen percent.

Take a couple of chances. Nothing nuts. You're not going to get hurt. Your big thing is, you never get hurt. That is your big thing. Yup. You never get hurt. Knock on wood. Any luck, you could be the Carlos Lopes of Atlanta. Already as fast as Frank Shorter.

Shorter always ran smart. You ran an ignorant race at the '92 Olympic Trials marathon. Faded in the heat and humidity, finishing seventh.

The '96 Games will be different. One thing Atlanta does, it equalizes the talent a little bit. Comes down to running really smart. If it were perfect conditions, and you had Kenyans and you had Ethiopians, umm, it might be tough, tougher, to medal. Dangerous weather, too dangerous for the biggest race of your life, this makes it easier to medal. Because maybe on a ninety degree day, somebody is going to get a medal with a 2:17 or 2:18. Somebody running smart. Somebody who's not Kenyan.

Charlotte, the Trials. The weather will be good, you're sure of that. Typical U.S. selection process, get a trio of athletes who can perform great when the conditions are perfect then send them to a heatstroke death march. And wonder why they don't perform. Won't be hot in Charlotte in February. Won't be anything like the Olympic marathoners are going to experience in Atlanta in August.

You have run the Charlotte course. Very hilly. You are a very good uphill runner. Teaching yourself to be a better, more relaxed downhill runner between now and that race. Have to do it. That's all there is to it. You didn't prepare on downhills at all and your legs weren't ready to take the downhill pounding they took. You didn't realize the course was as tough as it was. But now you do and you've made adjustments.

You are not afraid to give it all you've got for just one shot. Not afraid. Here's a question. Would I rather run superfast for a season or two or would I rather have a somewhat slower time and a career which goes on for decades?

If you are Chris Fox, you've had that debate quite a few times with your running buddies. For the last twenty years, if you had to be honest, you guess you admit you chose the long and winding track. But now you are getting a taste of the other end of the equation, the fast times.

Before hanging up your spikes, you would like to have both. Maybe a medal, too.

Bob Kennedy: In a Class By Himself
July 1997

Bob Kennedy finds himself an American alone in an event dominated by Africans.

You go to Coos Bay, Oregon. Over to a tidy home with a sturdy fence at 921 Elrod Street, where you are greeted at the front door by his parents, Ray and Elfriede, who serve coffee and cookies.

Later you open a door in the back of the house and go into Pre's bedroom. Pre's bedroom is much smaller than you might guess. But you can feel him there still. In the quiet. The Prefontaine Classic and The Pre Legend remind us the truly great ones come along only so often. Not truly often enough.

Bob Kennedy annually makes a pilgrimage to Eugene, the fabled track capital of Lane County. This year's 3000m is Kennedy's first serious race of the season, heading outdoors after an injury-riddled spring. You expect something special from him. But the race is routine.

Unchallenged, no Africans, he runs a meet record 7:39.22 and doesn't seem particularly winded. Head closely shorn, beard tightly trimmed, he prances through a victory lap, golden bouquet in one hand, waving with the other. Blowing kisses. He bows and smiles, playing to the crowd. He beams. Feels good to be fast.

"I know I am on track to have another great summer, another great season," he says quietly. Kennedy is only 26 years old, already older than Pre ever got to be. And faster. Much, much faster.

In the quiet, sitting with Kennedy, you get the sense – you feel it – he has greatness about him.

You can see the Prefontaine influence, sure, but the man Bob Kennedy reminds you of most is Tiger Woods. Woods is the first black man to win The Masters. Bob Kennedy is the first white man to run under 13:00 for 5k. The first non-African even. Integrating the lead pack of the world's great distance races, he is the Jackie Robinson of track's X Generation.

Among American runners, regardless of ethnic considerations, there is no one remotely close.

"You run under 13:00 and you're set," says Marc (Don't compare me to Dennis Rodman) Davis. "There's nothing you can't get." You can decide for yourself what that might be.

Kennedy ran 12:58.21 last year, breaking his own American Record 12:58.75. He is now the No. 9 performer of all time. He set a couple of records at 3000 meters, the faster at 7:31.69. He knows he will run faster still. Kennedy knows what he wants. Fast times and major medals, medals at major championships.

Thinks he is getting closer. He was ranked No. 4 in the world in 1994. In '96, he was ranked No. 6, but he was nowhere to be found in '95. "I was 11th or 12th. It was just a mediocre year. I was flat. Don't know whether I was resting on my laurels or whether my training was erratic. Whatever."

He ran 13:03 and calls it mediocre. "The event moved and I didn't move with it."

You are puzzled why he is the only American running with the Kenyans.

"I wanted to find out what it would be like to be that fast," Kennedy recalls. "In '94, coach Sam Bell and I, thinking to break 13:00 and do something special, set the goal of a World Record at 5k in '96."

"Two years later, right on schedule, I broke the mark that had been the WR when I set my goal. But by then the game had changed and suddenly I am 14 seconds back."

Kennedy is behind the curve on the international scene and as much as a decade ahead of his countrymen. You have some questions.

Fourteen seconds. What's that worth? Haile Gebrselassie's world record is a full second faster per lap.

"I looked at it as running 61 seconds per lap. That's not unrealistic." Kennedy is the fastest man never to have trained at altitude. He trains in Australia and London and Indianapolis. He has trained with Kenyans but never in Kenya.

12:58? "It doesn't feel any different, no different than 13:05 or 13:50. It depends on if you are going for it all or not. I was going for it and it hurt. It hurt bad. It hurt from the second lap. No. It actually hurt on the first lap. You have to understand it's going to hurt and hurt bad, so you accept that and move on.

"To be honest with you – and this may be part of the problem with the sport – all these races are really time trials. You run as fast as you can and that's where you end up.

"A lot of times I find myself alone in no-man's-land." Can't always stay with the lead pack, too fast for everybody else.

Does Kennedy have a better shot at the 10k record? Is the 26:38.08 by Moroccan Salah Hissou a more realistic target? You can't help thinking, uh, that time is already craziness.

"I am going to race 10k. It's going to happen, probably in '98, probably in Oslo. The distance doesn't scare me. I've run 12k at Worlds Cross-Country." His 10k PR is a cross-country 29:10. He thinks he can go faster. It's okay to go faster.

"I honestly believe I can run under 27:00, maybe even my first time out. I don't mean to suggest it's going to be easy, but," he says with a shrug, "hey, it's two 13:30's." And how tough can that be?

Kennedy is a big Utah Jazz booster. His wife knows the daughter of the coach of Karl Malone.

It's okay to train fast. "I am always doing track stuff," Bob offers. "Even when I am running 110 miles weekly, I'd want to run 800m repeats in the 2:00–2:04 range. Nothing slower. Usually I don't do more than 5000m total in a track workout. Did a workout the other day: 2k in 5:15, 1600m in 4:10, 1200m in 3:06, 800 in 2-flat, 400m in 57. With a 300m recovery."

The Atlanta Games? "I have been on three World Championship teams and in two Olympics, and Atlanta was the first time I was ever really in the race. The medal is right there, it's not far away."

Kennedy was right there when he took the lead with a half mile remaining in the Olympics. The heroic blue U.S.A. singlet, bib #2373, chasing after a major medal. "I didn't do it just to get the applause. I have to put myself in the best position, the position that gives me the best chance to win the race. I knew if I waited until the final 400m, I had no chance. I went with two laps to go. Probably should have gone sooner."

That's about where Pre took off in Munich.

"No, he went earlier," corrects Kennedy. "Pre went with four laps to go.

That's probably what I should have done."

Pre did go early. That was one of his most compelling qualities. Kennedy placed 6th in Atlanta; he thinks gold in Sydney is not unrealistic.

Everybody wants to know if it's scary to go so fast. "You're lying if you say fear is not an aspect of what we are doing," Kennedy admits. Pre hated to lose, couldn't stand it. Pre feared losing. Kennedy loses many more races than he wins.

"I have handled losing well because I know what I am trying to do. I am patient. I can't be patient or complacent about my place on the event's totem pole, because I'm not. You do not want to find yourself falling into that trap." One measure of greatness is your ability to rebound from defeat.

"My fear is getting into a big race and running 13:40, that complete failing feeling," Kennedy admits. "My fear is not being competitive. Dealing with their fear is one of the reasons runners are either good or they are not good."

You can look at Bob Kennedy and see Pre.

"It's a different era, number one. He won more races. He had an aura that drew people to him. I don't know I have an aura like that. I understand people are looking to be entertained by what I do. Pre entertained," Kennedy points out. "His aggressiveness, the tenacity, the desire to win every single race, no matter what it took, that was what separated Pre from the rest."

Wonder why the American public has yet to embrace Kennedy. Guess he has to win some big races. A Nike ad blitz wouldn't hurt. "The thing about me is I'm boring," he admits. "My entire life is, has been, and remains, normal."

Kennedy is the highest paid American distance runner. "I make the most. There's a lot of money in the sport if you're one of the best." If you're slow, there's little dough. "There's no league minimum on the world circuit. They'll pay you how you run.

"Morceli might make $40,000-$80,000 per race. Kiptanui might go at $20,000-$50,000. The numbers go up obviously for a Michael Johnson. And that's just appearance money. Add shoe contacts, prize money... well, let's just say I paid a huge income tax bill this year."

Something Alberto Salazar said about Kennedy bears repeating: "He wouldn't do so much as spit without thinking how it might affect his running." You can look at Bob Kennedy and see Tiger Woods. Focused.

You are tired of hearing about focused, which is after all paying attention to paying attention. Simply paying attention, that doesn't always get it done.

The problem with American distance running is simple. U.S. runners need to learn to run faster. The rest of the world – and Bob Kennedy – knows it's okay to be fast.

Life is like breakfast. Really great running is all about ham & eggs. And you have to think of yourself as part of the meal. Are you a chicken or are you a pig? That's the question an athlete has to ask. Am I a chicken or a pig? A chicken is involved; it supplies the eggs. But his neck's not on the line. A pig is invested, he's committed, because it's a slice right off of his hide headed from the griddle.

Pre was fully invested. Salazar and Buddy Edelen were that way. Jim Ryun, too. Joan Benoit Samuelson and Mary Slaney and Lynn Jennings, the real deal. Tiger Woods is invested, so far. Bob Kennedy is invested.

"It's hard to run with the Africans," Kennedy admits, to no one's surprise. We never thought it would be easy. "It is real hard, the effort during training and during the race, the actual running, but the plan itself is a simple one. It's what everybody already knows. You take all you ever learned from your high school and college coaches and everything you've ever read and you come up with having an adequate base, speedwork, race, rest. Do more each year. Eat right."

He has never looked so slender. He has achieved the level of fitness that causes mothers – not just your own – to rush to the kitchen to cook you a decent meal for a change. 'Eat a burger, sweetie.'

"I am probably a couple pounds lighter than I have ever been. You need to be as light as you can be and still be healthy and strong. Let me caution younger runners, this is what is okay for me now at this time at this level. And it's the result of a lot of miles and good nutrition."

The road to greatness seems well mapped out, even adequately illuminated, for Kennedy, so he can't help wondering why more runners aren't following the same path.

"I am not so naïve I think the way I do things is going to work for everybody," he opines. "But it seems to me it will work for a lot of people."

Goal-setting is also simple. His goals are the same this year as last. A major medal at a major championship. "It's gonna happen. I'm there." The Kenyans can only run three men per event in the Olympics.

"Their dominance is not the Kenyans' fault, it's our fault. What are they supposed to do, go slower? What we have to do is go faster, learn how to keep up with them."

Kennedy is now coached by his London-based agent Kim McDonald, who manages arguably the world's top stable of distance runners. Many of them Africans. The mindset now is toward the world's top level. The peak of the pyramid.

"There are Kenyans who don't make it. There are more Kenyans who don't make it than those who do. But you never read about the guys who wash out. It's like pro basketball in the U.S."

The winner of the Donovan Bailey/Michael Johnson race should have to meet Kennedy over 2500m. "I am the world's fastest white man. I am the only one getting it done right now. But I hope there's a bunch of young guys in this country who can run 13:10. You don't have to run under 13:00, but we need to get people running under 13:20. That's a start."

The chicken doesn't get to fly with the eagles. The pig, if he stays lean and works hard, will eventually run as fast as his legs and dreams will take him. "A perfect example is what happened at the Pre meet," he offers. "When I was young, I was willing to test myself. At Pre I was in a race where the runners didn't even try to go with me."

Bob Kennedy finds that sad. "I do have something I want to say. The U.S.-only road circuit is ludicrous. Why pay for mediocrity? That's really stupid, now isn't it?"

What else?

"The million dollar marathon prize is exciting; it's exciting for its possibility. There's a realistic chance somebody might actually do it. I might drive up to Chicago to see Kempainen or Williams take his best shot." Kennedy wouldn't run a marathon right now for $5 million.

Kennedy dominates his generation in the U.S., but Kenyans rule the world of distance running. The 5K is probably the most competitive event in track right now and Kennedy might as well be an alien from a distant foreign planet. Or even Indiana.

You watch him run with the Africans and you realize he fits right in. "There's not much that separates us," he says. "The Kenyans respect the way I run. I race hard. I train aggressively. When I train with these guys, I am not merely hanging on. Just as often I am the one pushing the pace."

You try to imagine Kennedy actually is African. Sometimes it's the only thing that makes sense. "I only know about three words in Swahili. I know 'hello', 'good-bye' and 'faster.' That's in case the rabbit is Kenyan, which they almost have to be when you are running a 13-minute 5K."

He has made you a 5K fan again.

And you are wondering about something a friend said. Suppose rocket science is easy, she said. We have just been convinced it's difficult, and it's really not so tough. Suppose we have placed such limits upon ourselves that we are afraid even to try.

Suppose it's not as hard to run with the Africans as we think it is. Bob Kennedy is doing it.

He has opened the door to possibilities many others only guess at. Like Pre, like Tiger, Kennedy makes a profound contribution. In raising the bars of expectation, he serves as an example. Follow me.

Where are the rest of you?

Keith Brantly is PR-Driven
June 1998

Why write about a guy who runs 2:12:31? A hundred-thousand reasons. Simple as that. Or maybe not. Keith Brantly wins the national marathon championship on "a bitch of a course," runs a PR, and all anybody wants to talk about is the $100,000 he earned.

Brantly could care less about the money: "I'm really stoked I got a personal record. I haven't been in the right place at the right time and done the right thing since 1993."

The 36-year-old erstwhile 5000m specialist ran his first – and until Pittsburgh, last – big PR of 2:12:49 placing 5th at New York in '93. "That's much easier in terms of effort," he reports. "I'm a better athlete today, smarter and stronger."

That he is racing at all is something of a surprise. Forget the money. Heck, forget the PR. Brantly is just happy to be running without pain: "I was injured most of '97. I tore a hamstring tendon at Crescent City. I thought my career was over. Injuries. That's the reason most athletes get out of any sport. Very rarely are we in control at the end of our careers. I always wanted to be the one who decided when I would get out."

He can make that decision now. He can afford to. "I was really behind the 8-ball. I started back in full this past January. Trained with Jerry Lawson for 7 weeks – not all at once, 7 weeks cumulatively. I'd train with him for a week, then home, spend some time with the family, then head back to Jerry's. I never went above 100 miles per week. I ran 90-95M weekly."

He feels no urge to get into triple-digit mileage, analyzing, "You can always get into triple digits if you measure by kilometers. I've tried higher mileage before but I just end up ragged. Logging a lot of slow miles just to log a lot of slow miles doesn't make much sense unless you need to build a base. Everything I did for Pittsburgh was fast."

Brantly earned his Pittsburgh fortune the old-fashioned way. He worked for it: "The money is not my thing – I want to run fast. Think about it. Took me almost five years to shave 20 seconds off my best time. You have to temper dreaming with realism."

On this day, realism meant a bold move just 11 miles into the race. If this race was a trial run on the Olympic Trials course, would he make a similarly bold move in 2000? "Eleven miles, that's far enough into the race so, if you're an experienced marathoner, if you know the course, if you know yourself... Yeah, I might do the same the next time."

Brantly hasn't put the last Olympics behind him. Still. "I trained like hell for Atlanta; really busted my butt. I based all my preparation upon racing hard over the last 4 miles. Then when I went to press down on the accelerator, I discovered I was out of gas. The tank was empty." He still can't believe it. "I just came up with zero energy.

"Pittsburgh was more important for me than you know. I am so disappointed in my performance at Atlanta. Finishing 28th, I had a crappy race. I ran a good effort. That's the heartbreak of the marathon.

"To me, the marathon is not just a difficult race to prepare for or to run, it's a difficult race to predict. I was ready to go to Barcelona in '92. My family was ready to go. And I didn't make the team. Making the U.S. Olympic team in 2000, that's the sole purpose of my running life."

There are more than a couple of athletes, all faster, all younger, standing in his way. "The bottom line with the Olympic Trials is nothing before that day matters, absolutely not a damn thing," offers Brantly. "I absolutely refuse to believe just because somebody has a PR that's five minutes faster than mine he is going to keep me off the team.

"I want to retire after Sydney. I have other things I want to do, like be a father."

And another big payday? "Everything in my athletic world is running PRs. Money has never been a factor. As corny as it sounds, you cannot give me enough money, absolutely not enough, to replace a PR.

"A PR is better than gold. Or cash money. A PR is tangible evidence you have gone beyond what you could do in the past. It shows you that you have achieved. I like to challenge myself. The money will be long gone but the PR and satisfaction will last forever.

"I realized long ago," continues Brantly, "that money can't buy happiness. A $100,000 can buy me a lot of things but anything I need I already had. You can't purchase time. You can't purchase freedom."

Then there's the road topic *du jour* – Kenyans. "People think I don't train as hard as the Kenyans. I've trained with them, because I wanted to know for myself," Brantly explains.

"And I found out – I do train as hard. I'm simply not as talented. I'm driving as hard as they are, but I don't have as big an engine. They just have bigger engines. Big, big engines."

He doesn't want to see special purses for American runners, explaining, "Frankly, it would be embarrassing for me to win more money than somebody who beat me. I am not interested in being the first American. I am interested in being the first guy to cross the line."

And he isn't interested in being the Fastest Blond Floridian: "It is embarrassing to be mentioned as the first American to cross the line in Atlanta. It's pathetic if you have to reach that far for your accolades. I'd have much rather finished 15th and been the third American."

Keith Brantly runs without pain. A national champion. He is faster than ever. More importantly, for any athlete who yearns for greatness, he has his head screwed on right and tight.

He has all the money he needs.

If he just had a bigger engine.

Chapter Three
Some of the Women

Doris Brown-Heritage (#4) leads a pioneering group at the 1970 AAU
Cross-Country Championships. Francie Larrieu is #83, Beth Bonner #56 & Janet Bristol #29

Same story, different gender. Newsmakers? Back in the day, the ladies were nothing less than great explorers, seeking the outer limits of, well, their limits. Who knew how fast they could go? Who could have guessed how many millions of women would follow?

I remember thinking early on – this is how crazy I am – if I was a female, I would be the 13th fastest marathoner in the world. Not long after, the only way I could keep up was by riding the press truck and getting a head start.

Patti Catalano:
USA's Top Woman Road Runner in 1980
January 1991

Hard work and a lucky clover leaf create a winner

Patti LaTora was a damn good runner. Patti Lyons was even better. Patti Catalano is the best.

Whatever the name on the finishers' list, there is usually no question about the position – Patti Catalano, at age 27, is America's top road racer.

Just look at the record book, which now reads like Catalano's 1980 schedule of appearances. She holds the 10k mark, having won the Bonne Bell Championship in 32:24. She became the first American woman to break 50 minutes for 15 kilometers, winning the Cascade RunOff in 49:42. She set the 10-mile record of 53:40 in winning the Bobby Crim race.

She covered the very hilly Elby 20k (uncertified) in a world-best 1:08:37. And, of course, she set an AR in the marathon in winning at Montreal (2:30:58), then broke that mark in New York City (2:29:34), where she became only the second woman under 2½ hours.

En route times at Bonne Bell (5 miles in 27:04) and Montreal (30k in 1:45:24) give her unofficial, but accurate, national bests. Add her 1979 half-marathon AR of 1:04:04 – a time she missed by only ten seconds this year – and Catalano's records speak for themselves.

Although records don't come easily, Catalano often makes it seem so. Her racing tactics are the simplest: "I just go out and run as hard as I can for as long as I can." The rest of the story is a little more complicated.

There is a joy about Patti Catalano. An atmosphere of sheer exhilaration, an attitude of unrepressed happiness that flows from her very pores. She has an endearing quality which almost shouts, "Hey, look at me! Wow! Isn't this fun?! Can you believe how well I'm doing?! Can anybody be this happy?!"

Every time she wins a race – something she does almost weekly – Patti acts as if it is her initial success. Teeth spread across her face like the grill of a 1958 Buick, she is beside herself with the surprise of the moment.

At first glance an observer might think she is hotdogging it. Acting amazed, the way the smart girls in high school always did when they received superior grades. In Patti's case, she *really* is shocked. She still remembers the fat girl who smoked, and she is simply overjoyed not to be that way any longer. She is ecstatic about being the best road racer in the United States. The "best" of anything is heady stuff.

Such rapture seems childlike. Perhaps it is. Patti has been quoted that she is finally having her childhood. She is experiencing the play that was denied to her as a youngster.

The eldest of nine children, Patti ended up caring for all of them. Both parents worked two or more jobs, so she became both mother and father to her siblings. It was not a carefree life. It was a toughening experience, giving her the self-discipline necessary to work day after day after tiring day.

Work? This woman has always worked. Running is play, even if it is 150 miles per week.

That mileage total is not a misprint. While Catalano does not run 150M a week routinely, she did exceed that amount in preparation for the 1980 New York City Marathon. Ordinarily, she will average 130 miles before a marathon. Even during a recent winter lull, she was covering 13 miles daily, close to 100M a week.

Once a week, there is speedwork. "Nothing short," coach/husband Joe relates. "Usually, we'll do long intervals – repeat halves, 1320s or miles. For instance, we'll run 6-8 times a mile at about 5:25 mile pace."

Of course, since Boston remains a big goal, there are some more specific workouts. Frequently, she will run the legendary Heartbreak Hill 10 times, covering the 600 yards at a 1:46-1:48 average. Remember, she is accustomed to hard work.

"She has so much energy that running alone doesn't use it all up," Joe tells us. It's not surprising then, to learn Patti also does Nautilus weight training thrice weekly.

While Joe and Patti believe this supplementary exercise is probably a contributing factor to her recent progress, they do not attempt to hide the fact that the lifting is not just another way to burn up Patti's excess energy. She *cannot* be allowed to train as hard as she wants.

Patti Catalano's transformation from an obese barroom habitué to world-class athlete has been frequently recounted. A transformation that melted the 150 pounds on her 5-4¾ frame down to 106.

Quite simply, she became tired of wasting her dollars and her time – as well as her life – and decided she had to make a change. She began to run.

Donning a sweatsuit, her most comfortable street shoes and a skin diver's weight belt, our tubby heroine circled a cemetery for 7 miles. The next day, feeling as if she should be planted in her training venue, she couldn't get out of bed.

Two weeks later, she could finally walk again without limping. In another week, she ran again. She was still smoking, but she was a runner. That was less than five years ago.

In September, 1976, Catalano (as Mrs. LaTora) made an important career move – she bought her first pair of real running shoes. She also stopped smoking. The next month she ran her first marathon, winning the Ocean State race in 2:53:40.

Despite this impressive debut, Patti wasn't yet committed to the sport. The weight became to return. She resumed smoking. After a seven-month injury-induced layoff, she renewed her athletic career in June of 1977 and ran 2:47:20 that fall.

Another injury, and the cycle began again – smoking and gaining weight. Then, not quite three years ago, Joe became her coach. When he told her what a great runner she could be, he sounded serious. So, she became serious. The rest, as they used to say in the past, is history.

In 1978 (back to her maiden name of Lyons) Patti lowered her marathon PR to 2:41:32, rated 5th best in the world. She was the No. 3 American Road Runner. In 1979, she dropped to 2:38:22, was rated No. 6 world-wide and rose to No. 2 among U.S. Road Runners. Now she's No. 1.

The breakthrough probably occurred in an event she did not win – the 1980 Boston Marathon. Jacqueline Gareau was the victor in that race, but Catalano's 2:35:08 for 2nd was another PR. More importantly, that race showed her she could be great; she *could* be the very best. That's all Patti Catalano needed to know.

Less than two weeks later, May 4th, she won the prestigious Midland Run, covering 15k in 51:58. Among those in her wake was Gareau.

On May 18 – pausing the day before to marry Joe and affect another name change – she set a since-broken 5M American Record of 26:14. And the next week she set her 20k world best. Keeping up the heavy schedule, on May 31, she chased the incomparable Grete Waitz at the L'Eggs Mini Marathon. Waitz set a 10k WR of 31:00, with Catalano finishing with her fifth PR in six weeks.

Patti also came up with one of the year's better quotes. Asked if she wasn't discouraged to see Waitz so far ahead – Catalano had finished two minutes in arrears — she said, "I wasn't discouraged to see her so far away. I was happy to see her at all."

Catalano is one of the few women in the world who can keep Waitz in sight. She can come closer to the Norwegian than most because of her ability to endure more work than other women. She has also developed the unique ability to avoid injury while at the same time competing frequently.

Finally, she has maintained her enthusiasm. Day after day, mile after mile, race after race. This bespeaks talent and intelligence. Much of it can be attributed to Joe. Few people have the guts and determination of Patti, but no one else has Joe, and he is clearly her greatest asset.

Joe Catalano has been running for 17 years. He has enjoyed modest success as an athlete, covering a marathon in 2:23:22. Yet his best performances are as his wife's coach.

Joe answers the phone, handles the press, negotiates with race directors, plans Patti's training, times her intervals and accompanies her on runs.

In short, he handles every problem that arises and avoids others before they have a chance to interfere with his wife's running. All (?) she has to do is concentrate on putting one foot in front of the other as rapidly as possible.

They play their roles perfectly. "I'm giving 100% of my energy to her, and she gives 100% to her running," Joe points out. "That's our deal and it seems to be working."

One look at Patti's obliteration of the record book in 1980 shows such teamwork is indeed working. There is no end in sight. In addition to winning the Boston Marathon in 1981, the goal set by the Catalanos is to improve all of Patti's times. "The way Patti has been improving, I just can't see any limit," offers Joe. "In the marathon particularly, her potential is unlimited."

Maybe. Maybe not. But how much better does she have to get? Really, she just wanted to lose a few pounds. All that's left for Patti Catalano is to cross the finish line and wait for Grete. With Joe's help, she might just do it.

In 1980, Patti Catalano raced from January into December. Of sixteen races, she won twelve, finished second in three. Five of those races were marathons. Now married to Dan, Patti Dillon had one of the greatest years ever, male or female. Single or married. – JDW

Lynn Jennings: The Throwback
February 1988

A very, very young Lynn Jennings sets the pace

Lynn Jennings seems to be a runner of the old school. I don't mean Princeton, from which she graduated in '83 with a degree in history. I don't mean high school, where she was three-time Massachusetts cross-country champion.

I mean she reminds me of a saner time in this sport, when improvement was more important than a shoe endorsement, when running was *not* a social phenomenon, when Doris Brown could beat anyone in the world.

The greatest cross-country runner in America today (Pat Porter aside), Lynn Jennings races the roads like Bo Jackson plays football – it's a hobby.

"I want to be a track runner," Jennings states. "That's who I am."

Jennings' periodic forays on the road have been successful enough to rank her No. 1 in the U.S. "If I run four or five road races a year and I beat up on people," Jennings points out, "you seem to think that's enough."

It must be more than enough for her competitors. Jennings doesn't race often, but she does race year-round.

"I'm very selective, but I run track, road *and* cross-country," explains Jennings. "If I wanted to make money, I wouldn't run cross-country. I do it because I love it. It's a labor of love."

What Jennings appears to love most about running is *improvement*. Her goals for 1988 are simple – "stay healthy and improve." She's looking for personal records at every distance from 1500m – 10k. With a 4:10 best in the metric mile, Jennings knows she must become quicker to go faster.

"It's not good enough to break 32 [for 10k]," she says. "To be competitive at a world-class level, my times at the shorter distances have to come down. Those Europeans are great at *all* distances."

After finishing 6th at the World Championships, Jennings has some sense of what it might take to win a 10k medal at Seoul. She learned a lesson at Rome.

"There comes a point in an intense distance race where you have to make a decision," she notes, "and I made the wrong decision. And I know why. First, I had no idea what pace I was running. I thought I was running 33:00 and I was discouraged. Secondly, it was an error."

The next time the lead pack tries to pull away from Jennings, she's going right with them.

"I've learned," Jennings confides, recalling Ingrid Kristiansen's back growing smaller. "It's just so rare to run a top quality 10k with women. It's a different feeling racing with traffic all around you all the time."

Jennings learned something else at the '87 World Championships. "I learned I could run a 10k on Monday morning," she says, "in hot weather, and come back four days later to run another quality 10k. That experience will be invaluable this year."

This year is an Olympic year, and Jennings knows her options are many. "The 3000 looks wide open. Too bad there's not a 5k. I think the 10k is wide open, to be honest... in an Olympic year, *everything* is wide open."

One of the reasons, one of the *main* reasons for such wide open spaces, is the intensity and dedication required to fulfill the Olympic dream. It don't come easy.

Jennings has a plan. "I spent nine months getting ready for that one day last year, the World Championships," she explains, in a tone that makes you believe she gave it her best shot. "I made some mistakes, but I know where I can improve."

Jennings doesn't rely too much on the watch. ("Because then you start questioning yourself.") She sets up a schedule, plans where she wants to be, then improvises as she goes.

"I play with my own ideas," she says. "I'm self-coached and I train alone. And I'm definitely woman enough to take two easy days in a row if my body requires it."

Jennings definitely makes sense. She has no plans to run a marathon. "I ran Boston in high school," she remembers, as if speaking about another life. "I feel I have plenty of time. Maybe when I'm 32 or something like that. I haven't even begun to achieve what I want to yet on the track."

Jennings begins to achieve each time she slips on her running shoes. That marathon back in 1978, no more than a childhood lark, was a 2:45. Gives one pause.

Today, Jennings is still much the child. She's queen of the gang in her neighborhood, one of the guys on a street lined with the homes of numerous first-graders.

"I consider myself very young athletically," Jennings offers. "I didn't really have a collegiate career in the sense of scoring points in major meets. I'm still a neophyte."

Jennings uses words like that. Still much the woman, she points out that "improvement is definitely the runner's aphrodisiac."

There's that word again. No, the other one, spike-breath! "Improvement." Jennings seems to use it more than an egomaniac uses the first-person pronoun.

She finished out of the money at the '84 Trials. What's the difference in her ability today? "Light years."

Jennings continues. "First and foremost, I wasn't fit... I deserved everything I got. That's why I'm a *very* hungry athlete, very hungry."

A vegetarian, Jennings points out that in the last four years she has "worked on everything I can work on... mental fitness and physical fitness and all the parameters in between."

So, what about Ingrid and what about the next time the World Champion makes her break?

"I will race very aggressively," Jennings says slowly in a voice that reminds me of Gary Cooper in *High Noon*. "Next time I'm gonna go. And I am going to prepare myself for that specific eventuality. When it comes time to do it in the Big Banana, I'll be ready for it."

Jennings will get ready by finding competition that demands her best, even when she doesn't know what that is. "I can find that competition at 3000m. And I'm planning on racing some 1500s. There are plenty of people in this country who can outrun me..." – she pauses to correct herself – "who have better 1500m times than mine. I plan on finding those people and racing guts-out."

It's a simple philosophy. No secret formulae. Consistency, discipline, quality mileage in the mid-60 range weekly. In her own words: "There's no masseuse, there's no psychologist, there's no handmaiden to carry the spikes. There's no Team Jennings."

It's as simple as can be for Lynn Jennings. She gives no quarter and she asks for none in return.

"I let everyone do what they want and when they show up at the starting line, I race 'em."

Just like the old days.

Soon thereafter I received a handwritten note...

7 March 1988

Jack,

Silly me. I had assumed all along that women had the perceptiveness market all to themselves. You've forced me to change my opinion.

Thank you for a flattering and honestly written story. I feel honored.

Lynn

Sitting Down With Ingrid Kristiansen
May 1989

Talk to Ingrid Kristiansen: you hear in her words the same strength – the same intensity and dedication – that is so apparent in her every perform-ance.

Watch Kristiansen run. Her face is often tense, her shoulders cocked, always pushing, always pushing ahead. You see in her movement the same integrity, the same desire, the same sense of purpose that is so apparent in her conversation.

This woman, world record holder in the 5000, 10,000 and marathon, is Emil Zatopek's equal in more ways than one.

I recently talked to her at her adopted home in Colorado after watch-ing her stride to another impressive win, at the Boston Marathon.

JDW: Let's talk about Boston. What were your aims this year?

IK: Of course, going in, it was 2:20. Every year I go for 2:20.

JDW: Was there any special importance placed on racing against Joan Samuelson?

IK: She's a great runner, but it's been four or five years since she was really good. It's more history. There were other girls in the race.

JDW: Were you trying to reestablish your reputation?

IK: No, I don't think so. The sport is tough. You have no playback. It's not easy. You have to train and train and train some more. You have to keep on going if you want to be on top. I went to Boston hoping to beat the best. That's what this was all about.

JDW: Tell me about your preparation. You ran a number of road races – all part of a plan?

IK: Part of the plan, of course. I train a lot – 140 miles a week. For weeks. Most of it, the distance is really slow, between 4:15-4:20 per kil-ometer. [That works out to 6:50-6:55].

I do "test" training. If I want to run a marathon under 2:20, I must run 5:15-5:18 miles. I have to practice that. So, three or four times a week I do 10k–30k on a treadmill at that pace. I never go on the track to train for the marathon.

JDW: That amount of treadmill work would drive me to suicide!

IK: [Laughs] It's good mental training, especially for the women's races. Because the best runners go to different races, so you have to be prepared to go far and fast by yourself.

Half of marathon racing is to keep on going when you're tired. That's why it's so tough for track racers to go beyond 30k. It's a different sport, to keep going when you're that tired.

JDW: Are marathons and track races of equal importance to you? Do you favor one over the other?

IK: I enjoy both. I look at my seasons. Winter, I train for a spring marathon. Then I rest for two weeks. Then I train for track season. Then I rest a little bit. Then I start long runs again for a fall marathon. I like always changing. It helps my training to be more interesting, and therefore I am able to train better.

JDW: Back to Boston. Tell me about the race itself. You finished 26th overall. That in itself is pretty amazing.

IK: I was really prepared. I think it's a great race. I hoped Joanie would be in better shape. I hoped maybe Rosa [Mota] would be there. I hoped for better weather. It was too warm for a great race.

JDW: I saw you race at the Red Lobster 10k in Orlando in March. Liz McColgan was in a class by herself. Do those kind of days bother you as a competitor?

IK: I was really disappointed to be beaten by a full minute. But I was training for the marathon. I was not ready in February; this summer I will be ready and I hope to race her then. She's a woman who really wants to go for it. I like that about her.

It would be good if more of the better women could compete against each other more often. There can only be one winner, but it's much nicer with others to compete against, not just always yourself alone.

JDW: What are your goals, besides 2:19:59?

IK: I go for a new goal now, sub-30:00 on the track. I am training for that now. I think it's possible. It's just a half-second per lap. So, I'm training for that. Maybe Bislett. Maybe the middle of August. We'll see.

I am a person who wants a goal far ahead of me. To train as hard as I'm doing, you need a big goal.

JDW: Anything else?

IK: Of course, I would like an Olympic gold medal. And to win the New York City Marathon. I'm not sure about after 1992. I might take a year off.

JDW: Anything about the sport that you find bothersome right now?

IK: I am very disappointed I almost never get to run against the best girls. I don't think that's good for the sport. We almost always seem to each of us be at different races.

For several years I wasn't invited to the New York City Marathon. Last year they did invite me, but I was injured, so I couldn't compete.

In order for the sport to grow, I think we should do all we can to get the best together. That's the most fun. That makes all the hard work worthwhile.

JDW: What has been your most disheartening loss?

IK: Finishing 4th in the Olympic Marathon in 1984, because in that race I didn't use my head. I do another person's race and I lose the whole thing... [sighs] But that's a long time ago.

JDW: What was the impact of your DNF in the Olympic 10k?

IK: I was really disappointed. But it's history now and I don't think about it much. I have to look ahead to new races.

JDW: Did it take you long to recover from that disappointment?

IK: No, not too long. Two or three days. I did have to take a rest for seven weeks for injury, but I believe you can't use your energy to think about what might have been. I looked forward to beating my competitors in the next 10k.

JDW: How would you sum up your career at this point?

IK: Ahhhhh... I've been happy with most races. I have improved most years. If I had to do the life all over again, I would do it.

JDW: What do you think your greatest strength as an athlete is?

IK: I don't know, maybe... one of the things... I don't look behind. I try to look ahead, always ahead to new things. If I run a great race, I put it behind me the next day.

Here, it's tougher than in Norway. In Norway nobody tells me I'm a great runner. They keep your feet on the ground. Here, in the U.S., I have to be careful not to think of myself as someone special.

JDW: How do you prepare mentally for a race?

IK: For big races, like the Boston Marathon, when I'm training hard, I think about the race. I visualize the event. The same for a track race. I visualize what I hope will happen, how I hope I'll feel. I might run the entire race in my head twenty times before I actually compete.

JDW: Why did you relocate to Boulder?

IK: I like Boulder. It's not too big, it's relaxing. Of course, you miss home, but it's a nice place to train. My husband is getting a Master's in business and, even though we've only been here a little while, we have so many friends. It is also important to us to learn about America, and Americans, and the American style of life.

JDW: What about the altitude?

IK: Oh, yes, of course. One of the reasons we chose Boulder was the high altitude. I've been training for 20 years, and to move ahead you have to look for ways to do more. I think the altitude adds 10-15% more work without actually doing more training.

JDW: I'm curious about something. It was warm at Boston, yet I noticed you were wearing gloves. Any special reason?

IK: I always race in gloves. I wear contact lenses, and I use the cotton gloves to take away the sweat. Also, sometimes when it's hot, you can wear the gloves and cool your hands.

JDW: Your little boy, Gaute, is going to be six years old. It seems that when you returned to competition after childbirth, you were much stronger. So much so that other women were talking about getting pregnant just to improve their performances.

IK: I think you do get stronger, but you also have a child you have to take care of. You don't get as much sleep. You have to change your lifestyle. It's not so easy.

But at the same time, now, my life has more than running. There's more to give my life meaning. I just think about running when I'm training and competing. The rest of my time, I think about being a mother, and a wife, and...

JDW: And what's ahead?

IK: If I feel happy with my running, I will continue to compete. I'll really go for it, probably the last time, in 1992...

Maybe I could coach somebody one time.

JDW: Joan Samuelson said at Boston, "Anyone who doesn't think that Ingrid Kristiansen is the best runner in the world is only kidding themselves." How do you feel when you hear that?

IK: I feel it was really nice of her to say. [laughs.] I'm not sure she's right. I like Joanie because she is a really nice person, a nice personality. We have similar interests. We're both mothers and we both like to stay home.

You have to keep on training. I would like to show that I am one of the best.

Is Race Walking Some Weird-Looking Shit or What?
August 1995

Dateline. LaGrange, Georgia. October 1995.

I have race walked exactly once. The same number of times I have performed many another bizarre or chancy act.

Some things a person need not try but once.

Too many years ago to count, I was in college somewhere out west, at very high altitude, and it was the Campus Indoor Track & Field Championships. To score valuable points for my intramural team, Sisu Striders, I entered the one-mile race walk.

I am not too proud. Young, tremendously fit and not a little stupid, I figured, "How tough could it be, right?"

Thank God this happened before the advent of video cameras. I looked like a giant heron in heat, smoking meth, doing the funky chicken. Jurassic Stork. Kept wanting to break into a run. Take flight. Managed to gut my way around the many highly banked laps in less than ten minutes. Hips and knees completely messed up. The mere memory of that race stiffens my still aching back.

Is race walking some weird-looking shit or what? – JDW

Michelle Rohl rolls, just like her name is pronounced, over the women walkers in the United States. She rules. She holds the American record with a personal best of 44:17 for ten kilometers. Did that at the recent World Championships. She's a leading candidate for next year's Olympic team. Rohl is the reigning queen of her sport, you might say.

Queen mother. In her own home, the thirty-year-old needs all her stamina chasing after those two little tykes. Molly, an athletic four, and Sebastian, two. They're allowed to run. Walkers must, of course, always maintain unbroken contact with the ground. Mom not much bigger than the kids herself. She's small, tiny even at four feet and eleven inches.

Ninety pounds on a humid day.

Michelle is, in fact, a brilliant runner. Fast. Fifteen times during her collegiate career, track and cross-country, Rohl was named to the All-American team. Twice indoor national champ. Very fast. Rohl didn't take up race walking until after her graduation from the University of Wisconsin at Parkside in 1989.

"I switched from running to race walking for financial reasons mostly," Rohl admits. "I was trying to run fifteen hundred meters and having a hard time getting to races where there was good competition. I was going broke. I didn't have a sponsor. We ran our credit cards up to the limit. We just couldn't afford to fly me to any more races.

"It came down to my last chance to qualify for the national championships. Mike DeWitt, my coach, suggested I try to qualify in the walk. I could get to walking races. Where I was living then, there are a lot of race walks, and a lot of race walkers who would be competitive with me at that time. So I didn't have to travel.

"Also, I knew I had a better chance to make the National team. And if I did that, I would get more support. Not a lot more, but a bit. I had never even walked ten kilometers before. Never walked more than a mile."

She hit the qualifying time with a minute or so to spare. Went and placed tenth in the nationals. Which meant she was the tenth best walker in the country. A month after she became a racewalker.

Mike DeWitt is one hell of a coach.

Progress was swift. Less than two years after giving birth to her first child, Rohl showed up at the starting line of the '92 Olympic Trials.

"I wasn't completely sure I'd make the team, but I thought I had a pretty good shot," Michelle recalls. "It's easier to come back to walking than running."

Rohl brought the baby with her. "It was a big help bringing Molly," Rohl says. "She helped keep my mind off the race. I went out controlled and waited for people to fall back. Even when I was in sixth place, I was confident I could finish third. At the end, my biggest worry was not to get disqualified. I was warned twice during the race, so I had to keep concentrating."

Husband Mike attended the University of Wisconsin at Parkside on a racewalk scholarship. UW@P is the only college in the U.S.A. which offers an athletic scholarship for racewalking. You are not surprised. He is still walking. Still not surprised.

Today, Mike, a former cross-country coach at Wisconsin, is an assistant at West Georgia College, where he also pursues a master's degree in English. He's training, in his spare time, for a race walking berth on the U.S. Olympic team.

In August, 1993, the couple moved south to participate in the I Train In LaGrange Program. Which more towns should offer. The community is close to Atlanta, the venue of next year's Olympics. There's free housing in a little house on Fannin Court. And good coaching.

Southern hospitality seems intact. "We've had people show up at workouts with muffins for us," Michelle smiles at the memory. There is such a thing as a free lunch.

"LaGrange has been really good to us," offers Rohl. "It was lucky I was living here this year, because they provide physical therapy. These are things the top runners in the country have, but most racewalkers don't have access to. That's one of the reasons we have a harder time competing, because we don't have access to a lot of the help other athletes take for granted.

"Being able to get that therapy, I am sure made the biggest difference. If I hadn't had the PT available, I'm sure I wouldn't have been able to get through my race at World Championships. The town is supportive. If we ask for something, they'll try to do it for us. They'll help us with child care. Any little thing. If we're trying to get to a race that's nearby, they'll provide a van for us."

Michelle didn't get into the event for the glamour, prestige, wealth and fame, which inevitably avoids race walkers like they have some contagious disease. She works some twenty hours a week at the First Baptist Church nursery. Michelle needs the money.

"Actually, I've made more money from running than race walking." She laughs. "Not very much."

"Financially, it is very hard to train because you can't work full time," Michelle points out. "Living near Milwaukee was very expensive. When we decided to train for the Olympics, we made a conscious decision not to look for good paying jobs because a job like that would occupy all our time, and we would have to neglect training."

Because Mike must use the family car to commute to work, forty-two miles each way, longer than a 50k and 10k combined, Michelle has to be resourceful to get the kids around town. The Rohls' second vehicle is a Radio Flyer, a little red wagon she uses to pull the kids to the store for grocery shopping or to the library for children's story hour.

"About a mile and a half from our house is my limit pulling them in the wagon," says Michelle. Of course, the littlest Rohls grow bigger and heavier every day.

Just another training advantage motherhood bestows.

Technique is critical.

"I am mostly working on my form to be fast and to be legal," Michelle explains. "We have two rules. First, bent knee, which doesn't apply much to me. Bent knee means your leg has to be straight when it passes under your body. Lifting: you always have to be in contact with the ground. That's more of a problem, of course, when you're going faster. When one foot is coming up, the other has to be on the ground."

Most walkers get more lifting penalties than bent knee. If Rohl gets disqualified, and she has been, look for lifting calls.

"In a way, my size has hindered me here," Michelle suggests. "I have shorter legs, so I have a faster turnover, and a lot of these judges don't know what to do with that. They have a harder time seeing if I'm off the ground.

"When I was first starting, my coach said I was the only person he'd told to lengthen their stride. He's always telling people to shorten their stride for walking. He told me to lengthen mine, because the judges just couldn't handle it.

"I am a toe-runner, so it was really hard for me to convert to race walking which demands you move heel-toe," Michelle explains. "I have very strong calf muscles, which makes it hard for me to land on my heel and get my toes up. I really had to work at that when I was starting out. I have to spend a lot of time stretching my calves, making sure I can get my toes up.

"Usually, when people get called, it's not because they are purposely trying to cheat. Their form is breaking down. They are trying to go faster than they're ready to go. You get tired, mentally as well as physically. Mostly, lifting is physical. A lot of people get bent knees because they become injured and they start hurting in the later part of the race. Then they can't straighten their leg.

"If you lose your technique in the middle of the race, it's really hard to get back into it. It's just easier to keep walking, to do it right the whole way. If I don't concentrate my entire race about keeping my arms down and my toes up, then I'll start lifting. It's probably more of a mental thing with me, I guess, now that I think about it. I have to really concentrate my whole race. Keeping my toes up. Keeping my arms down. You wouldn't think the arms down would have much to do with lifting, but, for some reason, it does."

Is she maybe a little paranoid about her form? "I worry about the judges more than a lot of athletes do," she admits. "I think I am paranoid about the judges. Maybe not my technique. I'm paranoid about the judges in the U.S. I'm not paranoid about the international judges. It's kind of a political thing. Like any sport. There are certain judges who are going to like you and others who aren't. You just have to hope the ones who like you are going to be there. Most of them do like me these days.

"You have to pay your dues in this sport. In the U.S. I always like to clarify that, because in other countries the judging isn't like it is here. I think we have a problem with judging in our country. When I first started race walking, I had a hard time getting past the judges, because they didn't know who I was. I was up in the front and they're asking themselves, 'Who is she?' Next thing you hear, 'We don't know what she's doing wrong, but she couldn't possibly be walking that fast.' So, they give you a call."

Not all judges. "We have some good judges," says Michelle. "But it only takes three to disqualify you. That used to be frustrating. But once I made the Olympic team, I had a lot less trouble."

"My philosophy about judges," offers DeWitt, "is that you got to learn how to walk to please them. Whatever that takes. It might slow you down sometimes, but in the long run you are only helping yourself."

The Eastern Europeans are a couple of minutes faster.

"They used to be four minutes faster," Michelle rushes to note. "I've improved by a couple of minutes since I had Sebastian, I can still cut at least another minute off them. They never walk that fast in big competitions. Usually they walk those fast times at home, where they have judges who like them. Unfortunately, I don't have judges who like me at home."

She laughs. "So I can't do those times."

She walks seven-minute miles. A good judge can tell if you are using good form. The best men in the world go six minutes a mile. The judges can tell when the men are lifting.

"The rule is what is perceivable to the human eye. So, if an athlete is lifting and you can't see it, then it's not illegal," Michelle says. "Somebody did a study once at a major international race, and they discovered that everybody is actually lifting a little bit every step of the race, but you can't tell. It's just so minute, they're only off the ground for such a tiny fraction of a second, there is no way anyone could ever see it."

Sometimes the foot is quicker than the eye.

Michelle Rohl is a talent.

"Michelle is such a fiery competitor," notes DeWitt. Glows. Burns.

"She's exceptional," a totally unbiased Mike Rohl exclaims. "As a coach, having coached my own teams, I've not worked with an athlete as exceptional. She is tough. She doesn't think it, but she's so mentally cued into what she's doing. She may not be able to tell you how she trains well. 'I just do what my coach says,' she'll say. That's part of her mental toughness. She's tough enough in her mind and has enough trust to not question what she is doing. Just that her coach has said she can do this, so she believes she can do it.

"I'll look at the workouts and say, 'I don't even know if I could do this workout.' She'll say, 'I can do it. If Coach thinks I can.' Then she goes out and does it. And she does it by herself. That's a key factor."

The Rohls run cross-country in the fall. "When I'm in serious training, I can spend up to an hour and a half on technique," Michelle relates, "and forty-five minutes of stretching. Every day. I don't do it all together. I'll do weights every day, alternating upper and lower body."

Remember, she weighs ninety pounds. Boy, those weights must be working, huh. "The meat of my workout will take a couple hours, so I can train as much as five hours daily when I'm doing my serious training. Although I've kinda decided it's not worth training that many hours. A lot of it is technique work, where I'm going a hundred meters down, and a hundred meters back.

"On Mondays I do long intervals. Two miles, a mile and a half, one mile. All uphill. Tuesdays, I'll do a threshold workout, which is a mile easy, then three to eight miles at threshold pace, then another mile easy. As the season progresses, this workout gets longer. On Wednesday, I racewalk an hour easy. Thursday, I do short intervals. Fridays, an easy half hour or so, and Saturday, I race. Sunday, I go long, an hour and a half, or so. I don't worry about the pace too much.

"I train a lot less miles than most racewalkers train. I maybe do fifty miles a week. I haven't been keeping a log lately. I'm not doing morning workouts right now, just one workout a day. I'm going to start doing morning workouts next week."

One wonders what makes her special. "I am a good athlete," Michelle suggests after some thought. "The reason I've had success in walking in the U.S. is that most walkers are people who didn't have any success at running, they're kinda mediocre athletes who switched to racewalking, hoping for some success because the competition isn't as deep. My coach always says, people ask him how he made me an Olympian so fast. He replies, 'Give me any 4:20 fifteen hundred meter runner and I'll give you a forty-five minute ten kilometer walker.' That's where my success lies, simply the fact that I'm a good athlete."

She is coachable. "Michael says, mentally tough," Michelle agrees. "I am mentally tough. My coach will give me my goals and my race plan, and I don't like to not achieve them. I'm driven to always have things exactly the way they're supposed to end.

"Winning," she adds.

Oh, Michelle Rohl has had her broken moments, too.

She doesn't like getting disqualified. Not surprising. "This is a serious problem," Mike Rohl rues. "When she gets disqualified, it's very upsetting. She's not happy for a week or two. Last year, at the nationals in Buffalo, where she got DQed, the only time in the last two years, she was going to quit racewalking."

Michelle was in tears on the side of the track. "Her knee was hurting, her technique wasn't right," Mike Rohl remembers. "I had to tell her, 'you have to quit fooling around. You have to get over this stuff, it's part of the sport. Or you have to quit and go back to running. I don't care what you do. But you're not going to mope around, complaining about being a race walker, you're going to get on with it.' She decided to get back up and go train."

And she came back at a higher level.

"I find that amazing," Mike says. "I tell my athletes that Michelle is basically my hero, because she just does everything she's supposed to do."

Weird.

The Rohls do very little training together when they get serious, because she's preparing for a six-mile race and he thirty-two miles. "Also, if we don't train together, then we don't have to pay for a baby sitter as long," Michelle notes. "We really don't like to train together too much anyway. We get on each other's nerves."

She laughs. Mike laughs.

Is racewalking weird-looking or what? "I never thought it was weird-looking," Mike demurs. "Even when I was a freshman in high school and I saw it for the first time, I thought it was kinda cool. I always thought the racewalk was a graceful movement."

Surprising.

"We don't like to talk about weird-looking," Coach DeWitt says. "If people think walking is weird-looking, how weird is a guy racing, carrying a long pole and jumping over a bar that's twenty feet up in the air? Then dropping two stories, hoping the mat's still there. How about somebody throwing a bowling ball sixty, seventy, feet. Same thing."

Is racewalking beautiful then? "I don't know if beautiful is the right word," says DeWitt, a great walker himself. "When an athlete is walking with excellent technique on an excellent day, cruising along real good, I'll tell you what, it looks as good as anything else in track & field.

"As far as people giggling, this thought usually calms quite a few of the skeptical," adds DeWitt, "when we're doing a good long distance training walk, the top walkers will be covering a marathon in three and a half hours. Helps you appreciate it."

In training. Do the math.

I have this image of Michelle, the Olympian. She finished twentieth at Barcelona in the ten kilometer walk, first American, telling herself, 'slower, slower, don't run, slower, you're starting to run.' Is race walking weird or what?

Michelle claims she never has a big desire to just start running. "I have a big desire to start running when I'm not walking. I would rather run. Race walking isn't my favorite sport."

That's weird. "It's no problem, except the first couple of weeks after a long layoff. Takes me a while to get back into my race walking technique, and it's hard to stay on the ground. I am a good tactical racer, because Coach gives me a very detailed race plan, and it always works. I trust him. I know the plan he gives me is going to work.

"I think my race plan is the best; it works for me. People don't think it's going to work, people keep saying, you're not going to win that way, you're not going to get faster that way. But I keep beating them."

Basically, the plan is nothing weird. "I walk an evenly paced race. I don't go out above my head," Michelle says. "Especially in walking that's important, because if you go out too hard, your technique is going to break down in the end. So, even if you try to hang on, you may get DQed. I try to stay with the pack. It's better if you're in a pack, rather than walking alone, because the judges only have one person to focus on then.

"In walking, one thing that's different than what I was doing when running, is my kick, the finishing sprint, has to be a lot longer. And less obvious. You can't just wait until the last hundred meters and then sprint in, because there are going to be four judges on that last hundred meters, for sure. You've got to start kicking with like eight hundred meters to go. Slowly picking up the pace. You don't want anything to be noticeable when you're walking. A lot more discrete than running."

Did somebody say Olympics? "I really don't want to think about the Olympics," Michelle says. "I need to concentrate on getting to the Trials first. It's never a sure thing. Especially in racewalking." Take it just one step at a time.

"I've decided I am not going to change anything about my training in preparation for the '96 Olympics. Because right now I'm on top," Michelle affirms, "and it would be silly for me to switch things around, just because it's the Olympic year. It's been working for me so far. I'm going to run cross-country, because I always run cross-country. Then I'll walk the indoor season. I may go to Europe for a couple of races in the spring, because they put on better racewalking races there. Aim then for the Olympic Trials."

Step by step.

Is racewalking weird-looking or what?

"I guess you'd have to say it's weird-looking," says Michelle. "In Europe, it's different. There are so many more racewalkers. They love track & field over there and they accept racewalking as simply another event in a great sport."

On an even par with, say, the sledgehammer throw.

Mike Rohl developed his love for racewalking while attending Averill Park High School in Chatham, New York, back in the mid-Eighties. Back then, back there, race walking was actually a legitimate event in a prep track & field meet. Mike's first place finish in the walk helped his team, the Warriors, capture a conference title. "One of my claims to fame," he says.

A senior, undefeated that season, Mike beat his arch rival by a tenth of a second. "The race was, the two of us the whole way exchanging the lead. And if I won the race, we'd win the conference championship by two points.

"Looking back on all the things I've done, it wasn't really a defining moment. What was more memorable to me, was not that I won, but what struck me, this was the last time my arch rival and I were going to race where it mattered to the team. At the end, after the fierce competition we'd waged, all we did was catch each other. All we could do was hold each other up, because we were both so exhausted."

Know just what he means. A real competitor would do anything, even race walk, to help his team win. Or her team.

Race walking is not weird. Just looks, umm, a little out of step. And nobody laughs at a winner. It's a rule.

Interview with Michelle & Mike Rohl
October 1995

"I've been taking it easy since the World Championships. Nothing competitive.

"I had a lot of fun at the WCs and I had a real good race. I was really happy with it. They put on a nice event there. Our race was fast. Flat, fast course, I was happy with it."

The eastern Europeans are a couple of minutes faster.

"They used to be four minutes faster. I've improved by a couple of minutes since I had Sebastian, I can still cut at least another minute off them. They never walk that fast in big competitions. Usually they walk those fast times at home, where they have judges who like them. Unfortunately, I don't have judges who like me at home." She laughs. "So I can't do those times."

"We have two rules. First, bent knee, which doesn't apply much to me. Bent knee means your leg has to be straight when it passes under your body.

"Lifting is the other style rule: you always have to be in contact with the ground. That's more of a problem, of course, when you're going faster. When one foot is coming up, the other has to be on the ground.

"Most walkers get more lifting penalties than bent knee. If I get disqualified, it'll be lifting calls."

She used to be a fine runner. "It's no problem, except the first couple of weeks after a long layoff. Takes me a while to get back into my race walking technique, and it's hard to stay on the ground.

"Also, I am a toe-runner, so it was really hard for me to convert to race walking which demands you move heel-toe. I have very strong calf muscles, which makes it hard for me to land on my heel and get my toes up. I really had to work at that when I was starting out. I have to spend a lot of time stretching my calves, making sure I can get my toes up."

She never has a big desire to just start running. "I have a big desire to start running when I'm not walking. I would rather run. Race walking isn't my favorite sport.

"If you lose your technique in the middle of the race, it's really hard to get back into it. It's just easier to keep walking, to do it right the whole way.

"Usually, when people get called, it's not because they are purposely trying to cheat. Their form is breaking down. They are trying to go faster than they're ready to go. You get tired, mentally as well as physically. Mostly, lifting is physical. A lot of people when they get bent knees, it's because they get injuries and they start hurting in the later part of the race. Then they can't straighten their leg."

Lifting? "If I don't concentrate my entire race about keeping my arms down and my toes up, then I'll start lifting. It's probably more of a mental thing with me, I guess, now that I think about it. I have to really concentrate my whole race. Keeping my toes up. Keeping my arms down. You wouldn't think the arms down would have much to do with lifting, but, for some reason, it does."

Is she maybe a little paranoid about her form? "I worry about the judges more than a lot of athletes do", she admits. "I think I am paranoid about the judges. Maybe not my technique. I'm paranoid about the judges in the U.S. I'm not paranoid about the international judges. It's kind of a political thing. Like any sport. There are certain judges who are going to like you and others who aren't. You just have to hope the ones who like you are going to be there."

"Most of them do like me these days. You have to pay your dues in this sport. In the U.S. I always like to clarify that, because in other countries the judging isn't like it is here. I think we have a problem with judging in our country.

"When I first started race walking, I had a hard time getting past the judges, because they didn't know who I was. I was up in the front and they're asking themselves, 'Who is she?' Next thing you hear, 'We don't know what she's doing wrong, but she couldn't possibly be walking that fast.' So, they give you a call.

"Not all judges. We have some good judges. But it only takes three to DQ you. That used to be frustrating. But once I made the Olympic team, I had a lot less trouble."

She walks seven-minute miles. "A good judge can tell if you are using good form. The best men in the world go six minutes a mile. The judges can tell when the men are lifting.

"The rule is, what is perceivable to the human eye. So, if an athlete is lifting and you can't see it, then it's not illegal.

"Somebody did a study once at a major international race, and they discovered that everybody is actually lifting every step of the race a little bit, but you can't tell. It's just so minute, they're only off the ground for such a tiny fraction of a second, there is no way anyone could ever see it.

"I switched from running to race walking for financial reasons mostly. In '89, which was my first year running after college, I was trying to run 1500m and having a hard time getting to races where there was good competition. I was going broke. I didn't have a sponsor. We ran our credit cards up to the limit getting to races. We just couldn't afford to fly me to any more races.

"It came down to my last chance to qualify for the national champion-ships. My coach said, well, you can try to qualify in this race but there is going to be nobody within thirty seconds of you. Or you can try to qualify in the walk. I could get to walking races. Where I was living there are many race walks, and a lot of race walkers who would be competitive with me at that time. So I didn't have to travel.

"Also, I knew I had a better chance to make the National team. And if I did that, I would get more support. Not a lot more, but a little bit.

"I had never even walked a 10k before. Never walked more than a mile. But I qualified for nationals when I tried to do it.

"Actually, I've made more money from running than race walking. Not very much.

"5k PR is 16:38. I ran a 4:20 1500m. I ran everything in college from 400m to 10k. I remember my 8k PR is 27:17. My marathon PR is 2:48:55. My only marathon. At Columbus."

What's the impact of your size? "There are race walkers of all different sizes internationally. Seems like in the U.S., walkers tend to be tall and thin, but it doesn't seem that way internationally. In a way, my size has hindered me here. I have shorter legs, so I have a lot faster turnover, and a lot of these judges don't know what to do with that. They have a harder time seeing if I'm off the ground, I think.

"When I was first starting, my coach said I was the only person he'd told to lengthen their stride. He's always telling people to shorten their stride for walking. He told me to lengthen mine, because the judges just couldn't handle it.

"I just walked a 44:17 10k road AR at the WCs. I hold the track AR of 44:41 set last year at the '94 Goodwill Games. My PR for 5k is 21:59. That's kind of a weak PR for me actually. I walked almost that fast for the first 5k of my record 10k.

"There are *so many walkers* right now. It's such a fast growing sport.

"I am a good tactical racer, because my coach gives me a very detailed race plan, and it always works. I trust him. I know the plan he gives me is going to work. I would say, I'm a good strategist, but I'm very coachable. I think my race plan is the best, it works for me. People don't think it's going to work, people keep saying, you're not going to win that way, you're not going to get faster that way. But I keep beating them.

"Basically, the plan is nothing strange really. I walk an evenly paced race. I don't go out above my head. Especially in walking that's important, because if you go out to hard, your technique is going to break down in the end. So, even if you try to hang on, you may get DQed. I try to stay with the pack. It's better if you're in a pack, rather than walking alone, because the judges only have one person to focus on then.

"In walking, one thing that's different than what I was doing when I running, is your kick has to be a lot longer. And less obvious. You can't just wait until the last 100m and then sprint in, because there are going to be four judges on that last 100m for sure. You've got to start kicking with like 800m to go. Slowly picking up the pace.

"You don't want anything to be noticeable when you're walking. A lot more discrete than running."

Is race walking weird- looking or what?

"I guess you'd have to say it's weird-looking. In Europe, there are so many more racewalkers. They love track & field over there and they accept racewalking as simple another event in a great sport.

"On a par with, say, the hammer throw even.

"I'm running cross-country now. When I'm in serious training, I can spend up to an hour and a half on technique, 45 minutes stretching. I don't do it all together. I'll do weights every day, alternating upper and lower body."

Some of the Women

She weighs 90 pounds. Boy, those weights are working, huh.

"The meat of my workout will take a couple hours, so I can train as much as 5 hours daily when I'm doing my serious training. Although I've kinda decided it's not worth training that many hours. A lot of it is technique work, where I'm going 100m down, and 100m back.

"I train a lot less miles than most racewalkers train. I maybe do 50 miles a week. I haven't been keeping a log lately. I'm not doing morning workouts right now, just one workout a day. I'm going to start doing morning workouts next week.

"On Mondays I do long intervals. 2M, 1½, 1m, all uphill. Tuesdays, I'll do a threshold workout, which is 1M easy, then 3-8 miles at threshold pace, then another mile easy. As the season progresses this workout gets longer. On Wednesday, I racewalk an hour easy. Thursday, I do short intervals. Fridays, an easy half hour or so, and Sat. I race. Sunday, I go long, an hour and a half, or so. I don't worry about the pace too much."

Your strength? "I am a good athlete. The reason I've had success in walking in the U.S. is that most walkers are people who didn't have any success at running, they're kinda mediocre athletes who switched to racewalking hoping for some success because the competition isn't as deep. My coach always say, people ask him how he made me an Olympian so fast. He replies, give me any 4:20 1500m runner and I'll give you a 45-minute 10k walker. That's where my success lies, simply the fact that I'm a good athlete.

"I am coachable. Michael says, mentally tough. I am mentally tough. My coach will give me my goals and race plan, and I don't like to not achieve them. I'm driven to always have things exactly the way they're supposed to end. Winning.

"I've decided I am not going to change anything about my training in preparation for the '96 Olympics. Because right now I'm on top, and it would be silly for me to switch things around, just because it's the Olympic year. It's been working for me so far. I'm going to run cross-country, because I always run cross-country. Then I'll walk the indoor season. I may go to Europe for a couple of races in the spring, because they put on better racewalking races there. Aim then for the Olympic Trials. I really don't want to think about the Olympics, I need to concentrate on getting to the Trials first, because it's never a sure thing. Especially in racewalking.

"This year was very hard. I had illiotibial band tendinitis, it was very painful, and it was starting to get to where I was having problems locking my knee, so I was getting a little worried. But by the time I got to the World Championships, it was gone, because after Nationals, I spent a lot of time in physical therapy and I haven't noticed it since. That is a problem I can have, so I have to be sure I stretch my IT bands real well. Iliotibial band goes from my hip to the knee, on the outside of the leg.

"This year, I was very badly dehydrated at the Pan-Am games, then again at World Cup. So now I have to be careful I'm drinking enough, be-cause I've been told it's a lot easier for me to get dehydrated, since I've already been severely dehydrated. If I don't drink enough, I really notice it.

"I'm getting old, I going to be 30 next month. I need to spend a lot more time taking care of myself, stretching, getting in the whirlpool, al-lowing myself more recovery than I used to have to have. Right now, I am hoping I don't get Achilles tendinitis, because usually by the end of cross country season, I get that.

"LaGrange has been really good to us. We have a nice little house here that we live in that they've provided for us. It was lucky I was living here this year, because they provide physical therapy for us. These are things most of the top runners in the country have, but most racewalkers don't have access to. That's one of the reasons we have a harder time compet-ing, because we don't have access to a lot of help other athletes take for granted. Being able to just get that therapy, I am sure made the biggest difference. If I hadn't had the PT available, I'm sure I wouldn't have been able to get through my race at World Championships.

"The town is supportive. If we ask for something, they'll try to do it for us. They'll help us with child care. Any little thing. If we're trying to get to a race that's nearby, they'll provide a van for us. We have a course around a lake that's about 20 miles away, if people don't have a car, they'll give us a rental car.

"I have a problem with my wagon right now. One of the wheels is bro-ken. We still only have one car. Mike is done with school except for his thesis. That was a 42-mile commute each way."

The importance of Mike. "He's training for the Olympic Trails himself. The 50k walk will be held in LaGrange in April. He's had a really good year this year, a lot of PRs, got back on the national team. He's been off the

National team for several years due to injuries. He's finally healthy and back in the sport, and better than he's ever been. He's really hoping that next year will be a good year for him.

"The 50k is a race where the best racers tend to be older. So, even though he's 30 now, he's very young for a 50k walker.

"They trained together today. Don't usually do much together in our serious training, because I'm training for a 10k and he's training for a 50k. Our training is a lot different.

"Also, if we don't train together, then we don't have to pay for a baby sitter as long. We really don't like to train together too much anyway. We get on each other's nerves." [She laughs. A deeper laugh rumbles in the background.]

Is Mike available?

"He's right here."

I thought he might be.

Enter Mike. Give me some background, please.

"As a senior in high school, I was undefeated that season, beat my archrival by a tenth of a second. The race was, the two of us the whole way exchanging the lead. And if I won the race, we'd win the conference championship by two points.

"Looking back on all the things I've done, it wasn't really a defining moment. What was more memorable to me, was not that I won, but what struck me, this was the last time my arch rival and I were going to race where it mattered to the team. At the end, after the fierce competition we'd waged, all we did was catch each other. All we could do was hold each other up, because we were both so exhausted."

Is racewalking weird-looking or what? "I never thought it was weird-looking. Even when I was a freshman in high school and I saw it for the first time, I thought it was kinda cool. I always thought the racewalk was a graceful movement.

"I am a walker because I'm built to do it. My chances are better than fifty-fifty of making the Olympic team. I give myself sixty-forty. I need to train hard in the next months and not get hurt, and I'll have a crack at it."

Is there Allan James and then everybody else? "Well, Allan sure thinks that. I have shown moments where I've been able to stay with some of the top people. I love those moments."

Hold those memories. "I hope so. When I'm racing I remember many of the things I do in training. I'll recall being tough in a workout, that's the reason I know I'll be able to get through the next part of a race.

"Michelle? She's exceptional. As a coach, having coached *my own* teams, I've not worked with an athlete that exceptional. She is very tough. She doesn't think it, but she's so mentally cued into what she's doing. She may not be able to tell you how she trains well. 'I just do what my coach says,' she'll say. That's part of her mental toughness. She's tough enough in her mind and has enough trust to not question what she is doing. Just that her coach has said that she can do this, so she believes she can do it. I'll look at the workouts and say, I don't even know if I could do this workout. She'll say, I can do it. If coach thinks I can. Then she goes out and does it. And she does it by herself. That's a key factor.

"Oh, she's had her broken down moments, too. She doesn't like getting disqualified. This is a serious problem. When she does go away and gets disqualified, it's very upsetting. She's not very happy for a week or two at a time. Last year, at the nationals in Buffalo, where she got DQed, the only time in the last two years, she was going to quit racewalking."

"Michelle was in tears on the side of the track. Her knee was hurting, her technique wasn't right. I had to tell her, 'you have to quit fooling around. You have to get over this stuff, it's part of the sport. Or you have to quit and go back to running. I don't care what you do. But you're not going to mope around, complaining about being a race walker, you're going to get on with it.' She decided to get back up and go train."

And she came back at a higher level.

"I find that amazing," Mike says. "I tell my athletes that Michelle is basically my hero, because she just does everything she's supposed to do."

Weird.

While editing this book, I found myself one morning power-walking around the neighborhood, going as fast I could muster. Legs stiff from old age, arms slicing the air left to right, like a metronome. Or right to left, however a metronome works. And I realized what I was doing was curiously akin to racewalking. And it seemed anything but weird. It seemed normal.

Of course, I wasn't doing that hip thing. - JDW

Chapter Four

In Their Own Words

I have been studying running and runners for almost half a century. The subject is endlessly fascinating to me. And so when I have an opportunity to sit down in an intimate setting and have a face-to-face conversation with a great runner, I try to let them do all the talking. And sometimes the tape recorder is doing all the running.

Conversation with Gerry Lindgren
December 1997

While at Washington State, Lindgren won 11 NCAA Championships

I remember a scrawny high school kid from Spokane battle alone against a team of grizzled muscular Commie soldiers, tens of thousands of spectators, like a youth tossed to the lions. In the L.A. Coliseum no less. The tale of David and Goliath ever comes to mind. – JDW

He was never an easy man to catch up with.

A couple nights before the Honolulu Marathon, at a banquet held annually at the Oahu Country Club, a beautiful woman walks up to the table and asks me for my autograph. The room is full of famous people and I figure there must be a big mistake. Then I realize the woman is looking past me into a dark corner. Partially obscured by a large tropical plant is a little man, so quiet I hadn't noticed him sitting there. I look at the nametag on his scrawny chest: Jerry Lyndgrin, it says.

Gerry Lindgren! Some men are famous, others are legendary. Before Bob Kennedy, before Alberto, before Kardong and Boston Billy, before Frank. Before little Mary Decker. Pre-Pre even, there was Gerry.

A couple bright eyes beam out from the shadow of the potted palm. A napkin gets signed and the woman leaves.

"I have been looking for you for 25 years," I tell him.

"And now you've found me."

Lindgren lives.

He is so wimpy.

"When I was a kid, the things I hated most were my squeaky voice and my wimpy body," says Lindgren. "I mean, I hated myself. And the two things that allowed me to have an influence on running and get other people to run were my wimpy body and my squeaky voice. They'd see my wimpy body on the track and say, 'If Gerry can do it, then I can do it, too.' Later, I'd get on the P.A. system, or they'd hear me talk, and they'd say, 'Oh, he's just a wimp.'

"Pre, Steve Prefontaine, used to tell me this all the time. When he heard me talk, that's what got him started running... he knew he could run, too. Even though he couldn't make it in baseball or football, which is what you did if you were in Coos Bay. He knew he could be a good runner, because of me running that way with a high squeaky voice and a wimpy body.

"I knew somebody who knew him well. And one year, when Pre didn't make the baseball team his friends were on, he was so disappointed. I was visiting our mutual friend up the coast in Reedsport, about 15 miles away. 'Why don't you run down and say "hi" to this kid?' I didn't know who Pre was but apparently he had heard of me.

"So, I ran down and knocked on his door. He answered and said, 'Hey, you're Gerry Lindgren.' I said, 'Hi, you're Steve Prefontaine.' He says, 'I'm going to beat you. I'm going to beat you someday.'" Lindgren laughs at this memory. "He says, 'You're wimpier than I am.'"

The 52-year-old Lindgren, a breach baby, had to have his arm twisted to enter this world. His shy arm broken.

"My father was 6'7", 285 pounds." Lindgren remembers, "and the problem was he was an alcoholic. Like a little Vietnam War in my house. Three children in the family and all of us had our growth stunted. It was *so* bad. When all the other boys in my junior high school, voices breaking, getting deeper, mine refused to break and never did. After I shed my Dad, my sophomore year, I grew four inches, up to 5 foot 6. That's as far as I went."

At 126, he is six pounds heavier than in his high school days. Stop and think about it now, that's the perfect size for a distance runner.

Squeaky wimp.

But not a wuss.

"You can never judge courage," Lindgren offered. "I taught Pre you have to be aggressive from the beginning of the race. And your aggression doesn't come in the race, it comes in training. You can prepare for an opponent's tactic, but not the aggression he brings to that tactic. I could break everybody but Pre. Awesome his aggression. I used to get butterflies when I first ran against Pre. I used to hate his courage. I'd love it but I'd hate it."

Remember something Oregon coach Bill Dellinger once said, off the top of his head, he thought Pre was afraid of losing. Asked Gerry if he had been afraid.

"If anything, I was afraid of winning," he replied. "My original goal was just to make the cross-country team. The coach, Tracy Walters, told me I could help make the team better. How? By getting out in front and making them chase me. I was such a wimp, the other kids didn't want me ahead of them. I was never trying to win a race. I was always trying to make the other guys work hard."

No surprise, Lindgren is a good, maybe great, hot weather runner.

"I have always loved bad conditions. When you get into bad conditions, everybody feels it. But you can use the conditions to your advantage. I remember, against the Russians, it was 105 degrees down on the track. While we were warming up, every time they'd look at me, I'd wipe my brow, and act like I was burning up. They knew I was too young, but they were fascinated by me because I was such an unusual thing. And every time they looked at me, I wiped the sweat off my face."

Sometimes he wore his wimpiness like a weapon, a sharp blade.

"When we lined up to come down the steps for the big, grand entry, I looked over at them and said, 'Hot.' And they said, 'Yes, hot. Hot.' Which planted one thing in their minds. Hot. Hot. Hot. They are not thinking I am hot, too. So, when it comes time for me to take off and sprint, they have to decide, do we cover his move or do we quit? Because they thought it was so hot, they hesitated. They made a mistake. That momentary judgment, it was the wrong one. They forgot I was hot, too.

"In every race, there's a critical time where you have to make a decision: can I do it, can I not do it? I was always trying to find a way to get the other guy to decide he couldn't do it."

How do you help people improve by breaking away like that?

He shrugs his narrow shoulders. "After the race, they kick themselves. They say, 'I'll never do that again.' The next race they are going to have a strategy. They are going to go with the guy who makes the break. They will train harder, they'll learn to compete better. When I beat the Russians, you can't imagine the guilt I felt."

Hard even now to believe the kid won.

Lindgren was a competitor.

"One of my best-ever races, probably my favorite race, was against Jurgen May, *the Track & Field News* Athlete of The Year. He was an East German who jumped the Berlin Wall. A 1,500 meter runner, he was very fast. Switched to the 5,000 meters and he was undefeated the whole year. Awesome kick like I have never seen before. He could run the last 400 meters in 50 seconds, 49 seconds. Nobody could stay with him.

"And I had him right on my back with two laps to go. What could I do? With 500 meters left, I grunted, dropped my arms, and sprinted as hard as I could go.

"Well, he was coiling and tightening, tightening, tightening, getting ready to launch this 400-meter kick, which was so devastatingly awesome.

"When I moved... boom! He hit, like triggering a spring and he was moving like you wouldn't believe. I tried as hard as I could to stay with him and I was about 25 meters behind when he reached the final curve. All of a sudden, he fell apart. Because 500 meters was way too soon to launch such a sprint.

"I made him make the wrong decision. Even though it was a positive, aggressive move for him. If he had waited, he'd have killed me."

Sometimes you can be positive, aggressive *and* wrong.

Pre was in that race. "Before the race, I told Pre what I was going to do, except for the last sprint, which I didn't know myself until I was in the race. I told Pre I planned to go out in the fastest first mile he had ever run, under 4:10, which wasn't done back then. Pre was behind me at the mile. When they gave us the time in German, he hollered, 'Too fast, too fast.' Which made me feel good because I knew then I had him on the ropes.

"But I slowed down too much the second half of the race."

At least he tried. At least he did that. He also won, clocking 13:38.4 to May's 13:40.8 and Pre's 13:52.8.

Lindgren tried to make a difference.

"You have to have the guts to run *your* race," he says. "You have to have confidence in your training. When it gets to the point in the race where you have to sprint, even as fast as the other guy, you are going to have to plan. Every step of the way, you have a plan. *You are going to do something.* Seems to me many runners today have no plan. So, when something happens, they have to react, instead of causing the action. You have to make it happen."

Don't wait for it to happen.

"I used to talk to Pre before the races and I'd say, 'Here's what I am going to do. First, I am going to take off as hard as I can go.' I'd say, 'don't worry about it, because I'll die after the first mile.' But I have to let them know I am in control. Then we'll see what happens. The second mile, I'd try to hold the pace. By the third mile, I'll probably be having some trouble. I'll try to come up with something at the end."

That's a plan? 'I'll try to come up with something.'

"Sure," Lindgren professes. "Okay, maybe I don't know what I can do against this particular competitor. Many times your plan doesn't work. *You do have to improvise.*

"But when you are running a race, every step of the way, you have to be thinking, what can I do to ensure whoever wins has run his butt off. Instead of sitting there and waiting and waiting and waiting," Gerry says. "You have to be the one who makes things happen."

You have to train that way.

"When I was training," he continues, "I always took Ron Clarke along on my back. He was right there and I would try to break him. You have to go out and do yourself in.

"I don't believe in ability. We all have the same ability. Attitude is everything. You have to believe you can make a difference."

That takes a plan.

Lindgren's secret was no secret – hard work. Hard work is a gun.

"My big forte as a high school boy was the great mileage and that's what allowed me to run with the more mature internationals. I ran so many more miles that I could go longer and harder than most runners," Lindgren begins to sound a little like a track club bumper sticker. "They weren't putting in enough miles to get into really great shape."

The wimp could go longer and harder than all but a few.

"Tell you the truth, I feel better today than I did in the beginning. I don't know why, but running is more fun. Maybe it's my diet."

Lindgren is a vegan; he eats no animal products. That means, as I understand it, no barbeque ribs.

"As I grew older," Gerry admits, "I was getting cowardly because I didn't have the energy. Therefore, I didn't have the courage to do what I had to do." He quit meat.

And he's still running. "I have been running for so many years and I still love it like I did the first day. Just love to run. Love to compete, love to try."

He even loves the injuries.

"One of the best things that can happen to you as a runner is an injury. It's actually a blessing, not a tragedy. Because when you have a goal and you are running and getting closer and closer to your goal and suddenly you have to pull back because of an injury, something you wanted was taken away from you. And you want it back. Once you have had a chance to rest your body and recuperate, because every day you break it down, break it down, break it down. Your body needs to rest, that's why you have the injury.

"You have to attack the injury, do everything you can to get over that injury... ice, elevation, homeopathic, everything you know to get over it. Then you are physically fighting the injury while being forced to rest and wanting very badly to get out there and run.

"When you come back, you are a dynamo. You are rested, your attitude is right, you have much more going for you than the guy who was never injured and continued to run. Every time a guy gets injured, within two weeks of coming back, they are right up there with the guy who didn't get injured. It's a blessing.

"One of the reasons I was able to run so well was I was one of the most injured guys you ever did see. When I was competing, I was injured as much as I wasn't injured.

"I overtrained," he concedes, apparently no worse for wear. "I really did."

Wimp.

Lindgren outlasted men he wasn't supposed to outlast. He outran faster men. He must have been doing something right.

"There is no right way to train," he notes. "But a race should be easier than your training runs. If you want to race at a 62-second pace, you have to train at a 60-second pace.

"It all depends on what you are going for. Ron Clarke was a good tempo runner. He could hit a good tempo, he could hit a *great* tempo. But if you could stay with his tempo, you could beat him, because he was tempo all the way. So, he lost a lot of races. But he also won a lot of races and set an awful lot of world records."

Clarke said, if an athlete missed a day's training, it put him a month behind.

"The last couple of weeks I've come up with very sore legs," Gerry says, "but they are feeling better now because I took the week off. So, I worry. But I think that's the best way to go into a marathon, a little worried. Keeps you from going out too fast, you don't mess around for the first ten miles."

Training 90 miles a week, Lindgren is a coach now. Not that there's anything wrong with that.

"I had a group of 17 runners, 15 had never run a marathon before. The two who had, hadn't run better than 5:40. I got everybody in under 4 hours. They just loved it. But I trained them hard. They trained at 8-minute pace on the track.

"I do weird things. I put bells on their shoes. When you run a marathon, it's not a race you run with your body. You have to relax and you run through your feet. It's tempo, tempo, tempo.

"Never let your body do the work. You'll use too much energy. In your feet, you have 114 tendons and tendons that work like springs or a rubber band. They press, contract, and push you off. If you run through your feet, you're springing, bouncing off, springing, bouncing off. And you are using muscle energy to do it.

"It's really a cheap form of energy and in a marathon you can go far that way. If you are pushing with your body, sooner or later, the muscles will run out of energy and you're going to fall apart. I teach my athletes to run with the bells. Listen to the jingle, keep up with the rhythm. Tempo, tempo, tempo."

Lindgren's long run these days is 30 miles. "Another thing I do for the marathon is put my runners – from the very beginning – through a series of 30-mile runs. Depletion runs, where we run for five hours. We deplete the glycogen so you feel like you are just hanging on your bones. I believe your body responds by building better glycogen stores, so you have more energy. As we do this, down and up more, down and up more, you enhance your body's ability to conserve glycogen.

"I think it will work. I won't know until after the race."

Couple days later, Lindgren is the last finisher to complete the Honolulu Marathon within three hours.

A full half hour slower than his goal.

Gerry Lindgren, a name hard to spell correctly, may be legendary, but he is hardly famous. Never seemed to get much publicity.

"When I started, I had no ego. I am not a self-promoter," Lindgren concedes. "Just don't have it in me. I am not in the limelight, never have been, and it's hurt me." He says exactly what's on his mind. "I'd like to have a sponsor, so I could run full-time and attack the age-group records."

Records mean a great deal to Gerry. Perhaps that is why he fought for so many. "It is in approaching goals you find happiness in whatever you do," he says. "I had 37 races in a row where I was under world-record pace through the first half. Of those, I set one record and barely missed another. The record I did get was just because the week before, I was injured. I was too stupid to know I needed the rest, because we just didn't analyze back then.

"Last week I wouldn't let any of my runners train. They had to take a full week off two weeks before the marathon. When you do all that hard marathon training, you wear yourself down and you have to build yourself back up again. This week my runners have been looking better than they had before the rest."

Lindgren is feeling better. He practices that which he preaches. The biggest difference today than when Lindgren was competing internationally are the goals. The goals are different. Every generation has that problem.

"When I was running," Gerry offers, "the goal was 65-second quarters for 5000 meters. Now it's 60 per quarter. And back in those days, the best I could think of was maybe 62.5. Maybe I could do that if I had a good day and I had a lot of great training. Before we die, they are going to be looking at 55 seconds. Because they will need to."

Most American runners are still looking at 65 seconds per quarter.

"*You have to look at the 60.* Not only that, you have to believe, not that you can win a race, but you can make a difference. So that whoever wins the race, you have to ensure that guy has to show heart in order to cross the line first."

The Kenyans do that so well. "It's fun to watch them run," Lindgren brightens. "They have so much guts. In Barcelona, there was this Kenyan guy in the 5000. After the second lap, he took off and got a great big lead on everybody. And, oh, how much guts that must have taken!

"I was crying as I watched this. Because that's the kind of runner I think an athlete should be. And, as he got closer to the finish line, they were catching up and catching up. At the end, three people passed him and he ended up 4th place. Didn't even get a medal. But the courage that guy had. The guts and the courage and the stamina. He just gave his heart. That was the highlight of the Games. Everybody is so interested in the gold medal. But to me, that man was the real winner.

"I never thought I was the best runner. I just thought I could bring out the best in other people."

There *is* something wrong with running in the USA today.

"The purpose to running has been skewed wrong," believes Lindgren. "We put too much emphasis on winning, on a gold medal. Too little emphasis on what running can mean. Runners change the world. They dictate how all people in the world are going to act.

"When I started running... I got arrested 17 different times for running, because it was something you just didn't do. Now, nobody even cares if you are running, because it's so common. They bike, they swim, they do so many things they never ever did back then.

"First there was the running revolution, then everything else followed. The runners started it all. Runners are the heart of our species. Running is so visible, and your courage has to come out so obviously.

"All of us learn from each other how to be human," Gerry Lindgren will say. "Runners set the standards."

He made a difference. Took giant steps. And left big shoes to fill. We owe the little wimp our gratitude.

The runt.

In The Words of Marc Davis (Honolulu '94)
December 1994

Wearing his re-entry shields, Davis wins another track race.

[Age 25 on December 17, 1994. Originally hailed from Oceanside, California, Home of Camp Pendleton, Northern beach towns of San Diego, went to high school in downtown San Diego. College at University of Arizona. 9/87-5/92. Redshirted 1990 track season after fracturing his foot in the 1989 Pac-10 cross-country championships.]

College started extremely slow. A big wake-up call as far as training and taking on 10,000 meter cross-country instead of 5000 meter. Just being away from home, experiencing new friends, new things to do. Doing whatever the heck I wanted to do. Beer. Staying out. Dancing four nights a week. Worrying about that more than my running and school. [He grabs his throat in a choking gesture.]

My sophomore year, things started to come around. Out of the blue, 19-years-old, I ran 13:32. Went on to win the NCAA's that year as a 19-year-old sophomore. So, things started to pick up. Unfortunately, in the fall, when everything was starting to come around, I was crushing course records in cross-country, I end up breaking my foot.

The next two to three years was constant nagging injuries, trying to get back into shape. Every time I would get back, it was with reckless abandonment, and usually severe shin splint problems, ankle problems, knee problems.

Finally, everything seemed to come together my fifth, my senior year, my last track season during the spring. I only had one class I had to take to keep eligibility and to graduate, a perfect time to concentrate on my training. Ended up winning the NCAAs in the steeplechase.

No injuries at all in high school, I hardly trained. If it was raining, I wouldn't run. Even if it stopped ten minutes later, I would just blow off the day. I was doing 20-30 miles per week tops.

[Davis then talked about his post-collegiate career and 1994, the season.]

Four nights later, came out and ran the steeplechase in Zurich, the meet of the summer, and I ran a race people haven't seen happen in a long time, where four Kenyans went out and I went after them. I mean, I didn't care who the hell they were. I didn't care who Moses Kiptanui was, who was in the race, Julius Kariuki, William Mutwol, I don't care who these guys are, I went after them. I'm not going to sit back and trying to reel them in, because they ain't coming back to you. These guys aren't going to fade. They outkicked me the last 200, but I don't care. I got 4th place. I ran 8:14. I was on a roll. That was a great high right there.

So I go to Monaco, three nights later after that, and jump into a 3,000m flat. Again, I'm a steeplechaser, what am I doing running 3,000m flat? I don't give a crap. I go out with them. Go out in 4 minutes the first mile, and just keep holding on. I run 7:38. My PR was 7:45 or something, even that was a major PR from a 7:57 earlier in the season. Within that one week I had just crushed my PRs as much as six seconds in every single race. This was July 29-August 6, 1993.

I got to calm down for two weeks after that until the World Championships in Stuttgart. It was good, I just went out there. Pow! Pow! Pow! Ran three good races and relaxed going into the WC.

The World Championships were an awful experience. My heat, first heat, not too bad of a heat. Got in there, running really well, Brooks Johnson talks to me a lot still, him and I are still really good friends. He's telling me before the race, stay out of the way, stay out of the way, run in lane three if you have to, just stay the hell out of the way. I'm in lane three the whole race. The one barrier that's on a curve, every other barrier is basically on a straight away, even the water barrier is straight, you jump over it, then the track curves.

The one barrier on a curve, a guy from England decides he wants to kiss the track, he does a complete somersault and - to be technical - the centrifugal force of his body throws him out into lane 3 or 4 and so I'm trying to step out of his way and he just sticks his arms as he's flaring out into my legs like a stick in a bicycle wheel. And I do a tumble that was just ugly. I rolled about 6 or 7 times.

I got up, I almost ran the other way. I'm down 50m from last place with less than a thousand meters to go, 900m to go in the race. I didn't hurt myself luckily. A good army roll. I'm going, Ohmigod, I just lost everything with hardly any time left, so I just sprint like crazy the next 300m and I get into 5th place. I know top 4 goes. I can see the guy in 4th place, he knows he's in 4th place, he knows I went down, he knows I'm coming on him.

I'm just kicking like crazy, but I couldn't catch him because I had just killed myself to get back up to that point. Got in 5th. Sat around, waited for the other heats. They take the top 4 times from 3 heats, plus the next

4 fastest finishers. 16 to run in the final, Sure enough I am 17th person on the list. I'm devastated, I'm just absolutely destroyed. I could not believe it. I mean, I didn't do anything wrong, why am I being punished like this?

So, we protest, we protest, we protest, two hours later, boom, I get accepted into the final. My mind is trashed, my body is trashed. There's no way in hell I'm going to do anything in the final, so sure enough, I get in the final. I go out with the guys, 1000m into it I just fall apart, I just kinda finish, get like 10th or 11th. I destroy my world ranking, I had, like, the 7th fastest time in the world, I don't even get ranked top ten. Run a pathetic time, I am absolutely destroyed.

I tried to make it up by going to a steeple in Berlin and hopefully finish the season right, get some of that back, but again in Berlin, I'm just absolutely wasted, mentally I'm destroyed. I go out and run another terrible race. I had another race set up and I told my agent, forget it, I'm going home. Tuck my tail between my legs and get out of there before I hurt myself any more. I've learned it's better to not run in a race in Europe, better to pull out than to race bad. A tough ending to a season that started off as an explosion.

I learned a lot. I partied a lot when I was over in Europe. After the Monaco race, I was out until 3 o'clock in the morning, drinking, diving into the Mediterranean buck-naked. Still reckless abandonment. I was still real young, didn't know what was going on, still wasn't realizing what I had and what I could do, so I wasn't doing it properly. That was probably another reason I was tired when I got to Worlds. I was partying, whooping it up, enjoying the limelight, all the attention, the money.

Fall '93. Didn't really do much, took a lot of time off coming back. About a month after my return, I started developing a knee injury that had actually begun back in '91 NCAA cross-country in Knoxville, Tennessee where I dropped out. Again a real big nagging injury when I was trying to come back from that broken foot. Loose cartilage maybe.

Major pain, major pain. I go and run for the U.S. team in the Eikiden in Chiba. Run a great leg, absolutely great 5k leg off of hardly any training. Soon as I got back to the States, I could barely walk. My leg's destroyed. I go see a couple people. Sure enough, we got to go in and do a scope. They go in there and find out they actually have to go in. My knee caps run out to the side, but because my left leg, my inside leg on the track, has gotten so much more abuse because it runs inside even more, they had to scrape the bottom of the kneecap.

Wasn't loose cartilage. The bottom of the kneecap was all scraped up from the side bones in your knee, smoothed the bottom of the kneecap, did a lateral release, they cut a small piece of the tendon which released the kneecap to come in a little bit more, so it wouldn't get damaged in the future.

Originally we were talking a simple scope, 2 or 3 weeks you're back jogging. I couldn't run for 2 or 3 *months*. I was out January, February, March. I had already lost the last half of November as well as December. So I'm out for another 3 months.

Again, I'm back to questioning myself. God, can I come back from this? But a lot of good cross-training. March starts rolling around, I start jogging, I start running, everything's going well. Hell, I come out a month later and run a 4-minute mile the beginning of April at a meet in Hayward Field in Eugene. I am thinking, God, it's coming together, but, you know, I'd start being real nice and patient. People are still wondering, questioning what I'm gonna do.

The '94 season

Early June, at the Prefontaine meet in the steeple, I bombed. Absolutely bombed terribly. I got crushed. I am thinking, God, what am I going to do at Nationals. Luckily, it was an off year.

I go to Nationals. I get to the starting line, I'm pumped up, I am ready to go. I'm relaxed, I calmed down. First of all, I won the semi-finals for some reason. I just kinda sprinted ahead and played around with some of the guys. I had a real easy heat. So, it was no big deal.

I was little worried about the final. My strength wasn't there. So, right before the gun goes off, I look over at Brian Diemer. I think to myself, this is the man. Wherever this guy is going, I am going. If anybody knows how to run a race when you're not ready to run a race, [laughs], this is the man. I mean, this guy has been able to run beautifully.

So, I just stick on to him for the first mile. All of a sudden, I start feeling good. I just started moving, moving up on people, moving up on people. Next thing you know I am outkicking Danny Lopez for 2nd. Croghan is way out ahead, he's in great shape.

So, I get second place. Everybody is saying, God, that's the most beautiful tactical race I have ever seen. That's the smartest I have ever seen you run. Oh, my God, they're going, where did you come from? You weren't hardly walking two months ago. You were on crutches three months ago. What happened, people were asking.

I don't know, I don't know, I don't know what's going on.

Again, we decide to go on the same plan. Good training. Alberto Salazar sets me up at a training camp in St. Moritz, the Swiss Alps. I'm just loving it up there. Dieter Baumann, Yobes Ondieki, Rachid El Basir, all these guys, MAJOR studs, I am training away with them, hammering with them, getting into great shape.

Still, literally this time, absolutely no speed work again. Once again, absolutely nothing. There was a steeple I did in Europe first. Ran like 8:21 in Stockholm. Real relaxed, Went out easy, didn't try to stay with anybody. Played it smart, that's what Alberto and I wanted to run right then. I ran Nice, France, steeple. Again, ran relaxed, but ran a little bit better. Ran about, ah, 8:17.

People are starting to go, God, how are you doing this?

How are you just licking times off like this? I don't know, it's coming together, that's all I can ever tell anybody. So, I go into the Goodwill Games thinking, okay, the field is kinda weak, I'll try to run with Croghan as long as I can. He'll probably try to take it out. I get out there and I just feel great. I am just running incredible. With 800m to go, I'm saying, forget this, I am taking off now. I go after it and I win. Run 8:14, jogging the last lap, waving to the crowd. Saying "hi" to my friends, waving to the Mayor of St. Petersburg. Had a wonderful time.

Again, things are starting to come together in a short amount of time. Come back home a little bit, go back and I jump in a steeple in Zurich, the meet again. Thinking I ran 8:14 last year, I ran 8:14 two weeks ago, I should be able to run at least 8:10. Go after the AR. Just go after it.

Well, to make a long story short, crappy weather, broken down mentality once again. I just ran a crappy race. Just blew up. I didn't run very well at all. Kind of disappointed with my steepling. Starting to realize something that later on in the summer I was going to come to a conclusion about... Am I really a steeplechaser, or am I just somebody who is very fast trying to run a steeplechase?

There's a big difference between the two.

After getting away from the steeple, I jump into a 1500m. I run 3:36. Off of nothing. Literally nothing. I'm thinking, God, where did this come from?

Two nights later, I've got the AR in the two mile. All set up for me. It's right there. I go out with Khalid Skah and again everything comes together. I run away with it.

Who cares about the time? Who cares about the distance? 3,218.23 meters, or whatever the hell the distance is. Doesn't mean anything. It was a big win against Khalid Skah, somebody that just does not get outkicked. And I outkicked him.

I come back from that to a steeple. Blow up again. Run in Berlin, the infamous site of my final race last summer. Run terrible again. I don't think Berlin is ever going to want me back.

I sat down and I thought a lot of things about the steeplechase and about what I was trying to do, what I was getting from it, what I wanted from it. I got so wrapped up in going after the AR. I had proclaimed the year before, if I got the AR, I wasn't going to run the event anymore. Just something I was doing for the heck of it. I wasn't giving the race its respect, I wasn't giving it its due, as far as hurdling technique, whatever, like that.

And I got so mentally broke down from one week running 8:14 and the next week running 8:40. The fact I could run 8:12 over two miles, I should at least be able to run under 8:10 in the steeple a week later. I couldn't even break 8:45. I have a couple bad barriers and my whole race falls apart. I can't utilize that speed, because I can't hurdle.

You can work on it. You try to start a career like Croghan was able to do in college. He was a steepler all through college. That's why he's great now. I, just for the heck of it, started doing it at the end of college. Croghan has that eye coordination down, he's got the hurdling technique, he hurdles like Henry Marsh. He's great, he's incredible. He doesn't need to be quick. And he wants to be a steepler.

I don't want to be a steepler. I just want the AR in the steeplechase.

There's a difference.

As of now we've decided we're probably going to stay away from the steeple. We want to get back to the 5000m. With that 2M time and with what Bob Kennedy has proved can be done, that AR is well within reach.

You know, you run under 13 minutes and you're set. There's nothing you can't ask for, there's nothing you can't get.

I hate the 5000m. Twenty damn laps. You get 7 laps into it and you're saying, God, I've got another 1½ miles to go.

I swear to God, if there was a 3000m flat, I would run it every single week. I'd run 7:20. That's my distance. Always has been. That was my distance in high school. It was always my distance in college. I mean, I ran great in college indoor 3000. I ran a great outdoor 3000 a couple of times. I have just always ran well in it. I love it. Two miles felt perfect. Just the right amount of distance. I could have kept going another mile at a similar pace and probably run 13 flat, 13:05. I didn't have much more to go.

I just don't want to go any further. That's a whole 'nother four laps. A long ways. There's some good money, it's a good distance. I think if I get to a certain level, you run 13 minutes, trust me, it will be over quick enough.

People will come watch me run 3000m, if I am a sub-13 5k performer. You got indoor 3000. Look at Doug Padilla, how he dominated. Steve Scott has the AR indoors. It would be great to go after that.

Waikiki Mile

I have been doing 20-30 miles a week the last month and a half. Taking 4, 5 days off at a time. Haven't done a lick of speed work. Haven't done a lick of endurance work. Haven't done any intervals. Did one workout about two weeks ago, in pissing rain, that was my last workout. Couldn't even walk for two days after that. Hardly doing anything except jogging. Four to six miles a day. Couple of times running hard.

I would get up and I would go do an interval workout and it would be dark out and rainy and I would just walk home. The last two weeks running every other day.

It's not the coaching, it's not that I'm not running because I didn't feel like it. Basically, I couldn't do it. My heel has been really bothering me. My achilles have been bothering me, which basically led to the heel problem. Your typical fall injuries of coming back after shutting down after a tough summer.

Basically came to have a good time. Not really worried about how I was going to finish, more interested in how this race would show where I was at. If I've lost a lot of strength over the last month or so, because of a little heel problem. Basically crappy weather in Oregon.

You know, you go in, you have a couple guys help you out in the race, next thing you know... I mean, Christ, I ran 3:57. My first legitimate sub-four mile. Obviously, I've run the equivalent to it. It's on the roads, so this is not legitimate either, when you think about it.

It was a really really big surprise. Everybody else seems to think it was something that was supposed to happen. Alberto swears it was supposed to happen that way. My girlfriend swears it was supposed to happen that way. A couple of the guys thought about it. They call me 'The Doc'

Two or three days before the race I get a head cold, I'm all stuffed up. I've been traveling all around the place. Can't even breathe. I'm all achey, definitely not feeling well. So, I was basically blowing the whole thing off. But you know, maybe the adrenalin from your body fighting the cold. The incentive to go under four minutes. I guess we just kinda went after it.

It was a perfectly set up race. I had 58 at the quarter, about 2, 2:01 at the half. I did not lead until a 100 meters to go.

"I used and abused every person out there. They all know it. I know it," Davis explained, dripping from a post-race plunge. "Nothing they could do about it. Not a damn thing. Somebody could've taken off with a quarter to go, I would've gone with him and still sat on him. The biggest surprise in my life. I just decided I wanted it more."

[Undertrained and undaunted, Davis took home a check for $12,000.]

This is my off season, from June to August. This is all just candy to me. July and August is the roast beef.

Alberto's been coaching me since I moved to Oregon, right after the summer of '93. I moved up there and started working with him right away.

"I've run more than he has," his girlfriend interjects.

I was talking to Shorter about this last night about my lack of training. 'That's all we need another Bill Rodgers,' he said. [Davis laughs.] Some guy who doesn't know what he's doing, doesn't even do it, and goes out and kicks everybody's ass.

There are some guys who are elitists, they won't give you the time of day. There's some guys who sit there and just talk smack about other runners. You know, I'm gonna kick this guy's ass, I'm gonna kick that guy's ass. It never comes true.

I think I'm one of these people who says basically, 'hey, look, I am going to do this.' With the understanding it may not happen, but I am going to do everything I can. I will probably guarantee, 95% of the time, I will do it. The rest of the time, I say, 'look, this is me, black and white. There's no gray area there. This is how I am. I am not saying I am better than you. I'm just saying this is how I am. I am not saying I am a great miler, and you're not as good as me, or you're not a great miler, I'm just saying, this is how I am. If you want to beat me, bring it on.'

I encourage anybody who wants to go.

I never go into a race thinking any of these guys are ever going to beat me. I don't care if it's Joe Schmoe or Khalid Skah. I am going to the starting line saying, 'he's just a guy, I'm just a guy.' Come up to me, talk to me, don't think I'm not going to talk to you just because you expect me to do the cordial thing. Forget that. I'm going to hang out, go out partying every once in a while, hang out in the lobby, talk to people, rap with them, go out for a run with them. Never be shy around me.

I remember one time, I could see these people wanting to approach me, I said, 'come over here,' and they said 'we didn't think you'd talk to us.' Gimme a break.

I go to parties and I introduce myself as another person. People hear my name and they go, 'ohmigod,' like I'm a celebrity. I hate that.

I go up to them, stick out my hand and say, 'Hi, my name is Chuck.' Two hours later, they may figure it out by somebody saying, 'do you know who that is?' It's great, it's flattering, but let's be serious.

When I'm on the track or when I'm on the roads or the golf course racing, that's a totally different person. When I'm off, I'm Chuck. I'm Chuck, I'm just hanging out in Hawaii, drinking coffee, having a whiskey sour, watching *Love Boat*, not doing anything.

Also ran a 2M in Portland, we tried to go after the American Record there. Nobody was in shape. I absolutely bombed again, trying to outkick somebody for 11th place. I am running 8:50 for 2M. Who knew what was going to happen two months later when I was running, heh heh, a little bit faster, needless to say.

[The "conversation" turned to Pre.]

'Ladies and gentlemen, we're seeing the next Steve Prefontaine here,' a track announcer once said. Alberto tells me that. That's a real long story. I mean, living in Eugene, that's a real easy trap, especially moving to Eugene, not being from there, not going to school there.

You get moved there and everybody thinks, oh, great, another asshole coming here and he wants to be the next Prefontaine. I hear guys like Todd Williams say, he wants to be the next Prefontaine. Hey, I'm gonna be the first Marc Davis. If he wants to be the next Steve Prefontaine, that's fine. But I'm going to be the first Marc Davis and that's all I wanna be.

Steve, you know, it was a sad story. When it really comes down to is a sad story. I hate to see some people look up to him for the antics and some of the things he did off the track, because it's really scary to think about. I've heard some of the stories of the things that he had done and it's scary to think about that.

But all the same time I admire the hell out of him for his charisma and what he gave to the sport and how he brought people into the sport. He brought "The People" into the sport.

I think that's what it takes, it takes somebody crazy enough to run a mile, walk onto the beach, scream at 30,000 people, 'anybody want to join me in the water?' and take a flying flip into the surf. In front of everybody. I could give a crap what anybody thinks. People say he's crazy, he's out of control. People that I beat are saying, he's an asshole, look it, he thinks he's better than us.

How do they see that? If I'm in the water saying, I'm better than you, you guys suck, I'm number one, if I'm saying, you suck Marcus, you suck Bob, you suck Todd, if I'm doing that, fine, they have every right to stand there and say every bad thing about it.

But if I'm in the water, saying, 'YES! I love Hawaii, I love this, everyone is great, I love you all.' How they could have the right to look at me in a bad way, to say I'm cocky?

I'm just loud and obnoxious. I never do it to piss anybody off, and that's what Pre was like. Pre was cocky, he was obnoxious, he was confident, he was bold. He never did it to say, Hey, look, I'm great and you suck.

Never once really said that. Never flat out. It was all, this is how I am, I believe I can do anything. I'm not saying I believe you can't do anything, or that you can't do anything I can't do. All I'm saying is, hey, if you want to do it, bring it on. That's all it is. Simple.

Like Pre did. It was never against anybody, it was for himself. It was the way he was.

I was only six years old when Prefontaine passed away. I didn't even know who Prefontaine was until my sophomore, junior year in college. I started running when I was in 10th grade in high school, because I sucked at everything else.

I don't have your idols. I met Billy Mills when I was in high school, never even heard of the guy before. Guys talk to me about other runners and their PRs, Steve Coe Cram Ovett, whatever their names are, I don't know who these guys are. I admire people that have idols and someone to look up to, and I'm not saying these heroes aren't worthy enough for me to look up to, I just don't know enough about the sport to be a track fan or geek or whatever you want to call somebody like that. I don't get into it. I'm just me.

It's real basic, black and white. I probably would've honored Pre. I would've been a Pre geek, if I'd had the chance. I didn't have the chance, nothing against him.

I paid my respects at the anniversary of his death this year, I went up at midnight, the rock where it says, REST IN PEACE. PRE 5/30/75, the rock is starting to deteriorate, breaking apart, fading. So I went up there with some white paint and a little tiny paint brush and just neatly filled in. I didn't change it, I didn't put anything else, just cleaned it up. I sat there and paid my respects. Wasn't like I sat there and I prayed. "Oh, my God, you're the god of all running, I wanna be just like you."

I don't want to be just like him. People know what Pre was like and nobody wants to be just like him. People want to have the charisma and the enthusiasm that he had. That's the one thing that you have to keep a hold on, that you have to cling to, that's the one thing I'm sure his family clings to.

I met his parents, and that's the one thing I am sure they cling to, the spirit inside of him was incredible. The spirit is still well alive in his family, in his sisters. I mean, his sisters are just a riot. They're great.

It's really wonderful to have somebody out there, that people compare me to him. That's great and fine and dandy, but don't call me the next Prefontaine, Mills, Salazar, Chapa, whoever, Steve Scott. I don't wanna be the next anybody. You want to find similarities, fine, but I am me. I'll pay my respects to who I can. It's my time and I am going to do what I can do.

What's the big deal about Pre? His times weren't all that great.

[A reliable source repeated secondhand from an unreliable source that this country's most frequently compared heir to Steve Prefontaine was present when these blasphemous thoughts were uttered. I asked Marc Davis his thoughts. Like Pre, Marc is as quick with a quip as he is with his feet. Here he struggled a little.]

"If Prefontaine was running today, he would be destroyed just like a lot of runners. Some of the times he ran were respectable but there were also people back then running a lot faster. People saw Pre as somebody who could crush anybody. Hey, he got beat a few times.

Especially after '72, things weren't coming around as often as they were before the Munich Olympics. When he was killing everybody. I don't know if I really meant to say he didn't have fast times. I just meant to say it's not like its records I'm going after.

The only record I know Pre has is the American Junior Record in the five thousand meters. And I missed that, not by time but by two weeks. When I ran 13:32 at 19, unfortunately, I was turning twenty December 17th of that year.

I don't know who said that. It probably just meant he was a great athlete. I would rather just look at him as a great athlete, not as somebody who ran a certain time. I like to look at his charisma more than anything.

I don't even know what his PRs are. That's the way I like to be compared to Pre. Off of no speed work, somebody has ten meters on me like O'Sullivan almost had the other day, for me just to reel him back in. Knowing, I don't care what I have or haven't done or what the guys in front of me have done, I want it more.

That was Pre's attitude. He wanted it more than anybody. Didn't matter, if for some reason, they wanted it more. He didn't believe in that.

There's no reason to believe in that. I mean, I go into a race, saying, I want it more. I don't care if somebody says, no, I want it more than you.

How can you, I, say that? Maybe they do want it more? I don't know anything about maybes. Or what ifs. I want it more and that's the end of it.

That's what happened against Skah. Nobody outkicks Skah. I wasn't supposed to outkick Skah. Skah was supposed to run away from me. It wasn't supposed to happen the way I made it happen. Tough luck. I wanted it more and if I want it more, I'm gonna have it. Whatever he's gonna give me, I'm gonna give him back.

That's a big part of me and I think that was a big part of Prefontaine. He didn't care who was in front of him, or how far ahead they were, he was going to want it. If it could happen, it was gonna happen.

And even if it couldn't happen, most of the time, it was gonna happen. That's the philosophy I like to live by.

Chapter Five

Training and the Coaches

Successful distance running is most easily achieved with the assistance of a knowledgeable coach. Good coaches can be just as talented as good runners – knowing how to get the best out of a runner is a unique skill.... Greg Shank is such a coach. He was instrumental in the success of Chris Fox, a five-time U.S. Olympic Trials qualifier in events ranging from 5,000 meters to the marathon. Mike Spinnler was instrumental, too.

If you study how coaches work with their athletes, you will be more capable of improving your own running. That is the theory at least.

As the number of racers grows, the need for good coaches increases.

Interview with Greg Shank, Fox's coach
July 1995

[Prep for Sacramento?] For Sacramento we really had to, I assume you are aware Chris had to run a qualifying time at the last minute for Sacramento, so that was only, we lobbied to get that waived, which just doesn't happen in our federation, so when we had to run the standard, which wasn't that difficult, but we only had 10 days between, because he had just come off Bay-To-Breakers and we were having some scheduling problems and hoping at the last minute they would waive the 10k qualifying standard. He only had to run a 28:50, but he was having a good night and he just ran by himself, as matter of fact.

When he did that, he really only had a 10-day window between his 28:18 and the Nationals, so there wasn't really much to be accomplished at that time. My opinion is, he increased his fitness level that night when he ran the 28:18, which is all he needed for Sacramento. After that race, I knew we didn't need to do anything else.

There really wasn't a direct preparation. We were preparing all year long for Bay-To-Breakers, it was a pretty important race for us. We had prepared pretty well for Bay-To-Breakers in May in San Francisco, a road race, the USA championships which he won. Finished 3rd overall, got beat by two world-record Kenyans, but won the US champs relatively easy. That was not a breakthrough race, but it was what we're pointing to all spring. I mean we wanted to run TAC, but you never know about Sacramento and the weather, so we were not that concerned. It was really a bonus as far as we were concerned.

After that it was pretty much let's see if we can maintain into Sacramento.

[Prep for Bay-To-Breakers?] For Bay-To-Breakers... I've been with Chris now for eight years, I've known him since he was a 13-year-old kid, but we started to do a little bit different than we had in the past. Before we would do more mile repeats, when he was preparing for 10k. Since

this year, maybe a little bit last year, we've started concentrating on 1000m. 1000m is a good distance for him from a training standpoint, because he can still get good quality speedwork, meaning coming through the 800 in 2:07-08, and try to change gears the last 200m. And that seems to work really well for him. It gives him that balance between long enough interval and quick enough.

Really what we concentrated on for May was 1000m intervals.

TAC was a bonus from a standpoint once we found out what kind of shape he was really in May, all we had to do was qualify and get there. We felt pretty confident once he got there he could make the team.

[Now he's made the team and run 27:53 and he's going to Sweden for the WC's. The original plan was Bay-To-Breakers to the marathon.]

Bay-To-Breakers to the marathon is still the plan. That is still the goal with some selected road races in between. We always had TAC in the background. I am of the opinion that too much road racing is certainly not good and one of the reasons that he's been able to maintain his competitive running at this stage is because he hasn't run a lot of road races.

I also think that on the track, it's very stressful, mentally stressful more than physically stressful, you must learn how to concentrate, and I think that's one thing he's lacked in the marathon. The 10K at the Worlds, and what he's had to do, he's run three 10Ks in the last five weeks is really going to help him in the marathon in the long run. From a concentration standpoint.

Concentration is one of the things we've had a problem with. His PRs and everything else doesn't equate to what he's run in the marathon. I think that's one of the issues because when you are out there for 2 hours and 10 minutes, you have to concentrate and make sure that you monitor what's happening to you and what's going on around you. Some people need to be taught concentration and I believe the track teaches that.

Concentration may be the difference between some of these really good guys and some of the guys who are really great. I think it will help him in the marathon a lot. Alberto, I'm convinced, when he first stepped on the line in New York, he was so young, but he had just come off a real fast 10,000 he had set up in Eugene. I think that helped him a lot as far as concentration. Not that he wasn't the kind of guy who could always concentrate.

[Alberto is an animal and a maniac; I mean that with the greatest re-spect.]

Exactly.

[And I don't get that out of Chris.]

Well, it's different though. Over the years, if you could see him de-velop, six, seven years ago, he had the reputation of being a great work-out guy and a guy who would have great races, then some not so great races, or maybe some races where he didn't compete very well at all. He was a nice guy, one of the nicest guys in the sport. I always told him, some of these guys you're competing with, they aren't so nice. In some cases. You have to be, I think, confidently cocky, and he has developed that over the last 2 years.

That and the evolution of his physical fitness. He had really matured from a body standpoint, he's so small, I think all of that is working to-gether. Right now, he's not a wild maniac like Alberto, but we did a work-out yesterday in terrible conditions, 90 degrees and 90% humidity. He just, he not only ran the workout great, he was very aggressive during the workout, that kind of thing. Which I would've never gotten through to him three years ago. He would have put his head down and said let's do it an-other day.

He's been one of the lucky guys in the sport, from the standpoint he's never been abused. His high school coach, who I just talked to the other day, didn't abuse him. Never ran him in dual meets. Rarely ran him too many intervals, he did the long slow miles back then but everybody was. He didn't get abused at Eugene, and because he was at Eugene, he wasn't running on the roads, because those guys didn't run on the roads. They had a short season, then they went to Europe.

He certainly hasn't been abused by me. We've moved up to the mara-thon, but we've always been very, very careful. He's never put marathons back to back. We selected one for our year. He's just been in an evolution process that's been working out fine for him. He's been lucky, but he's also been in a situation where he's been allowed to develop relatively slowly.

[How does he run in the heat?]

That was an issue, when he first came to North Carolina from Eugene, he seemed to totally not handle it. I mean when he was coming back from his operation, he just didn't handle it well at all. But I can remember him being a very good heat runner when he was a kid, not that that always stays the same. And then when he started running some on the roads, he used to have some problems where he thought he could. I would say over the last four or five years, he's developed into a good heat runner and I believe he can be a much better heat runner between now and Atlanta.

We will get away, change some places where he is going to train. He has some great contacts still down at Auburn, which would be a good place to train. As long as we can get out of here for three or four weeks in January, we'll go south someplace, maybe Miami, and get some training in before the Trials, just a little bit. Between the Trials and Atlanta, assuming he makes the team, I am sure he can spend some time in Auburn, that area.

Everybody is complaining about the heat, everybody is complaining about the hills, and everybody is complaining about the course and the time of day of the Olympic marathon, but in my opinion it gives Americans a better chance. Certainly it equalizes some of these 2:08 guys. They are not going to run 2:08 there. Probably a 2:12. And I think it opens the door.

Right now, Chris is running as good as he's ever run, at the most important time in his life. He is the American equivalent to Carlos Lopes, who started coming around again at that age, of about 36 years old. Anything is possible. He's a very good hill runner, by the way. Always has been. He's not a great downhill runner, he's a very good uphill runner. And they are going to run the last 5 miles on the Peachtree course, and there are going to be some tough hills. I don't know exactly where they are going to come, but they're going to come between 20-25 miles. He should be able to handle that. Plus there's not any real steep downhills, there are gradual downhills. The steep downhills are at Charlotte and that's going to give him a little bit of trouble, but we're going to work on that this winter. We're hoping to build his quads up a little bit.

[Fox is talking about taking chances, chances which seem to contradict his entire career.] Absolutely. He's been kind of timid, as you know. And again, his reputation, and I am sure it was at Eugene with him and at the '88 Trials, you know he ran five races and all the guys told me, we never realized he had that kind of guts. He should have made the team in '88, he just didn't get to the 10K fast enough. He didn't know how to run a 10K at that point. He was physically, not quite as good as he is now, but he was good. He just wasn't tough.

Right now, I can tell you, he's tough. I am not taking credit for that. I think it was just a gradual improvement in his mental process, how he focuses. He doesn't care about money anymore, literally doesn't, certainly he likes to make money. I know he's been in races before where he's said, okay, if I make this move I might cost myself a couple of grand. There's pressure to do that when you are trying to make a living. I might win an extra grand or I might lose two or three, that stuff never enters his mind anymore. He is just at a different level from a competition standpoint. Very aggressive. Very aggressive.

Right now, he's a front runner. He had a lot of trouble in Montreal last week holding back early. The rabbit didn't do a real good job the first mile and Chris was getting antsy, and bunching up behind the rabbit, not a very good rhythm. He didn't like being there.

Looking forward to the marathon trials, in that race, in the past race at Charlotte until he had some problems at 23M, he's probably the kicker in that race. He shouldn't have any trouble outkicking guys in that race, quite honestly. The good guys, like Kempainen, Brantly, Eyestone, those guys, they can't finish with Chris. Anything can happen in a marathon, but if you were out there on a flat course with 600m to go, whether it was 10M or 26M, people would bet on Chris.

Brantly was scared of his kick last year in the Charlotte race. He made that comment to me right after the race was, 'all I worried about the last 5M was getting rid of Chris.' Brantly thought he could outkick everybody else and he did.

[Chris ran a 62 to finish his 27:53; 62 is that not quick?] Quick by American standards maybe, by international standards, no. Which is the one reason the marathon is where he needs to be, because it's going to take a 57 to medal in the 10,000 probably, even in Atlanta. We all know that, depending upon the pace.

His marathon PR is 2:13 in Columbus. I know he can do 2:10, probably 2:09. I think Chris could run 5K in 13:18–19 right now.

That's the one thing while he's on this roll that he's missing, he'd like to take another shot at the 5000, but we don't have time for that. It would be a mistake to run a 5K before Worlds. There's a possibility he could run one afterwards; if for some reason he didn't make the finals, he could run one afterwards. But if he has to run two 10s, then that's dumb. He'll go to Falmouth then, maybe.

[*Did he run Crescent City this year?*] No, and he would've won Crescent City, I'm telling you, it was so slow. That was when he pulled his hamstring, that's why he couldn't run the 10K at the Penn Relays. He pulled the hamstring at William & Mary in the 5K running with Peter Sherry April 1st. That was what really set us back for two or three weeks.

He never gets seriously injured. Very seldom. He was playing around with Sherry, instead of waiting until 400m to go, he went from 700m. Ran about a 30-point 200, maybe under that, and just strained it a little bit. He got away with it, but it took about two weeks before he could train again.

[*How does he avoid injury?*]

Certainly his body build helps a lot, he's so small. His form is so much better than it used to be, he's always square all the time. We very, very seldom ever run on the roads. We have paths, dirt paths where he's at right now as matter of fact, we run on them at least 90% of the time since he's been here for the last 8 years, he has run on dirt paths, whether it's on the mountain or along the river. If he's doing a 10M run, he might run a mile to get to the river. I think that has a lot to do with it.

[*Fox almost quit running a few years ago. Why?*]

Emotional. What really frustrated him was the quality. I mean, he knows a lot of people in the sport, you hear a lot of rumors, he knows a lot of people now, and the workouts that he could do versus the workouts he felt his competition was doing or he had heard back his competition was doing. Not that some of those things aren't clouded a little bit, just made him frustrated a little bit. I think there was a time where he felt, I just can't transfer this to the competition. And he worked it out. I give him credit for that, he worked it out. We've been pushing him hard for a long time, but I think it was a gradual process, he sorted it out and said, like his attitude is today, yeah, I'm going to take a chance.

He's been doing that in road races. He's been leading, especially American races, he's been pushing the pace the last year and a half, every chance he gets.

[The last 18 months keeps coming up.]
He was very, very short on mileage when I got him, because they didn't do that kind of mileage out there *[read Eugene]*, it took him a long time to evolve into what I call a long distance runner. He was a 5000m guy and that's really where he wanted to be, He didn't like doing anything past that. Then he had some success.

I remember the first time I took him out for an hour and 45 minutes. I mean, I've been coaching guys for years, 2:20 guys who ran that far 30 weeks out of the year, and he had a lot of trouble. I mean, he literally fell apart at about 95 minutes. It took him a long time, a lot of years, to where he could handle that kind of mileage. He can now. He can handle, last year, we do things on 10-day periods, not week periods, where he was running 190 miles in ten days. Then backing off, going back to 170, then back up. Today he can do that type of thing with very little stress involved, just the right kind of stress you need.

It's much easier for him than it was three or four years ago. He's programmed, he doesn't have to think about what's happening, he just does it. Like I said, yesterday, in a workout that he would've had trouble with before, he wouldn't have wanted to do it, based on the conditions, but we were in a time problem here and he didn't question it at all. Actually seemed to relish in the fact that he had to run in those kind of conditions.

Yesterday, this is just to get him out of the race (last week's sub-28 10K), we did 3 x 5 minutes of fartlek, starting at 4:45, 4:35, 4:25 pace, coming through the mile in that time, a measured mile path, and we take 2 minutes. Then we did some fast quarters. He still had the race in his legs and we were just getting rid of that race.

[What's it mean to you as a coach to work with an athlete like Chris. Or vice versa?] We have a relationship that transcends merely the coach and the athlete. Maybe because I'm not worried about making money off of him. I knew him when he was a kid, we're friends. What he gets out of it is he knows I'm not using him for monetary purposes nor am I using him for credit. I mean, I've coached a little college and I've coached guys here for 20 years and I've had all the accolades I need to have from a coaching standpoint, so he knows I'm not using him to get something else or to get recognition or to get 50 guys lining up to coach, because I don't want those 50 guys. He feels unthreatened that I don't have some ulterior motive.

For me, it really means, certainly enjoyable. I've had 32-minute 10K guys that got down to 30:30, that means just as much to me as this. It's a chance to, an inner-personal chance to make sure you feel confident about what you're doing with other people. I look at it as, I got a big thrill the other night in Montreal, because he worked so hard, but I've gotten that kind of thrill, like I say, with 32-minute 10K guys before. And from my college kids. So, I mean, to me, it's just something we do together. And been doing together. Because we're, you know, we're friends. And I draw the line on that one, I have to. I used to have to do it a lot. We used to have to get mad at each other a lot, when he was having these little, I'm-feeling-sorry-for-myself-type periods.

But, recently, [chuckle] he doesn't have to be pushed much, he has to be held back. And that's the kind of guy you like to have. To hold him back, not have to make him do more. Or to question his guts. I don't have to do that anymore.

I'll tell you, I've been sitting two hours before a race, I remember specifically at TAC in '88, down in Florida in the 5000, knowing he was going to screw up. Not that he wasn't in good shape, but because he was nervous as a cat, scared to death. Looked like a deer with the lights shining on him. He was laying there on the track with guys he coulda beat. And that was frustrating. He almost quit that night, I can remember. He dropped out, no, he ran 13:55 or something like that.

It's been a long gradual process. And each time, each year, you get a little bit less concerned that something isn't going to happen mentally. If you can go in knowing the only limitations you have tonight are physical, that's a big step. A big step. You can coach the physical, but you can't coach the mental, in many cases. Takes a long time and they have to do it themselves.

A Second Interview with Greg Shank
September 1995

As Chris Fox's hair suggests, he looks fast even when standing still

The World Championships was a good learning experience, something that was a little rich. He [Chris] mentally handled it well, physically no problem. He went to Falmouth two weeks later and beat Todd. So he felt good about Falmouth, even though at Falmouth we could tell he was getting a little tired going in. He went to the lead a couple times there and had to hold back. Then he was pretty much running for American money. Another good experience. We needed to step back.

Since Falmouth, we've taken ten days off. Started 70 miles a week, one run a day, one day off a week. Maybe race once or twice in October. Waiting to Nov. 1 to start preparing for the Trials.

Instead of a 10-12 week build-up, we're looking at 14-16 weeks from October 29. Experimenting at altitude. Like to let him relax for a couple of weeks. He's put on 3 or 4 pounds. Ballooned.

He's hungry to train right now. I'm trying to hold him back right now. Make sure he takes a day off. Don't want him to get stale, go too hard too early.

When you make that commitment, November 1, October 29, whatever that Sunday is, everything from thereon is geared around Charlotte. Don't want him to make it too early, because I don't want him to get stale. When we do it, it's just balls out after that. All it is, is Charlotte, Charlotte, Charlotte, everything we do. Oh, we'll race a couple of times, but it'll be all Charlotte.

Can't tell you any secrets or they wouldn't be secrets.

We'll be making sure his diet is better than it's been in the past. We've got some interesting things we want to do from a distance standpoint. We expect to run 30 miles certainly a couple of times, which I think will work well with him. Which we haven't done in the past.

He's an old dog and he needs some new tricks.

Our philosophy is, we don't want to go in merely capable of making the team. We want to go in thinking this is for all the marbles here. We went to Charlotte last year for the Nationals, we were short, we knew we were short, we were supposed to be short. But we're not going to be short this time. We're gonna go right on the edge, hopefully, we'll hit it with a week or two to spare.

I've been through a lot with him, and we're to the point where I don't have to worry too much about the racing aspect as far as mental. He needs to get himself relaxed for 6 more weeks and then let it go. And when he lets it go, we're going to push it right to the edge.

We started a little bit of the downhill training, just so it's not a shock. We've got a couple of things I've done with a couple of other guys that I know he can handle. We expect that this will not be that difficult for him.

I personally think he can handle this 200-mile ten-day sessions like we've talked about in the past and never done. He can handle them a lot easier than he could in the past. He's mature enough. So we're going to pull out everything.

Falmouth, he was 10th, the only American in the top 17. He told me, when he went up to the front, about 4M. He was thinking, what the hell am I doing up here? He looked around at just a sea of Kenyans, and he dropped back and happened to bump right into Todd, and he knew Todd was in trouble. Knew he wasn't racing well. He thought at 5M, hey, quite frankly, Falmouth is a money race, put some away for the winter, so he went for the American purse.

His personal life is a problem, from the sense he has things he needs to work out. It's positive in many ways, too. I have to push him sometimes to solve these personal problems. It's not my job, but it is really, because we have to clean everything else out. He's just fine.

There is only one thing missing, he hasn't run 2:10:59, like Ed [Eyestone], or 2:11, or 2:12, like a couple of the other guys. But that, to me, is no big deal. Cause when you run 2:13 like he did in Columbus, five or six years ago, that shouldn't be an issue and we've dealt with that.

I don't think we could be in much better position. In my mind, a well-trained marathoner, if they're all trained the same, the 27:50 guy is going to beat the 28:10 guy. And that's where we're at right now. And we're happy about it. If everything's the same on a given day, that guy should beat the other guy. There's a big X factor in the marathon. But we're confident.

I'll be surprised if things don't go well. We haven't had too many opportunities where we've been in this position and we don't have to push for time. That's what we're looking for, to be able to take our time, we don't have to rush.

Interview With Mike Spinnler
July 1995

Chris Fox was something of a rebel in high school

Why has it taken him sooooo loooong? People ask me that about my writing career all the time.

Why did it take Chris so long to get to this level? Hmmm. Interesting. I have known him since we were in high school together. Personally, not to put him down, I always thought it was a confidence thing. I always thought he had the physical tools, it was just mentally he felt, you know, he was lacking something. He doubted himself a little bit. I thought since the early '80s he would run 2:09 and sub-28 for 10000m. He ran well, and he had a great career throughout the '80s and the early part of the '90s, but it seemed like a confidence thing.

It seems like he's really starting to believe in himself. What I saw up there in Montreal was a Chris Fox I had never ever seen before. Two laps into the race, he's putting his hand on the rabbit's hip and pushing him forward and yelling at him to go faster. And then when the rabbit wouldn't be pushed, Chris just took over by himself for a couple of laps. Actually, he pulled them through the first 1600 in 4:28.

I think it's just a mental thing. All about confidence. I think he really finally believes he's as good as these guys.

Wouldn't it be interesting to ask that Hispanic bunny what was going through his mind?

I talked to the other fellows we went up there with and I said, "That is not a Chris Fox we had ever seen before, that would do something that aggressive."

He was normally the type of guy who'd say, okay, this pace just isn't fast enough, maybe we will pick it up later. He just wanted to make things go, right then and there. I think he really had something to prove. I don't know if it was such a, you know, maybe... He told us, he says, he runs good when he is motivated by anger. I don't know who he was really angry at. I'm sure he's angry at the organizers in London for not letting him run there. But he was definitely angry on the track in Montreal.

That, with his newfound confidence, finally, he just believes in himself.

I am interested in the concept of fear as a barrier, as an opponent to be defeated. Dellinger said Pre was afraid. I had never heard anybody use the words Pre and fear in the same sentence. Got my attention. What I have noticed as a man and as a writer, I have been basically afraid all my life. Obviously, when you see people who are successful, it's not really tal-

ent, they're not afraid. Success is to be not afraid.

Well, you're right. I have to agree with you. Maybe he's just stop fearing. Maybe he just finally realized, and I am not saying this is what he told me or anything, but it just seems like he got to a point in his career where there is no sense being afraid.

He's already done... he's doing more at his age than anybody ever expected him to do. We all thought it was over in '92. At the '88 Trials when he didn't make the team, we thought he can move up to the marathon and give it a good shot in '92. But, after '92, I know for a few months, it was like, well, where do you go from here? You've got to go on with the rest of your life. It's folly for you to think you are going to make the Olympic team when you are 37 years old.

But he is physically gifted and he has taken advantage of all those physical tools, he hasn't abused his body. And he is probably the most consistent trainer that I have ever heard of or seen in my life. I'm sure that has a lot to do with it.

But the big thing I think mentally he thought, I've got nothing to prove to anybody and I want to ride this thing out just as far as I can.

At this point, jeez, he peaked. I'm not so sure but he's the American version of Carlos Lopes. Maybe he'll run his lifetime bests at age 37, 38. Who knows, even maybe beyond that. He's not putting any boundaries on himself. Like I've got to be done with this when I'm 39. Who knows, he may be 40 years old and running 27:30. I am not predicting, but I wouldn't be surprised at this point if he does.

Given the current crop of distance runners in this country, he could be making the team at 44. What an embarrassing phenomenon. I have a friend who started coaching after a 20-year retirement because he noticed today's top women are running the same times as his girls did in the early '70s. Ruth Wysocki, years retired, was sitting on her couch watching television and reading Track & Field News *Top Ten and knew right then she could still run with these kids. Placed 4th at The Nationals six months later.*

Not that Chris is one of those guys who came out of a five-year retirement or something. He's competed every year except the year he had his ankle surgery. He lost the '85 season. But every other year he's been out there, banging the roads, banging the track.

You can go back to '77 when he was on the U.S.A. World Junior team. That is quite a long tenure at the international class level.

He's a very quiet guy. Very modest. That's been his claim to fame up until now, he's been the guy who was ranked in the top 10, ranked in the 10000m, top 10 ranked in the marathon, but never a big star, but always consistent. Year in and year out. Named Mr. Road Racer.

Here's my premise. Let's just say, fear has never held him back but it's never let him get ahead. So, finally after 20 years, the guy finally puts it together. He goes to the World Championships and God only knows what happens there. That's probably the end of my story because I am running out of time. I would like to know how he overcame his fear. He didn't quit.

I think his hook-up with Greg Shank in '87 was a real great plus. And one of the reasons his career has been as long as it has, I think he might've been quits on the sport, if it hadn't been for Greg and, of course, the support he got through the shoe companies. I think the network of guys he's trained with when he came back here in '87 to where he grew up. It was like, one last year, blow it out until '88 and then you go with your adult life.

Then we made the decision not to do that. He got a lot of positive reinforcement instead of negative reinforcement. Other people weren't coming down on him, like you've got this Peter Pan syndrome, or what-ever. It was like, yeah, Chris, you've got the ability. You are one of the best American runners and who says you can't do it in '92.

I know he was very discouraged in '92. When he went off to Columbus for the marathon Trials, we all thought, this was his time. We knew he was every bit as good as Steve Spence. We thought he was better than Steve Spence. Steve is a great guy, we like him, you know, we love him, too. He lives about 17 miles from here. It was just something that really bothered Chris. Here's a guy I know I am physically more talented than he is. Steve got to see his dream come true and once again Chris had his dream crushed.

So, sometime between then and 1995, he just must have gotten tired of being second-string. And went after it.

At the '94 Penn Relays, up until what I saw him do up in Montreal a week and a half ago, those Penn Relays was the most impressive thing

I've seen him do. Even though it wasn't a major international breakthrough or anything, He ran 28:22 up there and he led that thing from the gun. It was a pretty decent field and John Sheer hung on him and outkicked him the last 300. That was the beginning of the new Chris Fox. That's when I first saw him go to the lead with a bunch of guys who were his equals, his peers, and just, say, dammit, I'm just going to run hard and if I die, I die.

It was a different Chris Fox than I had seen in a long time.

He said, hey, I want to run fast here and I am going to run fast here. I'm not going to sit in here and just get a qualifying time for the U.S.A. Track & Field Championships. I want to run fast. With no rabbits or anything else, you know. He went at it for 24 laps. He was cranking out the 67s and the 68s.

He might be changing. He used to pride himself on being a fast finisher. 3:59 flat in the mile, but that's a dozen years ago now. He sees himself as someone who can really put the pressure on you and hurt you.

That was his plan when he went to Sacramento. When Todd Williams went, he was going with him. He didn't know if he could go with Todd the whole way. But he figured when he did break, he was going to have a good enough gap on those guys behind that he wasn't going to have to worry about kicking. Actually, it worked out exactly the way he planned.

Everything except not getting the qualifying time out there. For which the weather wasn't too conducive.

Normally, before the '94 Penn Relays, he's the type of guy who tries to go with the pack and if the pack kinda whittles down... Like at the '84 Trials, he ran the 5000m final. It was like the pack whittled down and then he went to the fore with a mile to go, hoping to break things open. And, of course, it didn't work out perfect, but he still ended up finishing 5th.

But here was a guy two laps into it... AND RIGHT NOW. Dave Bedford style. Now. I am going to go.

Maybe it's a foolish thing. But it's aggressive, angry, not so young man.

Not too smart?

Maybe that's the way. I'll tell you, when he was a high school kid, and this is a zillion years ago, and I'm sure there are a bunch of stories like Chris'. He just went out at the gun and simply ran free-form. And they did better that way than they did when they'd sit in a group and you know watch things whittle away and play chess with the guys. I'm not saying he goes out and runs stupid, but if the pace is "smart", I think he is better off going to the front and doing it on his own.

When I look at Chris, I see him as a Ron Clarke type guy. Not that he's not a good competitor, but I see him as some guy who can go out front and do it on his own.

When he had to run this 11th hour qualifying time... The USAT&F wouldn't let him run in the Championships without a qualifying time, so he had to go out and get a qualifying time. We put this all-comers meet together. And he basically had to do all the work by himself. This guy ran 28:18 on a little high school track. Probably kind of reminiscent when Steve Prefontaine set that American Record for 2000m on his little high school track. I mean, it was an amazing performance. He was out there in a pair of racing flats, wasn't even wearing spikes. I started thinking to myself, this is the kind of thing Ron Clarke used to do. Just him and the stopwatch. Breaking his own wind. Pushing his own barriers back.

In high school, Chris and I weren't teammates, but we ran in the same conference. We ran for the same summer clubs, so I've known him since '74.

What's he like as a man?

He is very considerate of everybody else. You always hear that kind of stuff... couldn't happen to a nicer guy. With Chris, you hear that a lot of places. I'll tell someone I'm from Hagerstown, and they go, oh, do you know Chris Fox? He's running great and it couldn't happen to a nicer guy. But he's really like that. He is very concerned.

Maybe to the point where, you know, umm, he has a hard time transferring over from his regular-life guy, being really nice and really concerned about everyone's problems, to situations where he has to say, dammit, I am taking the lead and I am going to kick the crap out of you in this race. I think finally he is able to make that transition.

Where he is looking at these guys, and saying, enough is enough, these guys have been taking what's mine for all these years...

But as a person, he really is... He's always been the kind of person he's always been, these are all cliches, but he is an easy-going guy who doesn't have a temper and if guys start going at each other, he's the guy who's the mediator and has a way of getting them laughing.

In a way, he's a man and he's very mature, but there's a kid in him that's never grown up, maybe that's one reason he is doing so well still in the athletic world. It's still fun to him. He's kind of avoided a lot of the things that chased a lot of guys out of the sport.

The secret of his longevity?

Number one, he is very gifted. He's 6'1", 125 lbs. Not that he doesn't work very hard to keep that physique, but he hasn't taken the pounding maybe a guy who weighs 145 lbs. would've taken over the same 20 years of competition. He literally hasn't. He's like a ballerina. He's smooth as silk.

He's been gifted with very good concerned people who thought about his long term. Not just say, well, I'm gonna use this kid to try to win the state championship. Or we're going to try to be an All-American here. His high school coach was not abusive. I am kinda foggy on how things went for Chris down at Auburn. But I know he had a very good experience and he is still very close with them down there, so I imagine that was good for him. But I know his high school and post-collegiate guidance has always been excellent as far as getting advice.

He does a lot of running on soft surfaces, which I know the Europeans have been doing forever. I always thought the Americans were nuts to run on the roads as much as they do. In Hagerstown, we are lucky enough to have the C&L Canal pass run right through our county. He's on that on a daily basis.

He's really been conscious of keeping the machinery running right. Maybe this has always been his whole plan the whole time, thinking he was going to be someone who was going to have a 20-year world-class career.

After '84, it was like, okay, now I'll coach. And he did that for a while. And tried to keep his running going. Maybe there was always that allure, I didn't run nearly as good as I possibly could.

Eventually, if he does go into coaching as a career, he'll be super. He's helping a lot of open people as a advisor. After the '92 Olympics, thinking maybe it's time to go do that, he coached at George Washington for a year.

His running has always kept him back.

I think so. Seems every time he thinks, well, now I'll get a regular job and keep running whenever I can, all of a sudden, he'll start running super again. Maybe he just has a sense, I have to know.

Why hasn't he broken through sooner? I expected a long time ago, I thought when he was running as well as he was that first year or two out of Auburn. He graduated in '82, then he ran that 13:21 the summer of '83, I thought it would happen there. Maybe not '84.

You know, he had that setback, he had that cyst in his ankle joint that cost the '85 season and most of '86, '86 was like a rebuilding year for him, that had to set him back some. Maybe it would have happened in the mid-'80s, if it hadn't been that year and a half lost.

We were all pleasantly surprised to see his name show up in results again later in '86, even though it was really very minor regional road-race type stuff. Then in '87, he had a fabulous year. I think that's why he made the decision to go back and try to make the team in '88. That operation had to have something to do with why it took him so long to break through. He was off for a long time. As a matter of fact, a lot of people just wrote him off then. That he would never come back.

He did make the Olympic team. He's always been the guy who finished 4th or 5th, just missing. Everybody lived in Salazar's shadow in the early '80s. I always thought he was as good, if not better, than Eyestone and Spence. Maybe it was just a mental thing, not making it through at the big championships. Not doing well enough at the Olympic Trials to go on and do something.

Maybe he's unlucky. There are guys who were great runners who never made an Olympic team. Keith Brantly, although he may get that monkey here in a few months.

We can't all make the team.

Not to draw similarities with their personal lives, Chris reminds me of Barry Brown. He had this incredibly long career. Never made an Olympic team, but was always there. Got into his Masters and was still ranked at age 40. As a runner, I think Chris is closely related to him. Chris is even better. Although Barry ran a sub-4 minute mile, he didn't run no 27:53.

Best races?

When he won Cherry Blossom in 1990, I know that was a biggie for him. Personally, that was one he always wanted to win, too.

How fast is he?

I'll tell you, I think he can run 27:40. Just by looking at that 27:53. That night, if the rabbit had taken him through in 13:52 or 13:50, I think he was very capable of running 27:40 that night.

That's what he can do about now. I would like to think he will go to the World Championships and do better, but...

All of us are concerned, he's run a lot of 10,000s. The Pan-Am Games, the 10,000 qualifying for USA champs, the Nationals, the qualifying time for Worlds. So, he's run four pretty tough track 10,000s. I am hoping he is still on the upswing. I would be surprised if he ends up running faster at the World Championships. Because he has to run the rounds, I would be shocked if he ran faster in the finals. Considering they only have two days between the rounds and the finals.

He's almost due for a bad race.

I hope that doesn't happen. I hope he goes there, that the semis go the way he thinks it's going to go, that he can run his 28:20 or 28:25 without extending himself too far. Make it to the final and be able to run, you know, hopefully the race of his life.

He's going to have to run a smart race to make the finals.

This is going to be very difficult. I hope he can get away with running a 1:32 last 600m and that will be fast enough to make the final. I don't know how much faster he can go, unless the race is really pedestrian and under normal weather conditions.

And then you don't know who the other pedestrians are and what they're capable of. That 62 last lap at Montreal isn't all that impressive.

In Montreal with 600m to go, he looked back, the two guys ahead had broken away. I don't think he pushed. That's another reason makes me think he could've run 27:40 that night. I think he just basically finished that race. He wasn't going all out, knees and elbows down the last 200. He looked like he can pretty much run 62 seconds in the middle of a workout any time. Running halves or repeat miles. I think he can run 57 seconds, if it comes to that. Whether 57 seconds is going to be enough to do something for him in the final...

On the other hand, if he makes the final and lays down that 57 last lap to finish, say, 9th in the finals at the World Championships with a time of 27:40, you are going to have to hammer his feet into the pavement to keep him off the marathon team next February.

Yup. I think the marathon is where his next breakthrough is going to come. I was on the press vehicle down in Charlotte this past year, and that was a real heartbreak for him. He was really upset at himself. Because he saw himself no worse than 2nd in that race. Then as soon as stuff started happening, he was the first guy to go out the backdoor.

Why was that?

If you place a physical reason, he wasn't handling the downhills very well. Maybe it was the old demon like you've talked about jumped out there, "I don't know if I'm as good as these guys right now."

Maybe you can say it was the downhills, you were prepared for them, so you learned something. maybe you were a little short of mileage, blah, blah, blah. Maybe it was the old thing that poked its head up at the marathon trials in '92. Maybe he lacked that confidence, lacked the ability to hurt the way they were hurting at that point, or whatever.

I see him running under 2:10. Not down there at Charlotte. Not on that course and that will be his next marathon. I still see him running under 2:10. If he gets into a race like London, maybe Boston. He has the potential to break 2:10.

If he doesn't make the team at Charlotte, he'll change his focus to 10,000m. Without a doubt. Even if he does make the marathon team, I highly suspect he'll run a track season like he did this year and go to the Olympic Trials and run the 10,000m there.

He ran really poorly down at the Pan Am Games and he said he was just so overcome by the heat down there. He doesn't know how he stayed on his feet the last part of the race.

Right when the door opened on the track season, he went down to Colonial and ran that 5,000m against Peter Sherry, and I'm thinking, he's on a roll, he's really starting to believe in himself this year. He's not afraid to go to the front and make a hard move. He's just believing in himself.

We're a bunch of guys who have been hanging around with each other since we were teenagers. We're not really living our dreams through Chris, but we're just trying to let him know, if we can help him out in any way, we're there for him. If he needs somebody to ride a bike with him on a 20-mile run, heck, I'll sacrifice my run. We will help him out any way we can.

It's good for him to be around people who realize, and we feel like he is, what he is doing is important and worthwhile. Where he might not be getting that support from the same peer group someplace else.

I don't think Chris gets the credit for being that close to the top for that many years. For fifteen, sixteen years he's run 13:47 or faster. Not just that he's performed well, but what he had to go through to do that.

Even locally, I think people say, boy, he's a really skinny, talented guy. I don't think they see the little things he's always doing. Such as making sure he gets to physical therapy, making sure he's does the strengthening, the morning runs he's meticulously out for by himself. He doesn't get caught up. I'll toss out a name to you. A world-class runner in the early '80s from this area, Terry Baker. Terry had a hard time doing the little things and saying goodbye to the guys at 11 p.m. because he had to go home and get his rest. Chris has the discipline to get his rest.

He's a great motivator. My wife is on the downside of her career, she ran 33:51 on the track for 10000m, and she made it to the '88 Trials, which was one of her lifetime goals. And Chris was a big force in that. He shows interest in a lot of people that I think most guys at his level just run on by. Chris really gets into it. He gets into a kid breaking 10 minutes for the 2M, just as much as himself making the Olympic team.

He's great for the sport.

Shank is the same way. He's coaching 37-minute guys. He just likes to see people who want to get good, or want to be better at least, he likes to see them work hard. And he'll help him.

Shank is a big reason for Chris' success, at least for the last 8 years. Shank is a guy, he won't take a dime, he won't take a dime from you for his help. You see guys gets ruined by agents and everything else. And Greg Shank has never taken a penny. He wanted to help Terry Baker fifteen years ago. And when Chris came to town, and said, "Would you help me?" Greg never hesitated. Greg always has kept Chris focused on achieving his long time goals, not going for the quick buck.

After the Work, the Rest is Easy
December 1975

Dr. E.C. "Ned" Frederick wondering if he should call 911 after Jack's 2:46:07

What follows is the first article of mine ever published nationally. It appeared – probably – in the December 1975, edition of Runner's World. *Later reprinted in* The Complete Book of Marathoning. *Dr. E.C. Frederick was the originator of the piece, co-author and the source of anything scientific therein. Back in those days, Ned and I were the closest of friends, which is often what happens when two people run together daily. He al-lowed me to keep stride alongside... And the piece appears here with his permission.*

His doctors were upset at his determination to race. It appeared point-less. Not even Emil Zatopek could hope to overcome the debilitating ef-fects of his hospitalization in time to compete.

Zatopek had been bedridden for some two weeks with a serious stom-ach ailment. It seemed impossible he could be competitive after missing two weeks of training and in such a weakened state. Nevertheless, his de-termination won out and within an hour of his discharge, he was aboard a plane for Brussels and the 1950 European Championships. The rest is his-tory.

Zatopek nearly lapped second-placer Alain Mimoun in the 10,000 me-ters and captured the 5000m by a 23-second margin. Distance running historian Peter Lovesey has termed his victories "the most decisive double long-distance victory in any major international championship." It seems only logical to add that Zatopek's effort was all the more amazing when we remember the two weeks of training he missed.

Or was it?

Most modern coaches and runners would have us believe that every-day training is essential for maximal performances. Equally well touted is the dogma that points to continuous hard work as the only path to high-level running achievement.

We have serious doubts about the truth underlying these ideas. If this training dogma were based on fact, then how could Zatopek, for example, achieve his decisive victories following two weeks of bed rest? A "fluke" would be the answer of the hard trainers. Or perhaps it could be explained away by Zatopek's overwhelming superiority or by speculating poor prep-aration on the part of his competitors.

These criticisms might be reasonable if the Zatopek story were an ex-ceptional one. The startling realization is that this pattern is not unique. Similar incidents have happened time and again.

Several years ago, Dave Bedford surprised the track world by running a world record for 10,000 meters. The surprise was not that Bedford had run that fast but that he had done it with only minimal training. Bedford had been nursing a hamstring injury, which hampered his running. Instead of his characteristic high-mileage weeks, which sometimes pushed 200 miles, he had barely averaged 25 miles weekly for a three-month period.

Bedford did have the benefit of three weeks of accelerated training following this light period. But few serious proponents of the hard-training dogma would consider three weeks enough to put the athlete at a world-record peak. The answer has to be in his rest.

Dick Tayler, 1974 Commonwealth Games competitor, was in a similar situation. Torn ankle ligaments allowed him only three weeks of hard training before the Games. He won gold in the 10K with a time of 27:46.4.

Another Commonwealth Games competitor, 800-meter silver medalist Mike Boit, also had little training before the New Zealand competition. After a month's layoff, he trained only two weeks before running 1:44.4 in the final.

A not so dramatic example is supplied by Craig Virgin. Virgin was unable to train for more than a month due to severe tendonitis. In early February 1975, he began training again, and on February 11th he ran an indoor double. While his times of 4:12.5 and 8:51 are not world-class, they were, at the time, strong performances for Virgin.

Emil Puttemans missed 14 days of training six weeks before the '72 Munich 10,000 final. Yet he ran 27:39 to win the silver medal.

Dave Wottle missed 31 days of training between the Trials and the Munich Olympic Games, averaging only about four miles a day during that period. Yet he had the strength to come from behind in the 800-meter final and win the most exciting race of the Games.

The examples go on and on at all levels of competition. The pattern repeats itself again and again: *Hard work + rest = success.*

We can learn from these examples. They teach us that our ideas of what constitutes an effective training program need some revision. We need to take a closer look at the function of rest in a running program. But, before doing that, we need some perspectives on the use of rest in modern training programs.

Over-trained runners are much more common than under-trained runners. Observing this aspect of the problem, you would think runners were generally uninformed about the importance of rest. Ironically, this does not seem to be the case.

Engage a group of runners in a conversation about rest, and you'll find most agree rest is important. Most will also agree they probably don't get enough of it. Perhaps a number of them will even admit to having given more rest some serious thought. But in all likelihood, only a very few will ever have done anything about it. At least not voluntarily.

Rest is much like stretching exercises in that respect. A lot of lipservice is paid to its importance, even to its *necessity.* But few runners actually incorporate stretching into their training programs. We are creatures of habit, and our bad habits (or lack of good ones) are firmly entrenched.

Realizing the worth of something, intellectually, does not guarantee a constructive change will result. Cognition is one phenomenon, application another. Most often, the bad situation will persist, and the new realization will fade into the background.

This seems particularly true when dealing with ideas that relate to the body and health. How many people do you know who wish they could lose a few pounds or give up smoking but "just can't"?

The reason so many runners have neither stretching nor rest built into their training programs can only be apathy and/or negligence. The reason they don't care is largely an attitude we have developed about natural things and their relationship to the will.

What enforces this attitude is a lack of any clear conception of why rest is needed and what rest does. Further, many runners have no idea of how much rest is needed or just how to go about resting.

Our Western concept of the path to success doesn't include rest. Instead, the formula contains liberal doses of persistent hard work aimed at overcoming resistance – the resistance supplied by natural physical limits, intellectual capability, financial constraints, etc. It seems like it is always man *against* nature – man overcoming himself. When we get a headache from overstressing, do we stop and rest? No, we take a pill and forge on. The body is just another obstacle on the path to success. All too often, we see our own bodies as objects of conquest rather than cooperation.

This brings to mind a story about the first ascent of Mount Everest. There are some enlightening parallels with competitive running.

When Edmund Hilary and Tensing Norgay returned from their successful climb, they had different ideas about what had just taken place. New Zealander Hilary spoke triumphantly of conquering the mountain. Norgay, a Sherpa, saw things differently. He stated humbly, "The mountain and I together attained the heights."

More often than not, runners see their bodies as Hilary saw Everest – as an obstacle in their paths. When a runner does well, the impression one gets is that success has come in spite of the body, rather than *because* of the body.

Apparently, many (if not most) runners have lost touch with the simplest of realities. They have lost sight of the fact it is the whole organism which achieves and not just the power of will. Most runners are too busy conquering themselves with high-mileage weeks to see the profound significance of this idea.

If we could only realize we can gain more (in the largest sense) by co-operating with the body than by trying to conquer it, everything would fall into place. We would begin to see running as a means to develop the body to make maximal performance possible. Words like "nurture, coax and develop" would replace "thrash, push and force." The necessity of rest would be dramatically obvious.

Running is an exercise in destruction. Each time we run, we tear ourselves down. Muscle tissue is torn. Mitochondria, the powerhouses of the cells, swell grotesquely. Metabolic wastes accumulate. Blood-sugar levels drop. Dehydration occurs and, along with it, excessive losses of electrolytes upset the delicate balance required for efficient muscle and nerve function. We become overheated. Muscle glycogen is depleted. And, as the intensity and/or duration of the workout increase, this damage becomes more pronounced.

In the period between runs, the body attempts to recover and to rebuild. Torn muscle is repaired. New mitochondria are formed, metabolic wastes are flushed out of the system, blood-sugar levels are restored. We rehydrate and replace lost electrolytes. Any damage to muscles and to the nervous system due to hyperthermia (high body temperature) is repaired. Glycogen is replenished.

These two phases – destruction and regeneration – *together* constitute conditioning. And the two can never be separated if conditioning is to proceed in a positive direction.

In any program of running, then, the body is systematically broken down and rebuilt. And each rebuilding leaves the body a little stronger than before. These incremental increases amount to the development of a progressively stronger body, capable of more and faster running. That is, if the rebuilding is done correctly.

If the body is not allowed to complete the rebuilding phase of training for lack of time (rest) or materials (nutrition), the destruction will eventually exceed the body's ability to repair itself. Conditioning will proceed at a slower rate or not at all. In extreme cases, conditioning can actually deteriorate.

On the other hand, if the breakdown phase (the stress) is not optimal, then progress is also retarded. Since we all have become experts at the "stress" phase of training, nothing needs to be said about effective training methods. But the rebuilding phase – let's call it "regeneration" – does need some elucidation.

Some aspects of the regenerative phase take longer than others. All depend, to a certain degree, on the intensity and duration of the stress. For example, glycogen depletion, mitochondrial destruction and extensive muscle tissue damage all take about 48 hours to be completely reversed. Eating properly, getting plenty of rest and a little exercise seem to promote regeneration. Still, the time period needed to completely return to the status quo is well over 40 hours.

To understand how this information fits into a running program, we must juggle different intensities and durations of runs with the frequency of runs.

First of all, no one runs all day every day, so we have, say, 21–23 hours of non-exercise time during each day to recover from the physical havoc created by a daily run. It should be obvious the greater the amount of time spent in intensive rest (e.g., sleep), the more effective the rest time is. It should be obvious the more and faster we run, the more there is added to the "regenerative load."

This regenerative load is the product of the speed and distance of workouts, and is also influenced by the quality and quantity of rest during the same time period. We can, therefore, regulate this load by controlling the relationship between our daily dose of destruction and our daily capacity to regenerate.

Let's say, we take a hard 20-mile run in the afternoon of day one. If we do nothing on days two and three but rest and recuperate, we should be completely regenerated by the afternoon of day three. But few runners would be willing to do no running for such period of time. So, they are going to contribute to the regenerative load by running during this recovery time. If, however, they do only light workouts, get more rest than usual, and eat a diet rich in carbohydrates, protein, vitamins and minerals, they should regenerate on schedule. Or possibly they will need 72 hours to recover rather than the usual 48-hour period.

By tuning into such body signs as stiffness and soreness, lack of energy, cravings for sweets, etc., it is possible for a runner to determine the period required for rebuilding from a particular workout. Workouts, rest and diet can then be adjusted to promote quick and total regeneration.

However, if runners do the opposite, if they continue hard workouts and make no concessions in the lifestyle, then they will be delaying recovery from the hard run. Indeed, if high-intensity training is maintained continually, then the body never catches up with the regenerative load, and eventually staleness & overstress symptoms will result.

In this way, workouts can be varied in intensity and duration from day to day to promote regeneration. Running hard or long only every 48 hours seems to be optimal. In between, workouts should be short and/or easy. And one's life should be adjusted to maximize regeneration. Plenty of sleep is certainly important, but what one does with the waking hours is equally so.

This "cycling" of workouts is nothing new. Enlightened students of distance running, like Bill Bowerman and Tom Osler, have been preaching such cycling for years. Its efficiency at producing optimal training effects has been proven time and again by the high proportion of world-class runners who have flourished on this type of program. So there should be little doubt this type of training schedule is effective.

Much has been written about the structure and application of hard-easy training programs, so in all likelihood we wouldn't be able to contribute anything worthwhile. An area that does need to be developed, however, is the application of rest in this type of program. The resting phase is just as important as the running phase, and just as capable of being refined and perfected to produce maximal effects. Let's take a look at some regenerative techniques with an aim to maximizing our gains from this phase of conditioning.

Rest can be divided into two types: "passive rest" and "active rest." Passive rest is what we normally do, or actually *don't* do. In short, passive rest is inactivity. We do nothing in particular to promote rest, but instead give nature time to run its course. Passive rest certainly is important and effective. Such rest has its place in a program of regeneration.

But there are other activities we can *do* which will enhance regeneration and will multiply the effectiveness of rest. We would lump these activities under the heading of active rest. In other words, we are doing things to more effectively utilize the regenerative effects of rest.

After a hard run, activities such as light stretching, meditation, a sauna or a massage will cause regeneration to proceed more quickly than if we simply took a nap. These sorts of activities are regeneration promoting. Liberal doses of active rest can quicken and deepen healing, and thereby enhance the rebuilding of the body after a destructive run.

Yoga-type stretching exercises have been shown to stimulate circulation in all areas of the body but particularly in the exercised areas. There is also an enhancement of oxygenation of the tissues, not to mention the physical effects of the stretches on the muscle fibers themselves.

Meditation has been studied by a variety of researchers, and the majority of them have found meditation to be an intense form of relaxation and rest. The physiological state achieved in meditation is thought to be deeper even than sleep.

Sauna baths and steam baths are cleansing and often produce an intense relaxation, a relief of tension. Swimming and massage have similar relaxing qualities and have the added effect of promoting deep circulation.

These activities also have a soothing effect on the psyche, something which we have neglected so far, but something which is of equal or more importance than the physical factors we've mentioned. We can regenerate a psyche which has been damaged or overworked by a long or hard run using the same positive approach we have taken in healing the body.

Do something unusual. Take a walk somewhere you've never been before, read something different, sit in a bus station and watch the world in action, catch a Walt Disney movie, take a long drive over a back road, stroll in the rain, visit the ocean, go to a museum, make love. Not necessarily in that order nor one after another. In short, do something that will increase your awareness, stimulate you, generate new interests and ideas. It is just as important to have a fresh, healthy interest in your running as it is to have a sound body to do it with.

Bedford, Zatopek, et al., have stumbled upon the secret of this relationship. They have all followed long months of intense work with extended rest and then gone on to achieve superlative performances.

Their long months of steady intense work with only minimal regeneration produced a maximal stress load accumulated over time. The result was either sickness or breakdown beginning a period of enforced rest. During this prolonged rest period, their bodies were given the time and materials to completely rebuild – to adapt to the maximal stress which they had accumulated during months of intense training. In short, the body had time to catch up. The results were impressive.

Actually, what they were doing was no more than an expanded version of what every runner should be doing constantly. Using the running-regeneration cycle on a day-to-day basis is a much more efficient way to accomplish the same goal – maximal adaptation.

Even the most conscientiously designed balance of running and regeneration is bound to produce an accumulation of stress over a long period of time. For this reason, runners should cultivate an awareness of the signs of overstress and be prepared to take extended non-running rest periods from time to time.

For example, world three-mile record-holder Emiel Puttemans at least once yearly has a period in which he does no running at all. He overeats, gets a little sloppy, becoming the antithesis of his normal self. Puttemans claims these "rest" days are the most important part of his annual training pattern.

Ron Hill, a 2:09 marathoner, used to take at least a week's "vacation" during which he ran two workouts daily – two miles in the morning and two miles in the afternoons.

Although the idea of not running for even a day can generate tremendous anxiety in certain runners, we don't believe their fears are well founded. After all, look what rest did for Zatopek and Bedford.

Thoughts on Training
April 1979

Greg Meyer (#3) heading to victory at 1983 BAA Marathon

The legendary Jack Foster has said he doesn't train, he just runs every day. He does it well enough to have run a 2:11 marathon at the age of 41. Do not be misled by Foster's disclaimer – he is most certainly training. Frank Shorter once pointed out, "You don't run 2:10 on good looks and a secret recipe." You have to train, and you have to train properly.

A runner cannot possibly train properly unless he knows why he is training. An athlete should think of his training as a jigsaw puzzle. Each day, every workout, is another piece. To successfully complete that puzzle, he must have a good understanding of what it will look like when he's finished putting the puzzle together.

Do you run to race faster, to lose weight, or to forget the stock market? Are you trying to run a half-mile PR or break 3 hours for the marathon? Unless you are running for the sheer thrill of the wind in your hair – not that there's anything wrong with that – you should know why you are out there. You should design your running to maximize the likelihood you'll attain your goals.

Perhaps the optimal design for a training program is according to the principle of *specificity*. Simply put, specificity means the best way to learn to do something is by doing it. A boy or girl becomes a good basketball player by playing basketball, not by bowling. An athlete who wants to race fast should prepare by running fast in training. Jogging slowly will make you a good slow jogger. (LSD training has demonstrated an athlete can indeed run slowly in practice and race much faster in competition. Remember, however, one does not necessarily follow the other, as does night the day.)

Specificity describes training designed to mimic the desired response. A runner who wants to cover 26.2 miles in less than three hours will not train by running repeat 100-yard sprints. He will, however, run long distances at a pace around 6:50 per mile. At least he will, if he knows what training is meant to accomplish.

Training is meant to cause the athlete's body to adapt to specific stresses. If a person trains by covering one mile in 5½ minutes, his body will modify its physiological functions to meet the demand. The runner will adapt so he will be able to run that distance at that pace.

A 10-kilometer race requires a 5% anaerobic effort. A marathon is about 99% aerobic, but there is still that 1% without oxygen. If that percentage correlates exactly – and I imagine it does not – then one minute and forty-eight seconds of a three-hour marathon require anaerobic ability. The runner who has not prepared in training to perform anaerobically is therefore handicapped. A marathoner who trains 10 miles daily can run just one fast mile weekly and exceed the 1% anaerobic level.

Specificity applies to factors other than speed. It makes sense to me, if you want to race long, you must train long. Why should a body that has never run farther than 10 miles in training be expected to go another 16 in competition? Certainly there are many marathoners who never run long workouts, yet they can cover the 26.2 miles with aplomb.

I myself have run a marathon personal best without a single training run exceeding 12 miles. That does not make it an intelligent scheme, however. Note well: my run was most assuredly achieved without aplomb.

I am unaware of any runners who perform well on hilly courses without having run hills in training. Uphill running is cardiovascular interval work. It's tough, and it must be practiced to allow the runner to adapt to that particular stress.

Once you go up a hill, you'll probably have to run down. That is not as easy as it may sound. The legs take a terrible beating on a downhill course. If you don't believe anything else you read here, please believe you had better practice downhill running before you compete at Boston or the Fiesta Bowl marathon. That is, if you want to be able to walk up a flight of stairs the next couple of days.

A few more words about specificity. Train at least once weekly on the surface upon which you plan to race. Although I would love to run a marathon with a slight downhill grade on a firm, yet yielding surface – preferably with a tail wind – I have yet to locate such a venue. I doubt you have either. If you are racing on hard macadam roads, it is important you occasionally train on them. The legs must be introduced to the stress they will encounter during the competition.

Beach runs are an excellent example. Since your foot goes "beneath" the plane of the surface, your Achilles tendons are stretched much more than normal. Anyone who races in sand should run on the beach several times before the actual competition. Clearly, additional stretching of the lower leg is similarly advisable.

If you expect to race well, you might think – strongly – about simulating race conditions in training. Long after your body has surrendered to the rigors of competition, your mind can continue to push and strive. I do not believe it is reasonable to expect such desire will naturally evolve from the race situation itself.

Training must be done in *doses*, and I mean that in a pharmaceutical sense. Two aspirins may cure a headache, yet a bottle of the same compound will most likely cause death. The same principle applies to training. 10 x 440 twice weekly might make you a faster runner. 10 x 440 twice daily might make you a golfer with a limp.

Many modern athletes seem to ask, "How much is too much?" Instead of trying to determine how little they need to succeed, they invariably see how much they can do before breaking down. You can only discover the answer to "How much is too much?" when it is too late.

Better training *is not necessarily more* training. Sometimes less can be more. More better. The athlete must evaluate his entire lifestyle, not just his running. Eight hours of basketball on a rest day is obviously not a respite from the physical rigors of running. Okay, it is a respite from running, but not from the "rigors." A sleepless night, or an argument with your spouse, must be acknowledged because this, too, is stress.

It is essential to purge your mind of the idea the more miles you run, the better/faster you will become.

Many runners count miles as if they were coins of the realm, each alike, each of the same value. An athlete may jog five miles one day, then race a five-mile personal best the next day; he will log ten miles total in his diary. The first run is seen the same as the second. After all, five miles is five miles, right? Wrong. Ludicrous, but many people count their miles just that way. Why? Because they evaluate their running by the total mileage accumulated.

The running community continually reinforces this "miles-are-everything" syndrome. Every profile of an athlete contains a note about his mileage totals. Runners are always comparing their weekly sum against that of others. The first thing non-runners ask is "How far do you run?" And don't you just love it? Your spine straightens, your chest swells: "Oh, I'm injured, so I've cut back to just 80 miles a week."

I actually said that once. Once, at least. And I hereby publicly apologize. (One of my fonder sports memories is hearing my non-running brother exclaim, with not a little bemusement: "You know, you put more miles on your legs this year than I did on my car.")

Let's stop comparing mileage. The next time you get into a conversation with another runner, don't ask how far he or she ran last month. Instead, inquire: "How many runs did you enjoy? How many times last month did you dread going out in the rain?" (Here you can insert your own climatological burden.) Compare something meaningful, something important, something real, if you must compare anything at all.

Those running magazines which publish training schedules could use this theory to great advantage. After all, who wants to emulate some star who dreads every workout? I would much rather see something like... Frank Shorter, 30 years old, 2:10:30 PR. Trains 10 great, 15 okay, 3 poor, 2 abysmal days per month.

This method of running measurement would do much to eliminate the unfortunate prejudice leveled at those people who run fewer miles. Just as skin color is no indication of one's worth as a person, mileage is no gauge of a runner. I know it is simplistic, but these prejudices exist.

Since mileage is not a rational indicator of one's running, ummm, worthiness, a three-mile a day runner can be just as admirable as the person who does twenty miles. The person who jogs seven great runs weekly is surely "superior" to one who runs faster but logs just a single great day.

And if you must compare mileage still, the first runner would run 21 great miles weekly, whereas the second could only manage 20. Less is truly more.

Hubert Humphrey often said that life is not to be endured, but enjoyed. You should apply that wisdom to your training.

I wrote these notes nearly 35 years ago. Probably after a 100 mile week. In those days, I often went out at 10:30 at night, because I needed to get in a few more miles. Needed to.

And what you learn about running and what you learn about life is... it's not the stuff you do, but how you do the stuff you do... that's what really matters. – JDW

Chapter Six

At the Races

Sometimes there are places to be. The Honolulu Marathon in early December is such a place, especially for one escaping the rain of Oregon. Oregon, home of world-class events like the Cascade RunOff and the Hood To Coast Relay. Sometimes there is history to be made. The first women's USA Olympic Trials in 1984 was historic because the sport finally came of age, an age of equality.

What a Boston!

April 1979

April 16, 1979 - "The King. The greatest long distance runner in the history of the world, the greatest runner alive today. Ladies and gentlemen - Bill Rodgers!"

Finish line announcer Tom Grilk may tend, when excited, towards hyperbole and redundancy but no one cared as Bill Rodgers bested a Boston Marathon field of perhaps 10,000 while establishing an American Record of 2:09:27. Fukuoka victor Toshihiko Seko placed 2nd in 2:10:12, while Bob Hodge surprised everyone by slashing over 16 minutes from his PR to finish 3rd in 2:12:30. Tom Fleming, who led for the first 15M, maintained a strong effort to place 4th with 2:12:56.

Twenty-one-year-old Joan Benoit of Bowdoin College and Cape Elizabeth, Maine, also set an American Record, winning in 2:35:15 (477th overall). Patti Lyons, who received a pre-race cortisone injection for bursitis in her right foot, finished 2nd in 2:38:22. Both shattered Liane Winter's 1975 course record of 2:42:24.

The 1979 Boston Marathon was a record breaker, there is little doubt. Fourteen men broke 2:15 (ten had done so in '78). Fifty-four went below 2:20, surpassing last year's record of 32.

Fifty-seven Americans reached the Olympic Trials qualifying standard of 2:21:54 - Frank Shorter, who placed 79th, missed the mark by just two seconds. The once formidable 2:30 barrier was breached by 286 athletes.

The women shattered some marks themselves. For starters, 520 females had qualified for the race by having run sub-3:30. Here, fifteen bested 2:50 and 2:55:23 was worth no better than 25th. Benoit's record was more than 35 minutes faster than Nina Kuscik's winning time in 1972.

Clearly, this year's April classic was amazing even before the gun sounded. Ten sub-2:12 racers were entered. Some 90 entries had broken 2:20, and 7877 officially qualified marathoners combined with, I don't know, two or three thousand shadow runners to form the largest - and the best - field in Boston's history.

As no less than a half-dozen helicopters hovered overhead, the starter's gun barked. Fleming burst to the fore, and the world-class front runners followed, while most of the rest jogged in place.

With drizzling, overcast skies, and temperatures of 42-45 degrees, the runners were in no mood to hang around Hopkinton. Australia's Elizabeth Hassell led the women through 5M in 28:00, as Mr. Fleming led everybody, passing 6.7 miles in 31:54 and 10.8M in 50:08 (4:39 pace).

Bob Doyle, unaware he would run a PR 2:14:03, recalled, "We went by 10M in 48:30. I looked up and there were two hundred guys ahead of me. I almost quit right there."

Fleming didn't quit. "I just figured I'd run as fast as I could for as long as I could," he said. "I wanted to see if they could catch me."

At one stage, the 27-year-old veteran from Bloomfield, New Jersey, had built a lead of perhaps 250 yards. Rodgers remained in the chase pack with such luminaries as Shorter, Don Kardong, Chris Stewart and Jerome Drayton.

"Tom was running a 2:08 pace and I knew it was too cold to run that fast," Rodgers said. "I figured he had to come back to us."

Fleming did come back. After passing the Wellesley checkpoint (13.75 miles) in 1:05:01, he finally surrendered the lead to Garry Bjorklund at 15M.

Here, Rodgers thought BJ would win. "Garry seemed very smooth, very strong," the defending champion noted. "But I just tried to keep things together, to stay close... I wanted to wait for the hills."

Wait, he did. At 19.6M, Billy - with Seko following as if on a leash - passed Bjorklund. Despite feeling sluggish, Rodgers relentlessly cranked up the pace, establishing a 50-yard lead in the next two miles.

The 23-year-old Seko, a 27:51.7 10K performer and history's 10th-fastest marathoner, was no match for Boston Billy. The Japanese star later lamented: "It wasn't that the hills were so big; it was just that there were so many of them."

There is only one Bill Rodgers. On the downhill side of Heartbreak, which sounds like a country tune, Bill displayed his incredible ability. By Coolidge Corner (24.12M, reached in 1:58:41), Rodger's third Boston victory was assured. He could savor his win this year, in contrast to 1978, when he was forced by Jeff Wells to sprint to the finish line.

"I was running easily the last three-quarters of a mile," Rodgers said. "I never knew how fast I was going until the last 50 yards, I saw the clock over the finish line and realized I had to sprint to become the fourth fastest in history. I probably could've gotten under [Ian] Thompson's 2:09:12, if I hadn't spent so much time waving to the crowd. Oh, well."

Oh, well, indeed. Even while relishing his victory and acknowledging his fans, Rodgers still managed to run the last two miles in 26 seconds less than he had while clocking his former American Record (2:09:55 in '75). More incredibly, he could read a clock, remember record lists, and then sprint, after demolishing one of the most impressive collections of marathon runners ever assembled. Clearly, Bill Rodgers is a man apart.

So, too, is his team, the Greater Boston Track Club. With four of the top ten finishers, one wonders if anyone even bothered to total point scores before awarding the team trophy. In addition to Rodgers, Bob Hodge was 3rd, Randy Thomas 8th, and Dick Mahoney 10th. As Rodgers himself said, "We didn't just win the team prize; we beat all the other countries. We could take this club and win the Olympics."

Such an eventuality might not be any more surprising than Hodge's breakthrough to the No. 11 spot on the all-time U.S. list. One does not really want to call Hodgie a "surprise." But, after all, the 5-8/125 Lowell graduate was wearing bib number 1066.; his previous best WAS a 2:28. Even Hodge described himself as "mildly shocked," since his goal was 2:15.

He was similarly shocked when he went past 10M in "47 and change" with 26-30 guys. Despite a slight lack of confidence in his training - averaging 99 miles weekly - Hodge never faltered.

"I knew I could race the hills, 'cause we had run them very hard regularly in training. I just decided to hang tough."

Hanging tough was what the 83rd Boston was all about. Bjorklund faded off the pace at 20M, but still hung on for a PR. "At 22 miles, I felt like someone had hit me with a hammer. I've never felt that bad." BJ was clearly not satisfied. "I ran a shitty race. What does 5th-place get you except tired legs and depression?"

Fifth will also probably get Bjorklund a shot at the Pan-American Games, if he wants to go. Both Rodgers ("I don't want to die!") and Hodge ("It doesn't exactly thrill me.") are unlikely to participate in the July marathon in Puerto Rico.

Rodgers plans to run the World Cup in August and "probably" New York City in October. Hodge, admittedly not a hot weather runner, is one who prefers his marathons few and far between.

Let us not forget the women, no one did. No one could. Benoit passed the mile mark in 5:42, way behind the leader. Lyons was leading at the halfway mark, as well she should have been - her unofficial time was a briliant 1:14. Consider that women's "World Record" is 1:15:01 and Patti was running on a sore foot.

Benoit, Boston Red Sox cap askew, finally caught Lyons at the base at Heartbreak Hill. These two marvelous athletes raced stride for stride, until

Joanie pulled ahead a mile later. She never looked back.

Her win slashed 15 minutes from her personal best (a 2:50 workout in Bermuda this January) and 68 seconds from the American Record (Julie Brown's 2:36:23 at Nike/OTC last September). The pixieish - the adjective, soon to be abused by reporters and despised by the subject, is nonetheless most descriptive - Benoit is now the world's 4th-fastest marathoner. Grete Waitz's 2:32:30, Christa Vahlensieck's 2:34:48 and Chantal Langlace's 2:35:13 are the only faster runs. Clearly, those marks may be in danger if Benoit applies herself to the 26.2M event, as she appears capable of a sub-2:30.

In contrast to the chaotic crowd situation of 1978, this year's spectators were a more ruly group. Certainly, the cool, dismal weather played a role, but more people along the route is almost unimaginable. No portion of the course was without its coterie of marathon aficianados. Obviously, the various law enforcement agencies decided to do an exceptionally professional job of crowd restraint. There were no problems, except for the few runners who fell in a heap after stepping in a heap left behind by a mounted policeman or, more precisely, by the policeman's mount. However, apparently, the best policing of the crowd was by the crowd itself. The people of Boston love the marathon, and the safety of the marathoners this year became a major concern.

The Boston Marathon has always been special because of the spectators' support. No one received more support this year than favorite son, Bill Rodgers. Few have so richly deserved it, or so spectacularly responded to the adulation. There have now been 22 marathons run at sub-5:00 pace, and he has run five of them. Grilk may not be exaggerating. Rodgers may just be the greatest long distance runner in the world today. Bill Rodgers may just be "The King." He would wear the crown well.

(I write about the 1979 Boston Marathon with some authority. My bib number was 2566. I was among the legions who jogged in place - took 48 seconds just to get to the starting line. Then, still no room to run. My official time was 2:53:18, which I noted in my diary had to be worth no worse than 2:50. - JDW)

New York City Marathon, October 26, 1980
October 1980

14,012 starters/12,620 finishers.

The Rookie. The very nickname speaks of youth and potential. Spectacular accomplishments which must merely preface an imminently glorious career.

The Mule. Another of the sobriquets to which this particular 22-year-old answers. This name an indication of his awesomely stubborn tenacity. His ability to push himself to the limits of his body - and indeed beyond - is already legend. This is, after all, the man who was packed in ice and who received the last rites of his church after collapsing in the heat of Falmouth in 1978. He tried very hard.

Alberto Salazar. The true name of the 7th-fastest marathoner in world history and 2nd-fastest American ever following his 2:09:41 triumph in the 1980 NYC Marathon. Not an insignificant effort by any measure, the result requires special acknowledgement since this was the University of Oregon senior's first race at the distance. Indeed, his initial venture beyond eight miles.

More experienced runners followed in his wake, as favored Bill Rodgers finished 5th. Mexico's Rodolfo Gomez, who had led the Olympic Marathon from 12 through 23 miles, finished 2nd in a career-low 2:10:14. Briton John Graham clocked 2:11:47 in his third ever 26-miler, edging 4th-place Jeff Wells (2:12:00).

Norway's peerless Grete Waitz, who placed 74th overall, cannot run 2:09, but already there is talk of sub-2:20. In the third marathon of her life - all of which have been in the New York race - she produced her third consecutive World Record. This latest, 2:25:42, cut the 2:27:33 she ran here last year. Which, in turn, reduced her 2:32:30 of 1978.

Patti Lyons-Catalano (116th overall) became the second woman to break the 2 1/2-hour barrier with her American Record 2:29:34. That lowered the mark of 2:30:57 she had run just seven weeks earlier in Montreal.

Waitz's teammate, Ingrid Kristiansen, took nearly 11 minutes off her previous best 2:45:15 with 2:34:25 in 3rd as the first seven women all set personal bests.

After Wells in 4th, no one else broke 2:13 on a course generally considered to be something less than fast with its many sharp turns and occasionally hazardous footing. The weather was a factor, but only a few agreed whether it was a positive or negative one. Forty-five degrees F. with a blustery wind seems somewhat less than ideal.

However, the bluster reached 35mph and originated at the runners' collective rear for most of the race. Call it a tailwind, which it was for about 20M, but then the course took a turn while the wind did not. As Gomez noted, and every marathoner knows, the 6M of headwind seemed much more of a handicap than the 20M of tailwind had been an aid.

More than 14,000 starters gathered at the Verrazano Narrows Bridge on Staten Island, many of them hours before the race and clothed in garbage bags to combat the chilling wind. Gary Fanelli and Fenk Nenshun led the hordes over the bridge and China's Fenk led through 4M (18:54). Salazar and Norway's Oyvind Dahl were among the most prominent followers. A green-and-yellow knit hat, with pompom above and 4-time race champ Rodgers below, bobbed in the middle of the group of leaders.

"Since this was my first marathon, I wasn't going to force the pace like I might do in a track race," Salazar said after it was all over. "I just wanted to hang with the leaders and get to a point where I could pick up the pace."

Salazar's coach, Bill Dellinger, later explained, "We wanted him to stay with the main group at the lead and each time it became a smaller group, he was to stay in contact... keep moving with them until 6M was left, a distance Alberto was familiar with. At that point, it would be a little more than a 10,000-meter race."

Many tried to get the best of Salazar. Dave Babiracki got the honors through 9M, but only by a stride. It was Steve Floto - he of the movie-star looks, shag haircut and 2:15:55 PR - who finally began to break up the pack. His job was made easier when misfortune struck down Rodgers just beyond 20-kilometers.

The American Record holder collided with another runner and fell heavily at that point, losing as much as 100m on the leaders. ("I hit somebody, tripped and went flying through the air. No, I don't know who it was," Billy said later.) He sprang back up and, despite a slight limp and a pair of well-skinned knees, sprinted to close the gap.

But the effort was too much even for the great Rodgers, who had raised some eyebrows by running in the Toronto Marathon just three weeks earlier. Bill narrowed the margin to 50m, but never got closer and eventually came home a disappointed 5th in 2:13:21.

At the same time as Rodgers was picking himself up off the pavement, Floto was making a move. He went through the halfway point at 1:04:42, some ten seconds clear of Salazar. By 15M (1:14:21), Floto's lead was down to 25m.

Then the legions reached the Queensboro Bridge, the site in years past of the world's longest carpet, which is laid on the rough metal grating of the bridge to protect the runners' feet. But an awesome deluge the day before the race (nearly 2" of rain and 50mph winds) caused race director Fred Lebow's decision to forego the carpet.

Floto surrendered the lead and Dick Beardsley emerged as the temporary leader until the group of Salazar, Gomez and Graham roared past. A three-man race had begun in earnest, with Wells lurking ominously in 4th.

By the 20M mark (1:38:58), Salazar - with his efficient shuffle-stride - and Gomez ran side by side. Graham trailed by 10m.

Here was where Alberto had planned to move and, when Gomez slowed at the end of an aid station for a cup of water, Salazar suddenly found himself with a 10m lead. He was off and now REALLY running.

At 35K (1:47:30), Salazar led by six seconds. He ran the 21st mile in 4:57, up a slight grade and into the wind. Gomez, a lighter, bouncier stylist, apparently found the breeze more debilitating. By 23M (1:53:47), Alberto led by close to 200m and was quite obviously in a class all his own on this day.

"I was pretty confident with about six miles to go," he said later. "I felt real good, but I was scared of Gomez. I thought he might be as fast as me.

"The last half-mile or so, I really started to hurt. My stomach started to knot up, but I kept telling myself, 'Everybody else feels worse.'"

Behind Salazar, the women's race had reached resolution much earlier.

Waitz plowed through 5M in 27:00, only a stride ahead of Lyons-Catalano.

Patti eased off, fearful of blowing up, and watched the greatest woman distance runner ever pull away. Waitz passed 10M in 55:25 and the halfway post in 1:12:30.

Montreal Olympian Don Kardong, loping along nearby, says, "There was always a group of men who wanted to run with her. They sort of closed in around her, but when she started to run the second half of the race, she left them all. There wasn't anybody who could stay up with her. But the greatest moment still was when she passed Lasse Viren at 10M." The Finnish immortal didn't finish the race and countryman Martti Vainio finished 196th in 2:35:20.

Waitz hit 17M in 1:34:10. A mile before, Patti left behind her husband Joe Catalano: "I just told her to go get'em," he said. "She put her head down and took off."

But Mrs. Catalano was running only to break her announced goal of getting under 2:30. Waitz cruised by 25M in 2:19:18, at which point husband Jack yelled encouragement. "I needed that," Grete claimed later. "I felt tired." But few who watch her run - and surely none who run against her - can fathom fatigue in the Norwegian star.

The 27-year-old schoolteacher broke her global best by 1:51 and later admitted, "I slowed down in the middle of the race because I didn't think I would be able to get to the finish. But I had more strength at the end."

After dropping out, Joe Catalano got back to the finish area just in time to sprint the final 200 yards alongside his wife as she sped to her American best. Patti finished with long hair flying, eyes closed and a grimace - surely a mixture of pain and joy - on her face.

Patti admitted later she had been less psyched for New York than for Montreal, where she met her Boston conqueror Jacqueline Gareau. But she was willing to take a shot at Waitz through the five boroughs of NYC. There may have been no chance for success, but Patti Catalano was willing to try. And that she did.

"I felt really good," said an excited Catalano afterwards. "But I couldn't get my legs to go any faster." But she found some extra energy at the awards ceremony: she jumped up and down so enthusiastically, officials could hardly get the runner-up medal around her neck.

Salazar admitted his victory didn't surprise him too much. "I think I proved something to people who said I couldn't do it, who think running a marathon is some mystical thing," he said.

"Some people told me that you have to run a lot of times to run a good marathon. I'm not at all sure that's true; it's just a race.

"Other people said, 'You can't be so confident about it because you're a 10,000-meter runner and a marathoner has to prepare differently.' But I have run some 10,000 races that hurt a lot more than this marathon did. Certainly I wanted to do well, if only so I wouldn't have to hear people say, 'I told you so,' if I didn't run well."

One who didn't question Salazar's ability to run a top-notch marathon was Dellinger: "First of all, you have to almost take it for granted that there isn't anyone in the race who wants to win more than Alberto. He has the talent of a 10,000-meter runner, he has a very efficient running style, and he has incredible mental toughness.

"The longer the race, the more time you have to think about it and that's where Alberto's toughness comes in. You have to want to stay with a killing pace and Alberto does."

Praise also came from Rodgers: "He beat a crackerjack field, a tough field. There were a lot of good runners out there today, but they all got nailed. It's phenomenal that he could win a race like this in his first marathon."

Of his own effort, Rodgers, the pre-race favorite, said, "I thought I was in 2:10-2:11 shape. I ran as tough as I could and I feel I proved I was in good shape. I know I can run 2:10 this year.

"Maybe I'm pushing myself into the ground, pressing my luck. It was frustrating to be the third American, I didn't come here to get 5th.

"But I have to congratulate Alberto. Now I'm going to train to beat him."

Rodgers may not get that chance very soon. Salazar said he may not run another marathon until next year's New York affair. His immediate plans include the TAC cross-country race in late November and then completing his final season of outdoor track eligibility at Oregon next spring.

Despite his stupendous debut - the fastest ever - Salazar said, "To me, the marathon is just another race." But he quickly added, "Under the right conditions, I can run faster."

In Salazar's New York victory, we may well have seen the man who can run 2:07. And now there is no more Rookie.

Remember when American Women Set World Records?
April 1983

Boston, April 18, 1983 - "A ridiculous time," a race announcer said, describing Joan Benoit's effort as she approached the finish line of the 87th Boston Marathon.

Destroying the World Record by 2:46 as it did, the 2:22:43 by Benoit was sublime at the very least. The 25-year-old Boston University women's coach has added, if not another dimension, then certainly another plateau towards ultimate athletic achievement for women. She is alone.

How "ridiculous" was Benoit's mark? Well, since World War Two, Boston's men's race has been won ten times with slower marks than Joanie's. Amby Burfoot earned the 1968 laurel wreath with a clocking just 25 seconds faster. The 1975 women's WR win by Liane Winter was nearly 20 minutes slower. Twenty minutes!

Even Benoit expressed some incredulity, despite secret pre-race hopes for a "2:23:something."

She confessed that passing 10M in 51:30 "scared me a little bit.". But Benoit runs how she feels: "I felt good and thought, 'What the heck?' "

She had been aware of her pace early on, surrounded as she was by men with very low competitor's numbers. Her 31:50 split for 10K has been bettered by an American only twice in open events - both times by one J. Benoit.

"The men kept saying, 'Lady, watch it, 'but I always felt in control," said Benoit. "I kept listening to what my body told me and I stayed in complete control all the time."

Despite blistered feet, she passed the half-marathon point in 1:08:23, faster by 39 seconds than her official American Record. The hard early pace - established in part to escape Allison Roe, but also to set up a new global mark – began to signal some rebellion in the Wellesley Hills.

A side stitch at 15 miles. "I slowed the pace down," Benoit recounted. "Then I took some water, collected myself and moved on". Onward into history.

Benoit's clocking clipped nearly three minutes off the 2:25:29, first run by Roe in the '81 NYC Marathon. Just a day before Joanie's WR at Boston, Grete Waitz had matched Roe's mark at the London Marathon.

"Allison called me Sunday to tell me about Grete," said Benoit. "I just told her that all I wanted to do was run the best race I was capable of running.

"I had heard that everyone expected Allison to be on my tail, but I didn't want to play cat-and-mouse with her. During the race, I heard people say she was behind me at about five miles, but I didn't hear anything about her after that."

Leg cramps forced Roe out of the race at 17M. Runner-up honors went to 1980 champion Jacqueline Gareau of Canada, who ran wonderfully - yet distantly - for a 2:29:28 personal record.

It was a journey not without pain for Benoit. "My feet are killing me," she confessed afterward. The blisters she developed didn't slow her record tempo, however.

Benoit added, "I ran those last few miles really hurting in general. All I could think of was last year's race when Alberto Salazar and Dick Beardsley sprinted at the end through all those crowds and all that noise. How did they ever do it?"

This was also a triumph of will for the diminutive Benoit. Operations on both Achilles tendons in December of 1981 relegated her to extensive exercycle workouts for almost half of 1982. But she returned last September with a 2:26:11 win at the Nike race in Eugene, the fastest loop time ever.

After that race, Benoit commented, not surprisingly, "I know I can go much faster.". This year at Boston, Joan – and the rest of the world – got a glimpse of just how much faster.

Whether TAC and the NRDC will accept Benoit's blazer here as a record is not cut and dried, as some detractors have pointed to "illegal aid" provided by 2:13 performer Kevin Ryan, who apparently ran the full distance with Benoit, giving her constant moral support, if nothing else.

Critics claim he went beyond that, keeping her on pace and carrying a water bottle so that she could skip aid stations.

Whatever the outcome of this alleged controversy, the fact remains Joan Benoit made it on her own two feet from point A to point B faster than any woman before.

Greg Meyer destroyed no World Record, although he put some heat on Alberto Salazar's course standard through 20 miles. On his way to a 2:09:01 triumph, Meyer passed 20M in 1:37:11, some 18 seconds faster than Salazar managed during his 2:08:13 effort.

With the win seemingly more important than the record here - the first three American finishers would claim places on the U.S. team going to the World Championships - Meyer lost some concentration. But that's all the 27-year-old Bill Rodgers Running Center employee lost.

Ten miles into the race, Benji Durden had assumed the lead, with Meyer, Ed Mendoza and Paul Cummings in close attendance. Meyer pulled alongside Durden by 19M and a mile later, Greg went for the win.

"Before the second hill, I threw in a fake," said Meyer of a fake surge. "But it worked. I'm sure Benji was tired. After that, I knew it would be hard for anyone to catch me, so I relaxed. I was content to be alone for the last four miles."

Behind Meyer, Ron Tabb ran the race of his life, biding his time before sweeping past Durden around 26M to come home 2nd in a PR 2:09:32. He is now #5 American ever, while Durden's career low 2:09:58 for 3rd place put him #6.

Perennial Boston hero Bill Rodgers, bogged down by a heavy cold, struggled home 10th in 2:11:59, the lowest placing of the five Bostons he has finished. "This may be my last marathon," Boston Billy offered. "There is a big gap between me and the top guys. It's frustrating."

And now there's a big gap, too, between Joan Benoit and the rest of the world.

The First USA Women's Olympic Marathon Trials 1984

May 1984

In healthier days, Joan Benoit enroute to victory at the Nike–OTC Marathon

There was the grey of the overcast skies and the hair of 54-year-old Sister Marion Irvine. There was the evergreen of Douglas fir and 16-year-old Cathy Schiro. There was the gold of the Scotch broom and the dreams of the top three finishers. There was the mystery and misery and mastery of Joan Benoit. There was the control and confidence of Julie Brown. There were the hopes of 238 starters. There was no tomorrow and there will never again be another first Women's Olympic Marathon Trials.

Balloons soared as the starter's gun sounded. The field chased thirteen lead vehicles through a mile in 5:44 and all the favorites were there – Benoit, Brown, Betty Springs, Lisa Larsen, Mary & Julie Shea and, off to the left, Patti Catalano. By 2 km, Benoit found herself in the lead, surprised at the ease of the pace but accustomed to the position.

Passing 2M in 11:30, Benoit seemed adequately warmed up and all but eleven challengers had already fallen away. "I couldn't get comfortable in the first two miles, so I moved out," Benoit explained of 3M and 5km clockings of 17:00 and 17:33, a 2:28 pace. "My body was telling me what to do."

Benoit's bod also was telling Springs what to do as the Athletics West duo began to pull away. Only Brown, Larsen and Jeanne Lasse-Johnson tried to maintain contact. They didn't succeed.

"I was aware of the pace," said Brown, whose only goal was an Olympic berth. "I knew they would come back to me. Well, I didn't know about Joan, but she didn't matter."

Benoit and Springs reach 4M in 22:30 and 5M in 28:09. As the Tumwater Thunderbirds Marching Band tuned up, Margaret Groos pulled into contention for third place. No one seemed to remember how many miles, how much time, remained.

The Sunset Drive-In advertised a youth-oriented double feature of *Footloose* and *Hard To Hold,* as Springs and Benoit passed 6M in 33:42. When they hit 10km in 34:54, the second pack – some 23 seconds back – was led by Carol Urish-McLatchie and Sue King. Larsen rambled in between. Thirty-eight minutes into the race, the leaders surged, opening a significant margin over Larsen as Benoit ran the seventh mile in 5:30.

Climbing the route's initial hill at the Olympia Brewing Co., Springs began to pull away. Benoit stepped rather gingerly, obviously favoring one or more of her injuries. By 8M (44:32) Springs was a stride ahead. By 8.4,

Springs was the clear leader, forcing the pace. Benoit and Springs blew by 9M in 50:18, a 2:26:30 pace. Julie Brown stalked along some 25 seconds back and The Royal Bananas, a one-boy drum band, banged away to the largest crowd of his career.

Miles in 5:37 and 5:41 did nothing to change the scene as Springs, not her companion, seemed to be the leader. Joanie and Betty hit 12M in 1:07:12 with Larsen 16 seconds back and a patient Brown another 18 behind the former Michigan swimming star.

Obviously, Benoit, all 5-3/105 of her seemingly held together by sheer determination, decided the time had come to win the race. At 20km (1:09:32) she had managed to build a two-second margin over Springs. At the halfway point (1:13:18) Benoit was pulling away as fast as Springs was dropping back. Every stride brought Benoit closer to the finish, the predators closer to Springs and Springs closer to an attempt at an Olympic berth at 3000m.

Benoit continued her drive, passing 25km in 1:27:01. Springs was still headed backwards. Larsen was going nowhere fast and Brown was saving both her move and her energy. At 16.5M Brown gained a spot on the team. When Benoit passed 18M in 1:41:05, Larsen passed Springs. Oh, for a finish line at 30km (1:44:54).

But this was not just any marathon; this was a damn soap opera. Could Joanie hold up just 17 days after arthroscopic surgery on her right knee? Would Julie try for the victory? Could Lisa hold her position against the pacers who must be about to arrive? Yes, no and, ahh, no. Yeah! Why should she? And, nice try, but the better woman won.

Benoit went by 20M in 1:52:46. Twenty-Sixth Avenue Northwest is the toughest part of the course and it was here the true test began for Ol' No. 1. "I was running pretty comfortably, but the last six miles were tough," Benoit admitted. "Cardiovascular-wise, I was fine, but the legs wouldn't go. I knew if the pack came up on me and it came to a kick, I couldn't do it."

She had already done it to the pack, as her 2:31:04 (the best ever by an American in an all-women's race on a loop course) gave her 37 seconds of breathing room over Brown, who was already mentally packing for Los Angeles.

"I came here to place in the top three and run as easily as I could," said the 2nd-place finisher (2:31:41). "I expected to have to run a 2:27 or 2:28 and I saved a lot. I held back until the 20M mark and was ready to race if I needed to. I won't hold back in the Olympics."

Larsen held back nothing except the challenge of 234 women. She held back everything they had. She held back the stunningly audacious charge of Schiro, too young to know she shouldn't be an Olympian, too fast not to try. Schiro held them all back for 25 miles. Still, her "fade" to 9th garnered a World Junior Record of 2:34:24.

Julie Isphording, a 22-year-old who graduated *in absentia* (and *magna cum laude*) from Ohio's Xavier University this day, is a special kind of woman.

She began to jog five years ago to improve her tennis game. Her running improved enough to earn the No. 45 seed in this race. Ten miles of racing put her in 3rd. "My plan was to go out with the lead pack, but they took off too fast for me," she recounted. "I had my doubts."

Those doubts didn't slow the charismatic darkhorse as she moved past one mile, one runner, one obstacle after another: "I knew when I was like 19th through 11th, but I had no concept from 9th to 3rd. All I concentrated on was mileage markers and passing people."

She moved from 6th to 5th in the twenty-third mile, but she was still 58 seconds behind Larsen. A 5:19 penultimate mile was more than enough to write the conclusion to this fairy tale as she lowered her personal record to 2:32:26 in gaining an Olympic berth and the No. 6 position on the all-time U.S. list.

But the end was only the beginning. For Joan Benoit it was a victory over her own body. For Julie Brown it was a chance to go to the Olympics after the boycott of 1980. For Julie Isphording it was a living dream. For Lisa Larsen (4th in a PR 2:33:10) it was pride. For Margaret Groos (2:33:38) it was a personal best and an alternate's berth. For 238 athletes it was the ultimate competition.

Women and running will never be the same.

Couch potato coverage of the 1986 Chicago Marathon
October 1986

I missed the start of America's Marathon, the one every runner calls Chicago. In fact, I missed the first nine miles.

You see, I live on the West Coast and the marathon was being televised "same-day tape coverage." And I thought I'd cover the race from the comfort of my living room. But America's sport - football - just wouldn't quit. These guys play for 60 minutes and it takes 3 1/2 hours to do it. Besides, how important could that game have really been? Not only had I never heard of the teams... I'd never heard of the cities.

The first words I heard of the marathon broadcast were, "The Americans are conspicuous by their absence." The tone was set.

Tanzania's John Bura leads a pack of Toshihiko Seko, Rodolfo y Jose Gomez, Ahmed Saleh, Gerardo Alcala - and somebody I forgot to write down past 9M. I missed the time. Guess I should've warmed up. Ingrid Kristiansen has already set herself apart for her competitors. She reaches 8M in 43:08.

Time for the first commercial interruption, and, boy, is it ever. "Now you're talkin' after work. Now you're talkin' good times. Now you're talkin' beer.". The next ad was for insurance and the third was selling financial advice. Makes sense. First prize is $40,000.

We return to find Jose Gomez in front as the leaders hit 10M in 48:32. There is no wind in The Windy City.

Since television's powers-that-be are convinced foot racing is boring, we switch our attention to one of those ubiquitous video sidebars. We learn about the Whistle Lady of Little Italy; we hear three dudes do a rap song about the race; we are introduced to Amy Chan, age 12, who created the marathon poster. We are bored.

Back at the race, the leaders have covered the 11th mile in 4:53. In-

Ingrid arrives at 10M in 53:58. She is tiring.

The pack reaches halfway in 1:03:41. Time for Toni Reavis to do a talking-head about the decline of America's marathoners. Toni knows the sport and notes that 80% of the prize money at New York City, Boston and last year's Chicago went to foreigners.

Fred Lebow, NYC's impresario, is asked for his opinion. Straight-faced, Freddy says, "Prize money is the culprit.". It's the most audacious thing I've seen in the sport since Frank Shorter made a break at 15K in the '72 Olympics. I thought Mr. Lebow invented prize money.

Joan Benoit Samuelson, covering the women's race, suggests the problem lies with the collegiate system. No surprises, no solutions.

Ingrid makes it halfway home in 1:11:04. Jose can't see the leaders who cover 14M in 1:08:08.

John Makanya makes a little move just past 15M (1:13:04). He's "breaking the molecule of the pack," Reavis tells us. Then Seko moves, checks his watch as he will do throughout the race, and takes Saleh with him,

Ingrid gets to 14M in 1:15:58. JBS points out, at every opportunity, the Norwegian's reliance on sports psychology.

Seko, still escorted by Saleh, reaches 16M in 1:17:54. Checking my notes, well, I must have grabbed a Pepsi. There's no entry until "18M 1:27:43. Seko & Saleh. Alone together, together alone." Ingrid's already laboring at 16M (1:27:16). The camera shows her taking pills from a man identified as her physician. "She looks frustrated," Joanie notes, and moments later, "I don't think she's having fun right now."

Seko and Saleh reach 30K (1:30:43). The contrast is physique is stunning. Those legs of Seko... in a word, the man is sturdy. At 5-7 and 132 pounds, he powers along a stride ahead of the deer-like Djiboutian's 5-11/119 frame.

Another commercial break. While we hear about "The Smart Move" credit card, Ahmed Saleh surges. As he goes by 21M in 1:42:24, he looks anxious. He should be. Seko is a stride behind, still checking his watch.

Reavis: "As long as Seko is there, Seko's your winner." Just what Toshihiko was thinking. The 30-year-old Japanese made his move, a smart one at that, at 21 1/2 miles. By 22M (1:47:22), Saleh was falling back.

Those of us in TV land missed this crucial point, of course. We were watching more commercial interruptions.

Seko has only been beaten once since 1979, that when he placed a disappointing 14th in the '84 Games. This striding samurai was never in trouble this day. The 23rd mile was a 4:45 and Saleh said sayonara.

Seko had run the first 5M in 24:01. At least I think he did. His slowest 5M split of 24:32 came between 10-15 miles. And you tell me, maybe marriage has slowed down this guy?

Seko is in the last mile, and we're forced to listen to Craig Masback telling us about scientific efforts to eliminate "THE WALL." I'd much rather watch Seko battle this legendary barrier than listen to Craig talk about it.

We return to the actual race at 2:06:35. Forty seconds later, Seko reaches 26M. He doesn't run a World Record. He has let down the audience, not to mention race director Bob Bright. Gary Bender is clearly disappointed as Seko can only manage a personal record 2:08:27. The 12th fastest time ever.

"Now you're talkin' good times. Now you're talkin' beer."

Ingrid is talkin' pain as she passes 25M in 2:19:49. We watch Kristiansen and we get the feeling - we are given the feeling by so much of the coverage - that she has somehow failed. Toni Reavis asks, "Is there defeat in victory?" Ingrid is victorious in 2:27:08.

Another ad. "Now you're talkin' good times."

There's an interview with Kristiansen. She's bummed because she couldn't see her split times because of all the television cameras in her way. (Oh, the irony.). I have some trouble being empathetic. In addition to the win at one of the world's most prestigious marathons, and the $40,000 first prize, Ingrid also received a $40,000 appearance fee and "travel and accommodations for an entourage of seven.". (Of course, television didn't tell me that. Wouldn't want to shock the viewers.) TV does pay some of the bills. Must be all those ads.

The news comes on. The World Series is delayed by rain. I slip on my shoes and go out for a run. It's raining here, too. Now you are really talkin' a good time.

Cascade Run Off, Portland, Oregon
June 1993

In 1979, the author finished the Run Off in 184th place (56:20) of 4900+ finishers

Real surreal was the beginning of the 16th Annual Cascade Run Off.

Moments after the gun sounded to start this challenging 15k, there I was, shoulder to shoulder with Rob De Castella, Steve Scott and Sebastian Coe, chased by the finest field in this storied event's history.

I looked at Deek, Seb and Stev, they weren't even breathing hard. Unspoken... a nostalgic longing to return to the fray; understood... those times are past.

De Castella, Coe, Scott! Golly, what a lineup, and that was just the press truck.

A small crowd passed 1M in 4:27. The lead pack of 17 reached 2M in 9:21 with defending champion Sammy Lelei already taking control. The lithe Kenyan farmer looked like a tour guide shepherding a flock of out-of-town guests, pointing to the local sights.

At the bottom of terribly testing, torturously tall Terwilliger Boulevard, terrific teen Lazarus Nyakeraka pushed the pace. Up they climbed, reaching 5k in 15:01.

Nyakeraka, Lelei, Alejandro Cruz, Godfrey Kiprotich, Jose Castillo, Xolile Yawa, Kipkemboi Kimeli and Gideon Mutisya pushed by 4M in 19:21. Still climbing. At the top, there were eight men left.

Eight men gone strong. History made. Never have so many runners made it to the top of Terwilliger together. A sight to behold. 5M passes by in 24:08.

"DANGER. 6% DOWNGRADE." says a sign at the route's summit. It's all downhill from here.

A boy still, Nyakeraka can't keep up on the descent. The magnificent seven pass 6M in 28:34. Cruz, bothered by a strained leg muscle, gives every impression of starting his finishing kick here. Castillo surges with him. At 10k (29:29), Lelei closes the gap; by 7M (33:02) Sammy has a stride lead.

That one stride, they were all fighting for it, and Yawa refused to surrender. At 7M (33:02), Lelei began a series of surges, Yawa began a series of responses. With a single kilometer remaining, Lelei bolted away to a 43:15 victory. The $4,000 first place check answers the question, what makes Sammy run. Yawa was left to ponder how does Sammy go so fast.

Carolyn Schuwalow grows more confident with every stop on her first American tour. Here the Aussie pushed hard from the starting line, shaking golden Valentina Yegorova in the early stages of a course that discourages come-from-behind strategies. You can't win if you're not there at the top.

Schuwalow increased her margin to a startling 51 seconds with a 49:15 clocking. A little startling in her own right was runnerup 18-year-old Kenyan Jane Omoro, those same seconds back at 50:06.

Three-time winner Anne Audain, legendary and retired like Coe, Scott and De Castella, marveled at the display of talent.

"Ten years ago, first place here paid $10,000," said the personable Kiwi who kicked butt throughout the Eighties. "I'm glad I had my career when I did."

Blown and Leied in Paradise
December 1995

The Honolulu Marathon is like a box of chocolate-covered macadamia nuts.

You always know what you are going to get.

To be perfectly honest, my pre-race strategy fell by the wayside the moment I saw this huge limousine driver holding up a sign. Sign had HONOLULU MARATHON WELCOMES DEREK CLAYTON written on it.

Right then I decided to tell everybody I'm Derek Clayton.

"Aloha, mate," I said, in what I imagine was an Aussie accent. Clayton comes from Australia.

"Mista Crayton?" The chauffeur looks like a U.P.S. delivery van in a double-breasted tuxedo. "Mista Delleck Crayton?" There is this gorgeous petite Polynesian princess with him in a grass skirt with a couple of coconuts, half shells, covering her, um, coconuts. Looks like Rae Dawn Chong on her best day. A banana in her hair.

A thought blew through my brain.

Like out one ear and in the other. You know what I mean.

I bet I'd get some real special treatment if they catered to me like I was a great runner, a retired superstar who, it is said, once got suspended for taking three hundred bucks for a world record performance. Paid his own way, predicted a two-oh-eight and proceeded to run the son of a gun.

"Are you Mista Delleck Crayton?," he asked me.

"Yes, I am."

Fruit Salad Woman swished her fronds over to me. She lifted her arms around my head and rung my neck with an odiferous orchid wreath. One hot pistil, she smelled good, too. She gave me a kiss on both cheeks.

A trifle young but sweet.

Then she stuck her tongue deep into my mouth and squeezed my buns. I gazed down. What the hell, I checked her coconuts.

The limo, a white stretch Lincoln with a wet bar and television satellite, was embarrassingly long while the ride to The Princess Holdontomiglani Hotel was frustratingly short.

Sleeping naked in an ocean-front suite with the open curtains of the lanai blowing in the cooling breeze. A basket of free treats, crackers, cheese and such, and a bottle of *gratis* champagne. Magic Fingers in the mattress.

Fantastic fireworks, radiant rainbows, pristine porta-potties, spectacular surf, hang-loose hospitality you won't believe, and, oh, yes, twenty-six miles, three-hundred and eighty-five yards of hard road.

And always a happy ending.

Used to be, you'd go to the Honolulu Marathon to party. Back in the old days, the race was seen as little more than a free ticket to a great vacation.

Last night's low, by the way, Pearl Harbor Day, was seventy-three degrees Fahrenheit.

Today it's windy as shit and there's a take-no-prisoners attitude at the front.

In a scene straight out of a Frederico Fellini movie, over thirty thousand marathoners toe the line for the somehow oddly appropriate five-thirty-in-the-morning start. Run *noir*. With nearly twenty thousand Japanese visitors entered, many first-timers carrying cameras, Honolulu is the second largest marathon in the world. The race another pre-dawn invasion.

This many Japanese can't be wrong.

A desire to have a good time is the only entry qualification.

Show me another race passing three such heroic statues. Past life-sized bronzes of Mohandas Ghandi and Duke Kohanamoku. Honolulu manages to live up to their reputations.

Turns out the third statue is really Jim Moberly, imagine Alan Alda on steroids, who fired the gun.

I see a man like that, a natural leader with the smell of cordite on his hands and I wonder why a forgiving millionairess with some huge trust fund doesn't snap this guy up in a big hurry. Some very wealthy nymphomaniac is missing out on a sure bet if she doesn't snag Moberly soon.

I guess I should mention here, it was Moberly, a member of the Marathon's hardworking and handsome board of directors, Moberly, the same man who first noticed I wasn't really Derek Clayton.

Moberly let me stay.

Africans Josphat Ndeti and Andrew Mao set the early pace buffeted by tradewinds swirling between the high-rise condominiums and luxury hotels of Waikiki. The leaders covered five miles in less than twenty-five minutes. The dark duo continued to push the pace into a stiff headwind. They reached ten miles at fifty-two or so, slowed by thirty-plus mile per hour gusts.

A large but informal chase group huddled together, content to follow leisurely twenty-two seconds behind. The wind so strong the runners knocked into one another, as if jostled by invisible spirits. Stealth elbows.

Honolulu: no longer a total holiday for the quick and the invited.

By five miles, the women's race had already become a toe-to-toe duel between Carla Beurskens and Eriko Asai. Lisa Weidenbach was thirty-two seconds back and losing ground with every stride. When the first ladies hit ten miles, Weidenbach was nearly a minute and a half in arrears.

"All I could do was hope they would crash and burn," admitted Weidenbach.

The wind grew stronger, the pace slowed. Would you believe a six-minute mile?

Ndeti and Mao were joined at the fifteen-mile marker by Joseph Skosana and Benedict Ako. The pack remained the same.

"We were watching the Koreans, they were watching us," Kenyan Mbarak Hussein explained. "Last year we let them go. This year we didn't want them to leave us. And they didn't want us to leave them."

The blustery conditions gave the elite runners every reason to play the waiting game.

Meanwhile, Beurskens, who knows the course like the top of her foot, was enjoined in a frustrating struggle with the wind as well as Asai. Tired of breaking the breeze, the diminutive Beurskens slowed to a jog, hoping the even tinier Asai would share the load.

No weigh.

"I was a little angry," admitted the otherwise perfectly charming champion.

When the two reached fifteen miles, Beurskens detected the slightest hint of a tailwind and plowed ahead. "I made one surge. I could see Asai was having a little problem. Then I made a second surge and I held that pace."

Asai hung tough, trailing by a mere three ticks as Beurskens passed twenty miles in two hours, forty-four seconds.

As the women battled alone, the men worked together. Four in front, fourteen in the chase pack. The predators took turns fighting the wind. One runner would take the lead, then gradually fall back as another athlete moved into the teeth of the wind. Like bike racers. In Hawaii Kai, a three-mile loop sheltered somewhat, the lead was cut in half.

The pack finally swallowed the leaders.

Skosana started sprinting, covering the next half mile in perhaps two minutes and fifteen seconds.

When Benson Masya, lone among them man enough, no surprise here, covered the move, surprise, Skosana stopped. Dead in his tracks.

Why?

Well, the answer, my friend, was blowing in the wind. It all happened just that fast.

"When the winds changed, I made a move. Just one move," Masya said. "I just went away and nobody came with me. I wasn't worried even when we were behind. I looked at the group and I knew I could run faster. I knew I had the speed."

Everybody else knew the former boxer and current checkers enforcer had the speed. There's much respect for this man. Estimates of the pace at this point suggest a four-fifty mile.

He was with the pack, then he wasn't. This off three weeks of twenty-two miles per day preparation.

With the wind now at his back, Masya, America's obscure King of The Road, cruised twenty miles a full thirty seconds faster than Hussein and Thabiso Moqhali.

"I saved myself at first because the wind was very strong," said Masya. "I never felt threatened."

"I was afraid," Carla said. Beurskens never got a break from Asai. "She is very strong. I must run fast, otherwise she beat me." Beurskens' time was the slowest of her eight victories here.

"The wind cost two or three minutes," Beurskens guessed, clutching two gigantic trophies and a check for ten grand. "Every time I run here I win."

Asked to explain his thinking as he climbed dangerous Diamondhead,

Masya with a shy chuckle replied, "A good place to visit."

Twenty-two years in the running, the Honolulu Marathon somehow remains an up-and-coming event. Bigger. Better. Racier.

****

The inaugural Nike P.L.A.Y. Waikiki Mile was the most obvious improvement. A surprising development, thousands of kids introduced to the sport, thousands of dollars for needy schools. Bingo! We have a winner.

Canada's Angela Chalmers waited until the final forty yards to launch her big-time kick.

"To tell you the truth, I don't think any of us were ready for this," said the Northern Arizona University alumna. Somewhat stunned by the stiffness of the competition.

"I was a little surprised everybody ran so well," explained Annette Peters, seventh in four-thirty-eight and change. "The impression I had originally was everybody was on vacation. Something changed when the gun went off. The money might have had something to do with it."

There's never been a four-minute mile on the Islands. Seemed unlikely here, with that wind and the one-hundred-and-eighty-degree turn.

"Who's in shape for a sub-four in December anyway?," wondered Bob Kennedy, who placed eighth in four-oh-six even. Slowed by a aggravated Achilles tendon.

The answer, offered savvy Alberto Salazar, is an indoor specialist, somebody like Marcus O'Sullivan.

Rabbited by Jim Howarth and Steve Ave, the men's field raced up crowd-lined Kalakaua Avenue, passing the quarter pole in fifty-eight seconds, then THE BIG TURN, worth a second or two, halfway in two minutes flat. That canny Irishman O'Sullivan in the lead as they pass thirteen-twenty about three even.

Eighty meters to go, Marc Davis, himself a tireless predator, pounced. A blurry *Roadrunner* cartoon tattoo on his calf.

Faster than you can say, BetchaBenson-BestsBoston, there it was, an instant classic.

Three minutes, fifty-seven.

Sub-four. One of those "Wow" races to watch. Haven't seen a kick like that since Decker Slaney lunged past the Russkies in Helsinki back in '83, wasn't it? Very ballsy.

Davis did it. The hell with the damn wind.

"I used and abused every person out there. They all know it. I know it. Nothing they could do about it," Davis explained after a finish line plunge into the sea. "Nothing I could do about it. I've been fighting a head cold. I've never broken four. I haven't been training. Absolutely no speed work. I was basically blowing the whole thing off. Suddenly, I just decided I wanted it more. Positively the biggest surprise of my life. I came here for a good time."

A great time. Undertrained yet undaunted, gifted with raw speed, Davis took home twelve large. Thousands of dollars to the athletes.

"This is all just candy to me," offered Davis, an international track competitor with a cellular phone, fax and a big-time agent. "July and August is the roast beef."

Talking about the summer. It's always summer in Honolulu. Like living every day on the beach here.

Back home summer seems so far away.

Back home it's cold and dark and icy. Back home my lady and I both sleep in long flannel shirts to our knees.

The tans already starting to fade.

"A good place to start a career. If I am to do only one marathon each year," Mbarak Hussein, who does only one, said, "I do Honolulu."

I KNOW JUST HOW HE FEELS.

Another happy ending.

I'm With The Van:
The Hood To Coast Relay With Big Berto
August 1995

The Hood To Coast Relay is a big race – bigger than you know. In the business world of sport, Hood to Coast (H2C) is real, authentic, and, in Portland, Oregon, it's big-time serious. Last year, Nike head Phil Knight gave Alberto Salazar a black BMW convertible for leading, and anchoring, his team to victory.

Berto isn't running this year. He ran 25 miles yesterday, his longest effort since winning the 1994 Comrades Marathon. "I am too slow right now," he confides, so he'll captain the team and manage one of the two vans the elite men's team will be using.

Terry Williams is the squad leader in van 2. "He's cool, calm and collected," Alberto says of the one-time Oregon star. "The kind of guy you need in charge of a race like this."

Berto is a maniac. I mean that in the nicest way. Berto is perhaps paranoid. Adidas, the dreaded, despised crosstown rival, is out to get him, and H2C is – I don't mean to overemphasize the conflict – well, Salazar is at war. He manages to stay cool and burn bright at the same time.

Last year, the top runners averaged sub-5:00 miles for each of three five-mile legs. This year's team must do better.

"We had some guys last year who didn't run in the fours," Berto notes.

"You killed them, didn't you?," I accuse.

"Well, they're not back."

At a pre-race pep rally, loudspeakers blare adrenaline-releasing tunes across the patio on Nike's campus. "Two years ago, I was coerced into running H2C, and it really got me juiced up for the first time in ten years," Salazar tells the assembled throng. "It may sound hokey, but our slogan, 'Just Do It', is what this event is all about. Fitness for us is not just a business. We have a true love for competition. Our pride is on the line here."

More than an race for elite athletes, H2C is all about participation. More than 500 Nike employees are involved, including guest teams from England, Germany and Italy. Twenty-eight Nike teams, such as "There'd Better Be A Finish Line" and "Lactic Acid Heads" will compete. "Six Buck Amazons & A Half-Dozen Little Boys" will contest the mixed corporate division, while "Not Tonight, Honey, I'm Running" goes after the women's crown.

This is the first year the women's race will be absolutely intense. Local running guru Bob Williams, another old Oregon star, was hired to put together an elite women's team after rumors had reached Berto of a big adidas effort forthcoming. The sagacious Williams melded six top locals and Nike employees with imported ringers like ultra-legend Ann Trason and, my goodness, Selena Chemir, an altitude-trained Kenyan.

Berto has his own altitude-trained Kenyan; you begin to get some idea of how far these shoe wars could go if things got completely out of hand. Berto gathers his 12 guys for a final strategy session. "Mambu Baddu" is their name. That's Swahili for "the best is yet to come."

"Even in the middle of the night, there's almost always somebody in front of you. You'll see their flashlight." Berto is worried his team might get lost. "I'm the king of getting lost," he warns. "Don't get lost. You make the wrong decision, and the race is over."

Berto is concerned about that first downhill. The initial three legs drop an average of 1,000 to 1,400 feet. "Be conservative," he tells the team. "I wouldn't be surprised to see some big names. You never know who is going to show up. Don't kill yourself on your first leg." You know he expects you to throw yourself on a live grenade if that's what it takes to win.

Each leg of this competition is essentially an 8k to 10k race. Ergo, there are 36 events, one right after another, and 815 runners in each event. With a dozen runners on a team, each runner runs three times: wave after wave, 20 runners at a time from 9 a.m. to 7:30 p.m. There are approximately 49 wave starts, one every 15 minutes – in all, nearly 10,000 runners. Not to mention hundreds of support vans and the odd journalist.

Abnormally hot when the slower runners started earlier in the day, temps have cooled off by the time the fastest folks heat up the action at 7:30 p.m. Seems like with each wave, the runners become more slender. Muscle definition improves. They get a little shorter, too, to tell you the truth. Towards the later waves, you see fewer Walkmans.

The shoe companies haven't even turned in their final rosters. John Gregorek is back for adidas. Nan Doak-Davis and Elaine Van Blunk are here, too. Rumors run rampant. This may be the biggest race of 1995 for the shoe companies. This may be the biggest race in adidas's history, but only if they can win it.

By the way he's acting, all juiced up, this could be the biggest race of Alberto's life – bigger than Boston or New York – but only if he loses. He can't really expect another important luxury vehicle for a victory. But if he loses, maybe they'll take his name off the building on the Nike Campus.

The first leg drops 2,000 feet. Remember the opening scene in the Stephen King movie "The Shining," starring Jack Nicholson – the car climbing and climbing and climbing and winding up and up through the drifts of snow? That's the road they are running down. In a word, steep; forbidding even in the summer. The record for the first mile is 3:44, and the guy was holding back.

Leg 1 is a rite of passage for most teams. A majority of the folks falling down the mountainside are first-timers – all quads, no brains. Rare is the athlete who does this leg voluntarily. Some teams, seeking an early lead, have been known to sacrifice their first runner; this means the second and third athletes will have to run four legs.

Fifty yards into this 195-mile race, Nike takes the lead. Fast Eddy Hellebuyck clocks a sub-4 opener. He sets a Leg 1 record, averaging 4:01:58 for 5.6 miles. At 5 feet, 2 inches, 105 pounds, the 2:11 marathoner is shaped like a water bug. "I am not a wimp," the smiling Eddy tells me, after building the biggest lead coming off the hill anybody has ever seen.

The difference in the race this year may simply come down to Eddy H. Last year, the Nike and adidas teams were neck and neck all the way into Portland. This year, we're concerned Eddy might have put the race way out of reach really early. There's some disappointment in the air. Berto doesn't notice.

"It's not nearly the way it was, not as intense," Jon Sinclair complains. The Nike team is waiting for a counterstrike that doesn't seem to be coming its way.

I see Dave Murphy, manager of adidas's "Rolling Thunder," – trust me, there's some backstory to that name – looking calm. "We're gonna run hard all the way," he says, ever the battler. He's surprised Berto's not running. I tell him why, 'he's too slow to make his own team,' and I watch Murphy's Adam's apple bob up and down in his throat.

After the initial leg, athletes can't run the tangent. Both shoe-company teams are assessed one foul for crossing the yellow line on State Highway 26, which isn't closed to traffic for the race. You gotta be crazy just to *drive* on Highway 26. One more foul, and Nike is out of the race. Try explaining that to Knight.

Every five miles or so, at the relay exchange points, the traffic is like the exit of a ball game, or the state fair emptying out. Some 2,200 vans are jockeying for position. The van drivers could easily be the most valuable members of the relay squads. They're like the bass players in a rock-and-roll band.

Salazar is riding shotgun, reading the map, hollering advice and encouragement out the window, giving directions, actually hopping out of the van at particularly obscure turns. Can't get lost. Whenever we get into trouble, Salazar flashes his Big Berto smile, and volunteers fall all over themselves to see how they can help. Hang around him long enough, you tend to forget he's a celebrity.

There's so much that can go wrong in an event like this. You could arrive too late; you could get lost; you could be a stranger in a strange land. In the dark.

It's 10:30 p.m. Van 2 needs a break, so Berto phones home. "Molly, hi. Look, some guys are going to come over and crash. (Pause.) Nine. (Pause.) I just found out about it myself. (Pause.) Sorry. Just let them in."

After seven legs, Nike's lead is so great, the major worry now is going off course. Some of the guys are without their eyeglasses. The markings are not so clear as a man running 4:40 miles – in the night through foreign territory – might like.

Sinclair, his 38-year-old head shaved like Mr. Clean's, explains a problem about pacing yourself in the dark. "I thought I was running much faster. You have no idea how fast you're going. I thought I was attacking it. You never know. There is absolutely no way to judge."

These guys are caffeine-inspired, pounding the van roof and screaming support. It's the one race of the year in which they don't compete against one another. The whole time someone is running, everybody is screaming for him. Together, they start telling stories about how Dan Held crushed

Gregorek right here last year. "He's got The Face on!," a voice yells.

"There is a performance aspect here," the event's founder, Bob Foote, explains. "You are operating on stage amongst a dozen of your peers. You don't want to show any weakness. The current strategy is, you run every leg as hard as you can."

The voice inside you that whispers you should quit is drowned out by the cheers of your eleven teammates. "You know that little voice in your head?" Sinclair asks. "Mine has a loudspeaker."

"You're racing here," offers Peter Fonseca, a 2:11 marathoner from Canada. "Like I'm not even thinking about adidas. You're just drilling along, kinda in your own world out there. Which is good. You know, that sensation you're crankin' along. Feels good, being alone, in the middle of nowhere."

After the first dozen legs, adidas's women are three minutes ahead of Nike's, and the Nike men are about nine minutes ahead of the adidas men. I notice Hellebuyck grimace after finishing his second leg. "Boy, my legs are screwed up now."

"This race brings out all your weaknesses," Sinclair points out.

"And all your strengths," Lewis adds.

"Everything you have that's a problem will hurt for sure in this race," continues Sinclair. "The first leg, it's annoying. The second leg, you're in trouble. Third leg, you're just hoping to avoid disaster."

In the middle of the dark Oregon night, way, way out in the woods, John Kipkoskei is running 4:36 pace and smiling. If you're anybody but the elite team, the elite team is chasing you. You're road kill, waiting to happen. You're out in the middle of nowhere, in the middle of the night, and suddenly all you hear is "pitter patter, pitter patter," soft footsteps getting louder and louder. World class comes out of the darkness, a flashlight and reflective vest moving through the black like The Invisible Man.

"We may not be the first team to the beach," Lewis says, noting the ten-hour handicap surrendered to the slower squads.

"It's all right," Held responds.

"It's not all right," Lewis answers angrily. "I want to be there first."

It's 1:50 a.m. I'm in the lead car now. "Somebody from adidas had to blow up," driver, H2C board member and raconteur Gregory Miller surmises. Suddenly Nike's 9-minute lead is rumored to be 20 minutes at 2:50 a.m. Maybe adidas got lost. Or run over. Or kidnapped by Bigfoot.

In the village of Mist, the fog rolls in, Nike builds an ever-bigger lead. It's 6:30 a.m. "Oh, man, I'm happy," Fast Eddy explains upon completing his final leg. Bored by the size of their lead, the Nike team members begin competing among themselves to see who can log the fastest legs or best their projected times by the greatest margin. The race is now a time trial.

"You don't want to be the guy who lets his team down," says Sinclair. "I went as hard as I could go."

At 8:20 a.m., Nike is supposedly 40 minutes ahead of the adidas squad. Rolling along Lewis and Clark Road to the coastal resort town of Seaside, Alberto begins to relax, ceases to look like Jack Nicholson. After 195 miles, there had damn well better be a finish line.

"You know the routine," Salazar announces. "We all finish together." Half the guys don't know the routine. They're stiff and sore. Lewis can't find his shirt; Held locates his hat (it was backward on his head); Sinclair is calm. Poor Fonseca: he can hardly move, and he's looking at 5:00 pace.

"Brad'll park the van the first place he can," Berto explains, "and we'll all run in with Tom."

You should see the look on Fonseca's face.

There's a vacant lot, and we've stopped, and before I know it, I'm the only guy in the van. At Nike, even the drivers are fast.

The event was 3.3 miles longer than last year's, yet Nike clocked a race-record 15:44:55, nearly an hour in front of Rolling Thunder's 16:46:26. *(Almost 20 years later, that record still stands. -JDW)*

Murphy's revenge is a record-breaking 19:04:19 performance by the women's division of "Rolling Thunder." Nike's elite women finish more than 25 minutes later. Nike went from kicking butt last year to kissing your sister this year. It's a tie, really. Nike men win, and adidas women win. It's no fault of Berto. Williams got the world's only slow Kenyan to run on his team.

"My impression of the H2C?" Williams asks. "What I thought it was? A demanding endurance event. Demanding, because of sleep deprivation. Endurance, because everybody runs 15 miles as hard as they can. With five hours of recovery. And some food; maybe not enough nutritious food.

"I was surprised our women, even though we knew we were getting beat, decided early on they were not going to recognize that, but hope like hell... Hope the adidas van would either run off the course or they'd get lost. Someone would get bad blisters, and they couldn't run. Someone would get sick and couldn't run. They'd get hurt or injured, and they'd have to flip-flop their runners. And they'd lose time, and we'd pick up the pace and catch them. And that's the basis by which we raced.

"And we raced well," Williams said. "We continued to compete against ourselves, hoping something would happen to them and we'd catch up somewhere. And even though we knew at the very end we couldn't, we still ran hard. Except for one athlete who found she couldn't do it."

In other words, Selena Chemir isn't an H2C runner, at least not on the first trip.

"Her first leg at night, she did not give up any time on Nan Doak-Davis, who just hammered," explains Williams. "She gained maybe 2 seconds. After five hours of sleeping and very little food, she lost a little bit of oomph for Leg 2, then she lost a helluva lot after that. Even if Selena had run up to our expectations, adidas still would've beat us by 14 minutes."

"Would you run again?" I ask Fonseca.

"It would have to be a long-term decision," he says. "Like, if I was thinking about it right now, I'd say, 'Oh, yeah, I'll do it.' And then you'd have to catch me really short term. Like a few days before. 'Peter, you up?' and without thinking, I'd say, 'Yes!' and I'd be back.

"But don't ask me after a marathon or some other race. It's better to be right on the moment than to be thinking about the race three months before. You don't want to dwell on H2C. If a workout's going great, you're loving it. If a workout's going crappy, you're thinking, 'I'm never going to do that H2C thing again.'

"Once you start H2C, it's fine," Fonseca continues. "This was my first time. Actually, my first marathon was probably my best marathon for quite a few years. Best to go in naive about the event, as far as the pain you are going to go through, the no sleep, sitting in a cramped van for so many hours. The thing is, you are sitting in there with some really great guys; that's the special part about it, you know – the camaraderie.

"If it wasn't for that, if you factor out those guys, you're thinking, 'This is hellish; I don't know if I'd do this again.' If you factor in the people I ran with, then I'd say, 'I'd do it for the rest of my life.' That's how I feel about the event," Fonseca concluded.

Sinclair heads for the airport. "It's going to take a while to get over this."

The best is yet to come, I remind him and start looking for a ride home.

The Race and the Spaces in Between
December 1998

Our correspondent steps into the elite roadie's shoes Honolulu-style and finds a paradisical connection between competition's heat and the calm surrounding it.

Imagine you are an elite athlete.

You are greeted at the Honolulu airport by a lovely young lady who gives you a kiss and a floral lei. Aloha. There is a stretch limousine with a wet bar and TV waiting at the curb. The driver, built like a Samoan shot-putter, helps you with your luggage.

You arrive at the Outrigger Reef hotel on Waikiki beach where you spy old friends – Mary Slaney, Alberto Salazar. Your room with a spectacular ocean view overlooks the pool.

The hospitality suite is open. More friends. Suzy Hamilton, Marcus O'Sullivan. A roomful of Kenyans is watching a video-tape of the Japanese broadcast of the Fukuoka marathon. There's a barely audible collective gasp when Olympic champion Josiah Thugwane breaks away, having an easier time of it than when he won Honolulu in '95.

You grab a couple of bottles of designer water, sign up for a massage and head for Room 490 to pick up your check. There's a line of athletes stretching out the door.

Welcome to major league road running.

Sent to cover the biggest Japanese marathon in the world, imagine my astonishment to find out the race was in Hawaii. Some 17,000 of the 30,000 entrants in this "Boston of the Pacific" hail from the land of the rising sun..

Whereas that island nation is teeming with hot elite races – Fukuoka, Tokyo, Nagoya, Osaka, Beppu – Honolulu is where the marathon-mad masses come by the jet-load to fulfill the dream of completing a marathon.

At a banquet in the Oahu Country Club, I prepare myself as a beautiful woman walks up to the table and asks me for my autograph. The room is full of famous people and I figure there must be a big mistake. Then I realize the beautiful woman is looking right past me into a dark corner. In the dark corner, partially obscured by a potted plant, is a little man, so quiet I hadn't noticed him sitting there. I look at the nametag on his scrawny chest. "Jerry Lyndgrin," it says.

Gerry Lindgren!!

I sit with Steve Holman on the bus and I work up the nerve to ask him about his vexing series of poor races, missing the Olympics despite being his country's top miler. He is gracious and candid. Not his favorite topic of conversation.

"You have no idea how deeply humiliated and disappointed I felt," Holman confesses. "No idea."

There is much more to any competition than what we see from the stands or read about in the magazines. Holman knows what he has to do. "I have to be more aggressive."

I tell this story to '64 Olympian Lindgren. "You can never judge courage," Lindgren offers. "You have to be aggressive from the beginning of the race. And your aggression doesn't come in the race; it comes in training.

"You can prepare for an opponent's tactic, but not for the aggression he brings to the tactic."

Lindgren is thinking about aggression: "I could break everybody but Pre. Awesome, his aggression."

At every turn, you bump into a recognizable face: Filbert Bayi, Russ Francis, Mark Nenow, Frank Shorter, Wang Junxia.

Bob Kennedy is here. He is the greatest runner in America today and you think you know why. Aggression.

Kenny Moore invites us to a preview of the new film he scripted, "Without Limits," the story of Steve Prefontaine. "A race is a work of art," Pre says in the movie. He wanted every race to be won by the guy with the most guts. He thought he was that guy. In aggression there is art.

Race director Jim Barahal is an artist. The runners are his brushes, the course his canvas, the memories his paint.

The bus to the starting line of the Waikiki Mile follows a motorcycle escort down the wrong lane of traffic. You sit next to Sonia O'Sullivan.

There is no conversation.

You get to the start maybe an hour before your race. Wait 60 minutes to run for 4. Sit on the grass. Watch the athletes you'll line up against. Check your shoelaces. Check your watch. You make small talk. Stretch. Check your shoelaces. Check your watch. The agents stand off to the side and stare. The Kenyans sit off to the side by themselves. Like they run.

Finally, it is time to warm up.

"This is like no other race in the world," former champ Regina Jacobs will tell you. "Hawaii rules."

Hawaii rules? Experience counts, patience prevails and speed kills.

The race obviously means the most to Jacobs, who looks unusually fit for this time of year. Though it is December, the deep off-season, Jacobs admits - after her winning with a course record 4:26.06 - "I actually trained hard for this race.

"I tried to keep the pressure on, but the slow early pace played into my hands."

And Wang's 5:16.23? There were 12-year-old kids in the Nike/P.L.A.Y. Mile running better times.

What did you think about Wang's performance? "It would hurt to run that slow," says Leah Pells, the runner-up in the mile. "I don't even train that slowly."

Steve Ave, who plays Mohamed Gamoudi in "Without Limits", pulls the men's field down crowd-lined Kalakaua Avenue, looking like he's doing all he can do to keep Martin Keino, Moses Kigen, Stephen Kipkorir and David Lelei from blowing by.

There's no resting in the next half mile, and the Kenyans – all but Lelei – fade. Obviously went out too fast. Impatient.

"You have to be patient," winner Graham Hood (CR 3:55.66) notes. "I wasn't focusing on any one individual. I was just concentrating on how I felt.

"I felt phenomenal," adds the Canadian. "I thought, if anybody catches me, they'll really be moving. You never know until you cross the finish line, but with 400 meters to go, I didn't think I could lose." He couldn't.

And for the win Hood picked up an $18,000 check.

Holman – whose focus is the summer track season – ran faster this year than last but finished a place further back. "I'm a little disappointed," he says. "The early pace was quick, which put me in debt early. I just didn't have the spurt in my legs I needed at the end."

"To be honest," Holman adds, "if you run well here, you can make a lot of money. If somebody trained hard for this race, I don't blame them."

More men run under 4:00 than in the previous three years combined. "No wind," Hood says. "A perfect day."

Another perfect day in paradise.

Paradise does not come to those who wait.

Once a busman's holiday with limited national importance, the Honolulu Marathon today is an international slugfest with a reputation as "the birthplace of champions." Men like Ibrahim Hussein and Cosmas Ndeti cut their teeth here. Lee Bong-Ju, the Atlanta silver medalist, won Honolulu in '93.

You leave a wakeup call for 3 a.m. and are actually surprised when the phone rings in the middle of the night.

Oahu means "gathering place," and the word is never more meaningful than when 30,000 runners line up at 5 a.m. to challenge themselves over 26M, 385y of hard road.

Cannon. Fireworks. A pack of Africans strides through the concrete canyon of high-rise condominiums and luxury hotels, so far ahead there doesn't seem to be anyone behind them.

Too dark to see much. Sixty-six degrees. In our lifetime, Honolulu Marathon race conditions may never again be this good.

Patience. Last year's winner Eric Kimaiyo smokes mile 14 in 4:37. Eight men still left.

There's a testing climb at 23M, and winner-to-be Kimaiyo (2:12:17) puts his head down and takes off on his way to a $30,000 paycheck. Aggression.

Women's leaders and training partners Svetlana Vasilyeva and Irina Bogacheva – elbows flying – idle away many miles repeatedly bumping into each other before Vasilyeva (2:33:14) sprints to the win.

"I don't like Svetlana running behind me and touching me," Bogacheva complained afterwards. "She was clipping my heels. She made me nervous."

After the marathon, you hot-tub with the bikinied ex-Soviet women. You look for bruises. You look closely. Very closely. They make you nervous.

My special only-at-the-Honolulu Marathon vision? I decide to take a jog through the park alongside the military museum. It's 7:00 at night, the sun has already set. And there's Alberto Salazar, baseball mitt in hand, playing catch with his son. Tirelessly. In the dark.

That night the race sponsors host a cocktail party featuring more sushi than is good for you. Liu Dong is wearing a miniskirt, so short.

Have to be more aggressive.

The day after the big event, a one-legged pigeon lands among Japanese marathoners baking on the sands of Waikiki. Seems everybody is limping.

There's more to racing than racing, more to running than just running. There's the before and the after. It's the space between the notes that makes the music.

Make a difference.

Jack & Donna Scaff got me to the Honolulu Marathon the first time or two. Years later, Jim Moberly was instrumental in me getting back.

An all-expense-paid week in Honolulu in December was a special destination for an impecunious Oregon scribe. Thank you and thanks to the HMA. – JDW

Chapter Seven

More than a Business

There is a rather hackneyed expression, do what you love, the money will follow, which I know for a fact is not a universal given. Running is an expression of one's self at its most elemental. To be great in the running business, you have to love the sport.

Jeff Johnson: The Reluctant Farmer
February 1995

A very young Jeff Johnson, afloat and victorious

Jeff Johnson, Nike's long retired first employee, makes Phil Knight, the company's notoriously shy and reclusive founder, look like a flashy extrovert.

There would be no Nike without Johnson, who provided the name. Without the full-length cushioned mid-sole, which Johnson invented from shower tongs, many of us would be on crutches today. He is the least known important figure in the history of the sport. And determined to stay that way.

"I want to write a story about you," I told him.

"You *don't* want to write a story about me."

"I want to write about your new club, The Farm Team."

"That's better."

Jeff Johnson has come out of retirement and begun to apply his genius to coaching Olympic aspirants. He saw the lack of training opportunities in this country and felt a sense of personal responsibility.

Phil Knight & Jeff Johnson; Two buddies, two track fans

"You need a decent climate with available facilities, where there is a dedicated, full-time coach and good people to train with," he explains. "Consider those four variables and you have about zero options. You are basically dealing with some serious compromise someplace."

Johnson watched a friend's vain search and became acutely aware of a grave problem.

"Watching his struggle to find a comfortable place, "I said, 'This can't be too hard.' Nike exposed me to great scientists, athletes, Bill Bowerman,

coaches. Been a runner myself. I can put the pieces of the puzzle together."

What became an itch to experience coaching at a world-class level
evolved into a sense of duty. "My goal," Johnson offers, "is to help athletes reach their goals."

Johnson also had a sense of leaving something undone. The same sense
any good competitor has.

"An athlete asked to join The Farm Team. He said he didn't want to
reach middle-age and look back and wonder what he could've done. He
wanted to come out here and play the hand one more time. The same
thing drives so many of us. That's part of what was driving me.

"I would have been disappointed in myself if I hadn't started The Farm
Team," says Johnson. "I am the perfect person for the job. I understand
what athletes are going through. When they train and when they race. I
am a party to the obsession they struggle under. I recognize where the
line lies between proper and obsessive training. I can try to exert some
influence on runners who may be inclined to self-destruct. I can help them
through that.

"Virtually any coach you talk to about his great athletes says his main
function is pulling in the reins. The real skill a coach brings to an athlete is
knowing when it's time to say, 'Whoa. You can rest now.' The athletes
may know this intellectually, but emotionally they are driven to run more.
Maybe they are afraid. The fear of not running is fiercesome. They need
somebody to shoulder the responsibility of the decision for them.

"I've lived there myself, in that obsessive world of doing too much. I
think I have as clear an insight into obsession as anybody. Maybe I can put
a harness on it for the elite athletes I encounter along the way."

The weather in the San Francisco Bay Area may be the best in the
country. Low rainfall, low humidity, high level of sunshine. Wonderful terrain to run on, hills, parks, golf courses.

There are eight universities within a 60-mile radius of Stanford. From
Santa Cruz to Berkeley. Athletes interested in graduate studies can
choose from a range of universities within a hour's driving time of practice. The Bay Area's freeway system actually works and the population
base presumably gives The Farm Team the best chance of finding jobs.

Johnson has the professional credentials. Super high school coaching experience. Four times his state's cross-country coach of the year. Success with three women's clubs in New England, the Liberty Athletic Club, Seacoast Striders and the Athletica Track Club. He's certified by USATF.

Tom Laris, a 1968 Olympian at 10,000 meters, also works with The Farm Team. President of a securities business in Palo Alto, Laris goes to work at 4 or 5 in the morning and feels justified spending his late afternoons at the track. "He's basically giving back to a sport he's participated in for a long time," says Johnson, doing the same.

Johnson and Laris make an interesting team.

"Like I say to the athletes, 'I've read the books, Tom has actually done it.' He's lived it, I've studied it." A former two-miler at Stanford, Johnson is humble. "I was so slow, nobody cared. I was slower than road kill."

He dreamed of going faster. "I ran for Pete Petersens' Southern California Striders briefly. We got off work and came out to practice and ran as a group and tried to do well. Pete had a bunch of Olympians running with us. Good runners, but they were basically amateurs, living in crummy apartments, working at crummy jobs, trying to extend their athletic careers another few years."

Thirty years ago, the opportunities for post-college runners were arguably better than today.

"In the mid-1960's, Ted Hayden had a wonderful University of Chicago Track Club. Mihaly Igloi had the Los Angeles Track Club. There were a terrific bunch of clubs in this country then and they have dropped by the wayside.

"We've come back to that situation," says Johnson. "Our athletes are real amateurs. They are struggling in part-time jobs, trying to make ends meet, so they can keep chasing their dreams. Talented gals and guys with degrees who can do other things, but the fires still burn. They want to go to that track one more time.

"The joy of it comes when we gather on the golf course in the twilight for group runs. Bashing through intervals on a Saturday morning at the track. With each other. It's a very clubby, monkish, religious, spiritual kind of quest. We are certainly not in this for the money or the glory."

And Johnson? Is he trying to set an example?

He laughs out loud. "My God, no. I am one guy with a club. If anybody is looking for an example, look at The Farm Team. We're only a few months old. We haven't done anything yet, but our athletes are in pretty good shape already, running fairly well. We are able to compete with other people. That's all we can ask."

A righteous running club is not osteopathic surgery.

"They weren't exactly clamoring for a high school coach nobody ever heard of. I said, 'I'm here.' And these athletes said, 'Okay. Can I come?' And I answered, 'Sure, why not?' That's our criteria: you have to ask. The situation is so desperate, show up, and the athletes come," Johnson notes. "That speaks to the need for a comprehensive club program in the United States."

The rest of us ask, what can be done to help the sport? How can we help talented young men and young women achieve their greatest dreams? We ask these questions.

Jeff Johnson provides an answer. The first to tell you he's nobody special, he has again set a noble example.

The Farm Team Roster

The Farm Team, sponsored by Nike, is open to both men and women athletes. Many members are Cardinal *alumnae*, although there's no association between The Farm Team and Stanford University. Stanford graciously tolerates The Farm Team's occasional presence in their facilities.

Jeff Atkinson, an '88 Olympian at 1500m, is one of The Farm Team's daily training mates. A 3:52 miler, Jeff is not a club member because he officially represents Foot Locker. Marc Olesen, a Canadian, has PRs of 3:39.26 for 1500m and 13:38.09 for 5k. Gary Stolz was second in the 1992 NCAA X-C behind Bob Kennedy. Stolz, hobbled since with Achilles problems, is coming back from surgery. He's run 13:51 for 5k indoors.

Fred Carter clocked a 8:45.92 steeplechase in '92. Ray Appenheimer from Colgate has run 13:59 for 5k. Jon Pritchard from Penn State raced 14:17 for 5k. He's attending graduate school in Biology. Rey Flores from the University of Massachusetts lives in San Francisco, so he doesn't train with The Farm Team on a regular basis. His best times are 14:19 for 5k and 30:10 for 10k. He's faster on the roads, where he recently ran a 1:06:40 half marathon.

Kevin Connor is thirty-years-old and still trying to break two minutes for the 800. "We're trying to get him under," Johnson says. James Cramton, a 46.6 quarter-miler, has never run a half mile but he wants to try. "Kevin and James to some extent measure the ranges of this club," says Johnson.

Two women now train with The Farm Team on a regular basis. Michelle Deasy from Cornell has run 16:37 for 5k and 34:39 for 10k. Michelle is a relative novice who started running as a junior in college. Angela Mogielski shows good range with a 16:50 for 5k and 2:10 for 800m.

At-large members training elsewhere include marathoner Brad Hudson and Andrea Green, a 2:07 half-miler and former ACC champion at the University of North Carolina. "She is the club's first qualifier for a national championship," Johnson notes proudly.

"We are grass roots and we're elite, and everything in between," Johnson concedes. "We may have an identity crisis if we get sixty people here all of a sudden. We may have to make some decision about what we want to do, and who we are. At the moment The Farm Team is just a really nice training group."

In a decent climate with excellent facilities and a dedicated, full-time coach. Jeff Johnson just did it again.

JOJ has been my friend for decades. Back in the day, we might eat dinner together. We'd go to T.G.I. Fridays in Beaverton and sit across from each other, drinking adult beverages. Each of us reading a paperback. Oh, those were some wild times alright. – JDW

A Conversation with Jeff Johnson
February 1995

The following is the source for the previous article. Some material is re-dundant, but enough is new to be valuable. The reader will find - through-out this book - a number of interviews which served as source material for articles, published and unpublished. I want you to hear the wisdom and insight of these special people without their words being filtered by writer or magazine editors or both. – JDW

JDW: I want to write a story about you.

JOJ: You don't want to write a story about me.

JDW: Right. I want to write about your club.

JOJ: That's better, but I don't trust you. [Laughs.]

JDW: You can trust me.

JOJ: Okay.

JDW: I haven't let you down too badly in the past.

JOJ: No.

So, Knight laughed, huh? He's having a good time?

JDW: Yeah. He admitted he's fearful.

JOJ: Sure. Aren't we all that way?

JDW: The good ones are.

JOJ: Fear drives us all. I don't want to let my athletes down. Herb Elliot was afraid. He was more driven by the fear of losing than by the desire to win.

JDW: That's true. Anyway, Knight looked absolutely normal and healthy and not at all as weird as I remember him being.

JOJ: I never gave much credence to the weird stories because weird had to be just a disguise he was hiding behind. I don't believe people change that much.

JDW: I think the fear factor is an aspect of a lot of people's drive.

JOJ: I suppose there are better reasons to be driven. But fear works good for me. Fear of letting somebody down. Or the fear of letting myself down or the fear of, mostly, the fear of letting other people down. I personally don't give a shit. [Laughs.]

When I get myself in a position where people clearly are depending upon me for something, I get personally, this has nothing to do with Phil Knight, I get very uptight about trying to make sure every little thing gets done. If an enterprise does fail, then I will have at least done everything conceivable.

That even comes down to affecting my personal life in ways where I just become a complete wretch who won't relax and won't go out and have any fun during the period when some issue is in crisis, that I am responsible for. I just won't take any time off. I won't go out and be with people who want to have some kind of normal interchange, because to me that could be the moment when something needed to be tended to.

I think this fear may have been a contributing factor to the break-up of so many of the families at Nike. We might have had a lot of people like that at Nike, driven by fear, who basically said, this is the thing that defines me and I have to take care of this before I can take care of anything else, including my own family, because if I don't take care of this then I have let so many people down, I am not worthy of my family or anything else. What happens then is they end up letting their family down.

The only guy who ever did that was [Jim] Gorman. Gorman was a trooper and a soldier just like everybody else, but somehow he managed to find time to keep his family together.

We were all driven. I don't know what drove everybody, but as much as anything, I just refused...

I remember when I was at Exeter, starting a shoe factory, being responsible for that, and having a clock running on how much money we could put into this before we went belly up. The need to turn it and make it profitable so we could stop putting money into it. Because we didn't have the money to put into it. Essentially, between you and me, and maybe it was covered in the Swoosh book, dragging our feet on payments to Nissho-Iwai in order to finance the Exeter factory. We could only drag those so long, because if we burned that money up we're weren't going to have the money to pay them ever. And that would have been the end of the company. I had to make that thing get up and be profitable and it wasn't my entire job. But it was my responsibility

I just didn't see there was any hope. I really didn't know how this could possibly work. I certainly didn't know what I was doing. I just took it one day at a time and said, it's not going to fail today. It may fail tomorrow but it won't fail today. The next morning, I would get up and say the same thing. We'll fake it until five o'clock.

This was people's lives involved here, too. It wasn't just Phil Knight we'd be letting down. We'd be letting down everybody else in the company. Mortgage payments, college, two kids' tuition, and everything else depended on this thing staying afloat. It was a *huge* responsibility and, of course, Phil has felt that responsibility all of his life.

Each one of us had the ball in our hand and you could fumble it or not fumble it. At one time or another. It was a game where you had multiple balls, anyone could fumble it, and lose the game for everybody. Gorman could have sunk us in Korea, I could have sunk us in Exeter. There have been several people at several points in time who could have sunk the whole enterprise and just sucked it up and didn't.

Or lucked through. Whatever. So much of that came from Phil. In the sense of our affection for him, or the unreasonable amount of trust he put in us, it inspired us not to let him down. If he had been a prick who micromanaged everything we did, you might have said, "Oh, fuck him. I have somebody else participating in here. I'll do my job, I'll put in my 9 to 5, I'll do the best I can." Basically sharing the responsibility, so if it fails, then you feel like you've shared the responsibility with the other guy. But Phil was so distant, so hands off, so remote, the whole thing was in your lap and you knew it. There was no dodging that. It was your own baby. If it sank, there was nobody you could go crying to, except your own ass.

It wasn't like you were going to leave and get a real job somewhere else. [Laughs.]

Even if I had another talent which has yet to be identified at this distant point in my life, I didn't have a whole lot of other interests. I might have been able to do something else, but I certainly wouldn't have had as much fun or felt as much in synch with it as I did with a running shoe company and athletes and chasing the three-stripe guys.

Now that was a mission. The quest for the holy-grail-type of occupation, that wasn't a job.

The quest came from Phil to some extent but it also came from the rest of us. All I ever cared about when I was a kid, even in junior high, all I ever cared about was running and racing and competition. Going into a job situation which was basically running and racing and competing against other guys who run and race in the sense of their products, it was just such a logical extension of all I ever cared about it. Some of it came from Phil, but much of it came from my personal background.

We were certainly used to getting our butts kicked. We could've gotten our butts kicked again, but we certainly weren't going to drop out of the race. If you want to beat the analogy to death. We might lose the race but, goddamn it, we were going to hang in there to the fucking finish.

JDW: None of you guys were winners.

JOJ: HAHAHAHAHAHAHA!!!! That's a good way to put it. A collection of losers, if there ever was one.

We were certainly able to take our lumps. Maybe the fact that we were losers sustained us, because there were some hard times, and there were some definite losses, and there were some turning points, like Tiger pulling the contract in '71, '72.

I remember guys who were with us then- I remember one in particular - who were really winners, really cool guys, really sharp, the kind of guys we really tried to feel we should be more like. They were professional, they looked sharp, they said the right thing. They combed their hair in the morning, they shaved, they looked sharp. Had the right shoes on the right feet, that kind of stuff, unlike the rest of us bumpkins. Whenever there was a major, major crisis, those guys left. They knew a sinking ship when they saw one, and they went out and got real jobs.

The rest of us sucked it up, accepted our beating, and went on. I guess we were used to that. The fact that we were losers, we could handle defeat. We didn't like it, but we could handle it and we could go on. It certainly never occurred to us to go out and get a responsible job, a real job, in a company that was stable.

That was the word we often heard, "you guys are just too unstable. I'm not comfortable here. Good luck. I love you all and you're great guys but this is just too unstable for me. I can't sleep at night."

Just another beating for us. We're used to it. We were resilient. When you are a 4:11 miler at Oregon, you've got to be resilient. That's what Knight was. You got to be resilient because there's about 900 guys better than you are. In the Bowerman era, 4:11 is the water boy.

And I was worse than that in college. I was on the hamburger squad at Stanford.

JDW: And then you found the finish line.

JOJ: If I had found a finish line, I wouldn't be out here. I am somewhat suffering because I am a creature of home and hearth. Basically, if I had found the finish line, I would still be in New Hampshire. I wouldn't be out here living in a dive nine months a year in a state I can barely tolerate, up to my asshole in people, and stoplights and boring unchanging weather when people are telling me how wonderful it is back in Lebanon all the time. My neighbors will call and tell me about the latest snowstorm, the latest wild animals... so definitely, I haven't found the finish line.

Or if I've found it, it's back home, and as nice as it would be to take a break and sit there and watch a couple more movies and take a few swims and go out for a walk in the woods, I haven't crossed the finish line yet, that's basically it.

Setting up the club was a sense of responsibility ultimately. A sense of recognizing through a young friend's experience, the difficulty of trying to find a satisfactory situation to run as a post-graduate. When you start to realize, you have to go to a decent climate with available facilities, where there is a dedicated, full-time coach, where there's good people to train with, you put all those four variables up there, you are down to about zero options. You are basically dealing with some serious compromise someplace.

My friend found a great coach in a very cold climate. She found pieces of the whole puzzle, but she could never put the thing together. Maybe she's found it now. I became acutely aware of how desperate the situation really is out there. I guess I'd known before, but watching her struggle, trying to find a place that was for her totally comfortable, I just said, "shit, this can't be too hard."

I have been so blessed by always being at those intersections, being exposed to Jack Daniels for all these years, and Ned Frederick and the whole Nike experience and all the athletes I've met and all the coaches and Bowerman and having been a runner myself, I just feel, you know, I could put one of these things together. I am not that great, but how great do you have to be? There's nothing out there. The Reebok Enclave is about it for middle distance running in this country. That's about it. And that's a great situation. There should be a dozen more of those.

So, I figured, what the hell, maybe I'll do this. What became kind of an itch to try to experience coaching at this very high level evolved into a sense of responsibility. I really had to do it. I would have been disappointed in myself if I hadn't done it. I mentioned that to [David] Chang once and he used the phrase, *noblesse oblige*, which I hadn't remembered or heard for ages and ages, but that's basically it. It was a obligation of the nobility, to the extent my life has exposed me to this all along, I am the perfect person to do it. I understand it. I get it. Pretty much. I think. At least as well as anybody else does.

I think I understand the sport. I think I understand what athletes are going through. When they train and when they race. I think I am a party to the obsession they struggle under and I recognize where lies the line between proper and obsessive training. I can try to exert some kind of external influence on the great talents of the world that maybe from time to time are inclined to self-destruct, and help them through that.

That's all they really need. Bowerman, Tom Fleming, virtually any coach you talk to about his great athletes, will say his main function is pulling in the reins. I think Dick Brown said the same thing about Mary Slaney. The only skill a coach brings to an athlete is knowing when it's time to say "Whoa. Stop now. Don't go off and run those extra quarters. That's not going to do you any good today." The athletes probably know that intellectually, but emotionally they are driven to run those extra miles because they think it makes them special.

Maybe they are afraid. The fear of not running, to take that responsibility on themselves to say I shouldn't do this, is too fiercesome. They need somebody to take the responsibility of the decision for them. I've been there. I've seen that. I've done that. Lived there myself, in that obsessive world of doing too much. I think I have as clear an insight into obsession as anybody else. Maybe I can put a harness on it for the elite athletes I encounter along the way.

JDW: So, who's on the team?

JOJ: I've only been out here four months and I came out with no fanfare. The first athletes we got are mostly people who were here. We have only had a couple people come in from the outside so far. Heavily laced with ex-Stanford athletes.

There's Marc Olesen, a Canadian, and a 1500, 5k guy. Mainly a 5k guy now. 3k, 5k. 1500PR is 3:39.26, his 5k PR is 13:38.09.

Gary Stolz, another Stanford guy, who was second in the 1992 NCAA X-C behind Bob Kennedy. He's been pretty much injured ever since. His career cut short by achilles problems. Finally had surgery for it and he's coming back. He's run 13:51 for 5k. Indoors.

Fred Carter, another Stanford guy. 8:45.92 in the steeplechase in '92

James Cramton, a novice half miler. He's never run a half mile but he wants to try. He has 46.6 in the quarter.

Ray Appenheimer, he's from Colgate. He's run 13:59 for 5k. He just came in 3 weeks ago.

Jon Pritchard from Penn State attending graduate school in Biology here, he's run 14:17 for 5k.

Rey Flores from the University of Massachusetts, lives in San Francisco, so he doesn't train with The Farm Team on a regular basis. His best times are 14:19 for 5k and 30:10 for 10k. He's run faster on the roads. He just ran a 1:06:40 half marathon.

Jeff Atkinson is training with us. He's not part of our club because he runs for Foot Locker. He's one of our daily training mates and part of our training stable, who wears a different uniform at meets. He's run 3:52.80 for the mile and was an '88 Olympian at 1500m.

Kevin Connor, a thirty-year-old kid still trying to break two minutes for the 800. We're trying to get him under.

Kevin and James to some extent measure the ranges of this club. Right now we are sort of grass roots and we're sort of elite, and everything in between so far. We may have an identity crisis if we have 60 people here all of a sudden. We may have to make some sort of decision about what we want to do, and who we are. At the moment The Farm Team is just a really nice training group.

We have two women who train with us on a regular basis. Michelle Deasy, she's a 5k, 10k girl out of Cornell. She's run 16:37 for 5k and 34:39 for 10k. Michelle is pretty much a novice. She didn't start running until she was a junior in college. She got out of college with only two years running experience. She was a walk-on at Cornell. Her coach had no idea she had any talent, so he wasted half a year with her, he said.

That isn't entirely true, but he didn't realize she could run on varsity until, I think, she finished second girl one day. Which is pretty unusual for a walk-on at Cornell, cause Cornell traditionally has one of the top five or six teams in the country in women's cross-country and she walked on to it. With no running experience whatsoever.

Angela Mogielski has run 16:50 for 5k and she's also run 2:10 for 800m so she has good range.

We have a couple of at-large people who aren't training with us. Brad Hudson is actually a Farm Team member in Eugene. Under what circumstances, I don't know. He just called me out of the blue and said Jacco Tuominen had said Brad needed a club. We take care of his equipment needs.

We also have a girl in North Carolina, named Andrea Green. She's a 2:07 half-miler, former ACC champion at UNC. Who's now out of college and continuing to run. She is our first qualifier for a national championship. She ran 2:08 this winter and qualified for the Atlanta Indoor meet in a couple of weeks.

JDW: Why these athletes?

Ask them. I just came out here, and said, "Here I am." And these people showed up. I mean, I didn't choose them. [Laughs.]

JDW: What's the criteria for being on The Farm Team? "Hello, here I am?"

I said, "I'm here." And these athletes said, "Okay. Can I come?" And I said, sure, why not. That's the criteria. I basically haven't said "no" to anybody.

We have a second coach. There are two coaches here. The other one is Tom Laris, who was a 1968 Olympian at 10,000m. He's the President of a securities business in Palo Alto. E-Trade Securities. Basically, as I understand his situation, he goes to work at 4 or 5 in the morning to catch the early morning stock operations in NYC. So he feels justified in leaving work around 3 o'clock, 'cause he's been up since about 3 in the morning. His late afternoons are at the track. He's basically giving back to a sport he's participated in for a long time.

JDW: Credentials?

JOJ: Thirteen years of high school coaching experience. I coached three women's clubs in New England, Liberty Athletic Club, Sea Coast Striders and the Athletica Track Club, overlapping those 13 years. I'm certified at Level 2 with the USAT&F's coaching certification program. Level 2 is the highest certification you can get right now. There's about 500 and something Level 2's in the country. Just means you went through the schools. You can still be at Level 2 and be horrid.

Laris and I make an interesting team. Like I say to the athletes, I've read the books, Tom has actually done it. That's the way I put it. He's lived it, he's done it. I've just sort of studied it.

Twenty years ago, the opportunities for post-grad athletes were beginning to tail off a little bit. Thirty years ago, those opportunities were pretty good. I remember in the mid-60's, Pete Petersens had a great group with the Southern California Striders. Ted Hayden had a wonderful University of Chicago Track Club, going great guns with Wolhuter and Ken Sparks, and Lowell Powell, whatever the guy's name was, remember him, the guy who ran with a beard. A terrific track club. Mihaly Igloi had the Los Angeles Track Club. Just a great bunch of clubs in this country then. All those things have sorta dropped by the wayside.

Seems to me there's a lot less of an opportunity now for people. Those clubs were very poorly funded, if funded at all. I see we've come back to that situation. Our athletes are real amateurs. They are struggling in part-time jobs, trying to make ends meet, so they can keep chasing their dreams here. To me, this is a very '60's kind of thing.

I ran for Pete Petersens' Southern California Striders briefly, so I know what that was about. We were just working and got off work and came out to practice and ran as a group and tried to do well. And he had a bunch of Olympians running with us at that time, Ted Nelson and Ron Larrieu, good people, but they were basically amateurs, living in crummy apartments, working at crummy jobs, trying to extend their running careers another few years.

That's what we've got with these guys. Atkinson and Oleson are talented guys with degrees and can do other things, but the fires still burn. They want to go out to that track one more time.

JDW: Speaking personally, money can be a problem sometimes.

JOJ: I don't talk to them hardly at all about their finances, I consider that kind of a personal thing, but I have heard that Atkinson saved his money from the time when he was really hot. And he fairly much banked that, back in the late 80's. I don't know if that's true. If you want to get into his finances, get into it with him, not with me, because I don't know.

They are monks, more than anything else. They have this very Spartan life of running, wearing hair shirts and sleeping on hard cots in a little cell somewhere. I think the joy of it is to gather on the golf course in the twilight for group runs. And bashing through intervals on a Saturday morning on the track. With each other.

It's a very clubby, monkish, religious, spiritual kind of quest. They are certainly not in this for the money or the glory. Nobody knows who the hell they are. It's just a very personal thing.

JDW: Why here?

JOJ: I was drawn to the Bay area by the climate as much as anything. If I had gone to Los Angeles, presumably I'd have another group and we'd be talking about different athletes. I like the Bay Area because the weather is about as good here as it is anywhere in country. It may be *better* here than anywhere else in the country. Very low rainfall, very low humidity, high level of sunshine. Wonderful terrain to run on. We have hills and parks and trails.

There is no association between The Farm Team and Stanford University. We don't work out with the undergraduates. Stanford has been gracious enough to tolerate our occasional presence in some of their facilities.

Beyond the climate, it's extremely easy to get around. This freeway system actually works here. I can get to San Francisco Airport in 30 minutes.

I figured there were eight universities within a 60-mile radius of Stanford. From Santa Cruz to Berkeley. The point is, if athletes wanted to come out here and do graduate studies, they could choose from an enormous range of universities and still be within an hour's driving time of practice. Also, a population base here that presumably might give us the best chance of finding jobs, too. Just seemed like this was a perfect place to come.

Of course, I did grow up here. That's somewhat coincidental, but I am a little more at home here. Not a lot because it's changed so much since then.

There was not a really high profile running club in this area and that just didn't make sense to me. Because this was the area that could best support a club, I thought.

Boston is another good area for a club. The climate is not as good. A favorable climate for distance runners and tons of universities and it is very easy to get around down there very quickly. Boston has had good success with running clubs in Boston in the past 20 years. Boston is a prime spot. Maybe Washington, D.C. is just as good. But this is an area that seemed to be primo. There were sprint clubs here, but there was no major distance club that I was aware of.

And it just seemed there should be. And could be.

Just show up and go, "Yo!" And people would come.

So far so good.

My goal is to help these people reach their goals.

I was in New Hampshire enjoying life, but having a sense that there was something more I needed to do. Or should do. Or could do.

I have always had a sense about leaving something undone. The same sense an athlete has. I had an athlete call me the other night, another Canadian, who is probably going to join us in a few weeks. He gave as a reason, he didn't want to get to middle-age and look back and wonder what he could've done. He wanted to come out here and play the hand one more time.

That's the same thing that drives so many of us. Part of what was driving me. I didn't want, at the age of 52 sitting in New Hampshire, to give it another ten years and get to the point where I was too old to do this and then wonder if I could have. Wonder, if I had, would I have had the chance to share an Olympic experience with an athlete. Would I have seen an athlete develop from an unknown to a known. Would I have some more old man stories, that kind of stuff. [Laughter.]

It came down to, I felt I had a responsibility to the sport, a responsibility to myself, I guess, ultimately to do this. Everybody does things for themselves first. I had to do this.

JDW: Are you trying to set an example?

JOJ: Ha! I would hate to be an example for anybody. I am one guy with a team. If anybody is looking for an example, The Farm Team should be an example. We're only four months old. So it's hard, we haven't done anything yet. The need is great and I am struck by how easily somebody like myself, whom no one has ever heard of... there wasn't a single athlete out here who was clamoring for me to come out from New Hampshire and coach them. No one had ever heard of me.

And nobody was too excited when they did hear about some high school coach coming across the country to open a club. But the situation is so desperate, you show up, say "Yo!" and the athletes come. A field of dreams, of sorts.

JDW: Start a club and you have a team.

JOJ: That speaks to the need for a comprehensive club program in these United States, where it is so easy to set something up and get it going.

Our athletes are in pretty good shape already. They are running fairly well. Marc got 4th in the Sunkist 3000, his first indoor race of the year. We are able to compete with other people.

And that's all we can ask.

JDW: You have downplayed your record. Four times you were named the state cross-country coach of the year. A former miler, two-miler at Stanford.

JOJ: "But I was so slow nobody cared. Like 4:25. I was slower than road kill."

JDW: How's your running now?

JOJ: "Pathetic. I am averaging about two miles a day, with a range from zero to four.

02/27/95

Many years ago, I came across a Japanese saying I found particularly meaningful: A great man does not let himself be known. I am proud to have known a few, if only a little. – JDW

Women... Running into the Next Millennium
August 1995

An interview with an old friend and outstanding business woman.

Who else but Helen Rockey of Brooks Sports, Inc., the first woman president of a major athletic shoe company, to predict the future of women's running. Who better than The Rocket? "Anybody else," she answered. But the mere fact the 30-something ex-Nike executive agreed to share her views is typical. She is very much herself, a woman of the future running.

When I was a little girl, the only time you would ever see a woman run was when she was chasing a toddler. Or maybe a bus. Women in running is a modern phenomenon. There was no girls' track team at my school. Gender equity in athletics didn't begin until 1972 with the passage of Title IX. In 1978, Grete Waitz produced an amazing breakthrough, the first sub-2:30 marathon by a woman. Women's running clothes, apparel actually designed for the female body, were impossible to find until 1979. Until very recently, women raced no further than 800 meters at the Olympic Games. Joan Benoit won the first gold medal in the marathon only eleven years ago. We have come so far so fast.

More women will have more choices available to them in the future, and I hope more women choose to run. A growing number of women see running as a component of an overall fitness program. And they are dragging their husbands or significant others into the sport for health reasons. Like, if you don't, you will die. Breathing better is powerful motivation. I hope we see greater cooperation among all members of the health and fitness community to promote exercise.

I would never call myself a runner. A jogger maybe, but not a runner. I played soccer as a kid. I have been skiing like a maniac most of my life. I started running as an adult, at Nike, because it was the only way I could get any time with my boss.

I get up early, five or five-thirty, and go for a run. I do a few arm weights and some upper body work. I do a lot of stretching. Try to get to work by seven-thirty. Twelve hours a day, six days a week is normal. I need one day away.

I am your 30-miles-a-week-no-matter-what-country-or-city-of-the-world-I-might-be-in kind of a runner. Running makes my day, but it's not as long or as much as I would like. Time is a factor, a fact of life. Women will not have more time in the future, but I am convinced more time will be dedicated to fitness. Hopefully we can interest more people in spending their valuable time feeling better about themselves. As a friend says, "Running does help you find that feeling better place."

We cannot talk about the future without addressing the safety of women runners. I don't have an answer, but it's an issue that makes me very angry. I really believe there is no such thing as freedom as long as you live in fear. The lack of physical safety or the advent of violence, to me, is a freedom issue. The solution will come only from women, because no one else has an incentive to solve it.

If we can't go outdoors, it doesn't matter what brand of shoes we're wearing.

I am so damn competitive I will push myself until I collapse. I finally realized I am never going to win a race and I don't think I have that many miles left, so I've got to save the old body.

I do see more women competing, more women having the freedom and the self-esteem to compete. I hope we'll see many more prizes awarded at races, greater opportunities for more people to go home winners. More fun for more people.

I did the St. Patty's race. I'm going to Bay-To-Breakers. I do the fun events. I compete when I can get together with friends and family and make a party out of it.

Susan Molloy and Vicki Mitchell, to name just two Brooks' heroines, personify the women we'll see in competition in the future. I personally claim zero expertise when it comes to an informed evaluation of women's competition over the next half dozen years. So, I asked Susan and Vicki, both Olympic-caliber athletes, to share their perspectives.

"I predict more traffic," says Susan Molloy, mother of two boys she's prouder of than a 2:39:34 marathon debut. "Which is not good for distance training. I foresee an exponential increase at eight o'clock in the morning of hostile commuters intent on vehicular homicide."

Susan has a sharp eye on the future. "I have noticed more and more elite athletes, people making good money as professional runners, are also working full-time," she says. "The typical woman athlete today does not rotate her existence entirely around running. A well-rounded life will lengthen your career. A narrow mind is not healthy. When I am with my kids, I am content. When I am running, I focus on my running.

"More and more mothers are running fabulous times," says Susan. "I know my body is more efficient from having children. I can feel it, physically there's something extra there."

Ten p.m. 25-year-old Vicki Mitchell is ready for bed, a night run followed a day of teaching and coaching. "I don't sit around and contemplate things like the future of women's running," she admits. "I don't think about other women running. I just go out and do it."

Vicki has run 33:01 for 10k and a 15:54 5k. She's preparing for the 1996 U.S. Olympic Trials. "Realistically, I am not ready for '96," she says. "Perhaps if I continue to improve year after year, I'll be ready for Australia in 2000." Vicki has a healthy attitude about competition. "My goals aren't outcome-oriented," she says. "I aim for performance and hope that will get me across the finish line first. If not, I know I have done my best."

(Back to The Rocket.) The sport is self-rewarding. You get back at least as much as you put into it, and women like that about running. Women like that about a lot of things.

I wouldn't be surprised to see the running shoe again become a fashion trend. Running is an individualistic, self-actualizing sport, like mountain biking and snowboarding, which will have greater appeal in the next millennium. There will be fewer places to get away from it all and more things from which to seek escape.

The industry will evolve, whether it wants to or not.

The consumer is changing. She is shifting to a new psychology of the year 2000, more embracing, more holistic, more involved with the complete dimension of stress and fitness and how it relates to an individual's well-being.

The best example might be the new Dodge Ram. Never in my life did I want a pick-up truck. Until I saw the Ram with those big rounded fenders, incorporating this whole mood of making a product a part of the overall person.

Modern products will reflect a holistic philosophy in style and the mentality of the design itself. If we can break out of the mindset "this sneaker is for this sport" and instead offer products that provide the benefits associated with the sense of well-being produced through sports and fitness, we will re-energize this industry.

I predict a breakdown of the barriers between suppliers and retailers. Retailers will play a bigger role in advertising and design. I see the day, two to five years away, when the virtual corporation, a partnership between retailer and distributor, becomes a reality. For example, an in-store boutique, with a Brooks designer on site, will create a new shoe, agreeing conceptually on product and display. Then the product will ship directly from the factory on a just-in-time basis.

Which begs the question, whither goest the shoe company of the future? A scary thought for some, I'm sure. But think of this. Prices might stabilize or even decline. The products could be specifically designed by the retailer for its local clientele. Which could mean a better and less expensive shoe.

There will be a shakeout at the retail level and the ultimate winner will be the performance-oriented consumer. The smaller retailer, especially the sport specialty shops, will see increased traffic. Women in particular will seek expert advice and outstanding customer service in a nurturing environment.

Consumers are tired of bells and whistles. In some respects, women don't want to know how the technology works. And they don't want to be responsible for figuring out how it works. They just want the product to do what they expect it to do. Surely that's not too much to ask of the athletic shoe industry.

People want performance. At Brooks, we have a new cushioning system in development. We're excited about some injury prevention breakthroughs. We continue to invest in technology, but not for its own sake, but as a total package that performs for the runner.

People don't buy products anymore, they buy experience. Runners choose their retailers like they choose how to spend their free time. And the brand, in essence, is their friend. The brand is who you decide to spend your time with. People pick brands and retailers and friends who are happy, fun, attractive and supportive. They want products and companions who make them feel comfortable and good about themselves.

With women in particular, the products they purchase – and the companies with whom they do business – need to have a certain amount of credibility. Companies will have to become more open and responsive, more personable.

There is, by the way, the misconception that all women have petite feet. Not true. I can imagine the increased availability of broader shoes for women. New footwear designs will take into greater account the importance of shoe angles just for women, the differences caused by hip alignment, for example.

I ran my only marathon at the Avenue of The Giants in 3:20. I was so excited as I approached the finish line because it was my first marathon and my thirtieth birthday. You know what it's like. You've trained so hard, run so hard, and then, the finish line in sight, you are finally achieving this tremendous goal.

You get to the end of the race and they announce your name as they see you coming over the last hill. I heard my name and then these cute, young boys ran out from the side and they were grabbing at me, trying to tear my I.D. tag off my number. I thought they were congratulating me, so I grabbed them back. I must have been delirious with joy and an overwhelming sense of accomplishment. I was hugging and kissing these boys but really all they wanted was my bar code.

The future of women in running, it must be noted, is not limited to training and racing. I may be the first woman president of a major athletic shoe company, but I will not be the last. Women manage running stores, serve as elected leaders of our largest running organizations, promote some of the world's largest marathons. Sometimes we forget. And, of course, women are often the volunteers picking up the cups at water stations or handing out T-shirts at the finish line. Sometimes we take them for granted.

I like to think of running as a "right choice." As we mature, we tend to make wiser decisions. We treat ourselves better. The next five years will see an incredible number of people coming face to face with their own mortality.

My friend Laurel James of Super Jock N' Jill, a running specialty store in Seattle, says, "I don't promote marathoning, but I do promote a time for yourself, a time for fitness." Then she goes out and does her first triathlon. At age 59. Why? Because it feels good.

I do promote marathons. After all, marathoners wear out a lot of shoes. But Laurel's concept of taking the time to be good to yourself will bring a great many women to running. Running makes sense. It's inexpensive, requires little athletic talent and it is good for you, too.

As a matter of fact, I wouldn't be surprised to see another running boom, bigger than the last. Much slower, of course.

With women leading the way.

Buck Naked:
The Adventures of Nike's Founder
February 1995

The young Phil Knight, smiling in otherwise empty stands. He must know something...

Behind every champion is the willingness to risk defeat at the hope of claiming victory. The willingness to try new things and accept new challenges. If you're driven to becoming the best that you can be, now is the time to follow your dream to Nike. – from a Nike employment ad in The Sunday Oregonian.

They called him "The White Mole" and now he is the most powerful man in sports. He borrowed $37 from his father to buy his first shoe samples and today he is a multi-billionaire.

He has amassed the greatest fortune ever from athletics and he doesn't like to talk about his money. He changed the face of entertainment, of culture, and he won't talk about his power. Which is not to say he doesn't like money and power. It's just that affluence and influence are not his finish line.

Knight and a really great tie...

256

The Chairman and Chief Executive Officer of Nike, Inc., hates talking about all that media trash, so we talked sports. We sat in a conference room on the company's stupifyingly marvelous Beaverton campus, which is, quite simply, a work of art. It must be noted: the NBA's Chicago Bulls were practicing in the company gymnasium.

Old friends call him, "Buck." Buck loves to win and he hates to lose. Hates to lose. We talked about why he loves to win so much.

"The best thing in sports is winning," Buck says, "and the second best thing is losing." Nike is about having fun. And losing is no fun. Winning, winning is fun. Philip H. Knight spent too much time of his youth watching the behinds of faster boys disappear, fading into the distance.

Knight plots global domination

Winning fuels the man. Nike is his revenge.

He wore Converse sneakers as a kid. His first pair of track shoes were emblazoned with three stripes. And the Nike legend goes like this. In the Beginning, there was Knight. Knight ran the mile for the Fighting Ducks, the Mighty Men of Oregon. Gang Green. His personal best rests forever at 4:10.

And Knight wrote a term paper at the Stanford School of Business for Professor Frank Shallenberger, on the subject of starting a small business. Buck received an "A" for suggesting athletic shoes could be designed in America, produced in Asia at low cost and imported into the United States. Where they could be sold at prices lower than the most popular athletic shoes of the time, made in West Germany.

Knight went to Japan, hiked Mt. Fuji, a trek the Japanese believe makes one wiser, and visited the Onitsuka shoe factory in Kobe where sneakers were made. In February, 1964, Buck took his first order of Tiger shoes. His new company, Blue Ribbon Sports, did $20,000 worth of business that first year, showing a $3,240 profit.

Headquartered in his mother's laundry room, selling shoes part-time out of the back of a station wagon to athletes at track meets, Buck finally quit his day job as a CPA *cum* university teacher in 1969. He was the best salesman Tiger ever had. By 1971, Buck's business booming, the partnership dissolved.

Knight was forced to create a new shoe line, one named after the winged Greek goddess of victory. Nike: a perfect brand name and a fortuitous symbol. Today, Nike's annual sales approach $4.5 billion. That's a lot of winning.

The fifty-six-year-old Knight claims he never did a crazy thing in his life until he founded Nike. Buck is not Nike, but everything Nike is reflects the man. Behind those dark glasses, Knight is a visionary. The man can see a long way off.

"This is one weird scientist," Michael "Air" Jordan once said.

Jeff Johnson, Nike's first employee, remembers Knight as normal as the next guy. "I never gave much credence to the weird stories," Johnson offers, "because weird had to be just a disguise he was hiding behind."

"The guy's weird. He's strange," offers Nelson Farris, Nike's Director of Corporate Education. "He is truly brilliant and every brilliant guy has his quirky side."

Knight has been called exceptionally private, reclusive, shy, enigmatic, spacey. He is a thinker. He is a big sports fan. The hour we spent together he laughed and laughed and laughed.

If I was him, I'd be laughing, too.

I hold the man in the highest respect. Knight is a stand-up guy with a deeply sentimental streak and a defiant empathy for the underdog. He is neither bully nor anyone to mess with. Loyal. Buck has long been a hero of mine.

And you can tell a lot about a man by looking at his heroes.

Bill Bowerman, legendary educator at the University of Oregon where Knight toiled on the hamburger squad, is the co-founder of Nike. The two men shook hands and each chipped in $500 for the first shipment of a thousand pairs of Tiger Shoes.

Bowerman brought jogging to America. And Nike's address is One Bowerman Drive.

"Bowerman was the best track coach who ever lived, which is covering a lot of territory," Knight says. "Bowerman was a great teacher, in the purest sense of the word, and he was the biggest influence in my life, outside my family. He taught me how to compete.

"Bowerman used to say, 'I am a professor of competitive responses, not a track coach.' His point was true. Focus on big events, prepare physically, emotionally and intellectually, and get the best of yourself. Best education I ever had came on Hayward Field."

Oregon's Steve Prefontaine, the greatest distance runner in U.S. history, was Nike's first endorsement athlete.

"Pre embodied everything a competitor should be. He was ferocious. He was the Bowerman spirit epitomized on the running track," Knight says. "We still raise Pre's name around here a lot. His is the only personality statue on our campus."

Joan Benoit Samuelson, America's fastest female marathoner, herself a winged goddess, is the first finisher in the first women's marathon in Olympic history.

"Obviously, you have touched on my very favorites. Bowerman, Prefontaine, Benoit," Knight offers. "Joanie's win in the 1984 Games is the single most moving moment in track and field for me. Right off the charts. We've been with her from the time she worked in our tiny research lab in

Exeter, New Hampshire.

"Joanie won that gold medal against big odds. She had surgery in the spring and there was some question, could she make the team? She made the team and everybody worried, could she stay with the Grete Waitzs and Ingrid Kristiansens?

"Well, Joanie took off on her own and never looked back. She crossed the finish line, the first winner, gold medalist, of the first Olympic women's marathon. Then she grabbed the American flag. It was enormously moving. That doesn't define Joan Benoit, but when you say Joan Benoit, that incident stands out above all the others. Talk about Nike and the pride it has in athletes who have worn the stripe in battle, she stands near the top of the list. We named the buildings here, and one was named after her."

Mrs. Samuelson's Nike building, home to the richly paneled Boston Pub as well as the employee restaurant and gift shop, is sometimes called The Student Union.

"Phil Knight and Nike have treated me like family," Samuelson says, "so it's like being invited into their house. I always feel included. Knight has honored athletes throughout the years. He's a man who went on a mission to help athletes and changed society. He never lost sight of his humble beginnings and the people who have touched his life."

Turns out Knight played more than a spectator's role when the single most moving moment in his track and field life unfolded.

Outside the Olympic stadium in Los Angeles, Nike artfully covered the entire side of a many-storied brick building with a colorful mural. Huge. The last thing the marathoners would see before entering the tunnel to the finish line. A mural of Benoit winning the Boston Marathon. More than just another shoe advertisement, the wall art was testimony to Nike's confidence in Little Joanie.

Nike's prayers, too.

"That mural symbolized my motivation," Mrs. Samuelson says. "I wanted to reciprocate to Nike and all the people who supported me. Like Phil Knight. I focused on that wall, and it helped me through all my trials. When I trained, I kept that image in mind. I never lost sight of what the mural meant, who it represented."

They also named an office building after Alberto Salazar. The Rookie,

America's fastest male marathoner, once the hardest working man in sports, is now a veteran Nike employee. Still hard at work.

"Knight's love for sports most strikes me," Salazar says. "Amazing really. Despite the level of success he's attained, he has never forgotten his roots. He is still really grounded in sports."

At its best, like sports, Nike is a mutual love fest.

"Alberto is a ferocious competitor who won't quit," Buck explains. "He is running a lot of miles and he still has high ambitions. Last year Alberto won the Friendship Marathon in South Africa over 53 miles. He's still running very well and competes as good as anybody."

The buildings on the monumental Nike campus are named after 35-year-old people. "They did a lot," Knight says simply. With conviction. There is, just an aside, a new building on the University of Oregon campus named the Knight Library.

Buck admires ferocity in battle.

"Someone once said to Jimmy Connors, 'You're a ferocious competitor.' And he said, 'It isn't that I like to win so much, it's just I am afraid of losing,' Knight explains. "I think they all have that."

How motivating is fear to Knight? "It's huge," he laughs heartily. "You set certain goals, but you really don't want to lose. I don't mean fear in the sense you're timid and shaking and unwilling to accept challenges. It's a situation where you're afraid of letting yourself down or letting down your friends and acquaintances and associates. The most horrible moment in any business, especially this business which revolves around a huge amount of emotion and emotional attachment to a company and its products, is when we have to lay people off. It's just," Buck searches for the right word, "it's just awful. Just rips at you.

"And that's a fear thing. I don't want to go through that again. Yet I know I will. Because you can't be aggressive and go after your goals, if you are afraid. You just to try not to overreach yourself.

"Talk about being afraid to lose," Knight continues. "I can remember when we went public in 1980, something like 7500 people bought stock in Nike. That original list sat on the top of my credenza for three years. That list was the last thing I would look at when I sat down at my desk every day. Every day, I thought, 'They put all their savings into this company.' He laughs heartily. 'My God, I can't let all these people down.'"

Mary Decker Slaney doesn't have her name on a building.

"She's worn Nike shoes and she's not worn Nike shoes. She's an athlete we are real proud of. Mary overcame tremendous adversity to set the records she set. I like her a lot. She obviously didn't get the gold medal she wanted and so, when most people think of her, they recall her fall at the Olympics, but she accomplished an enormous amount. She held, what, every American record and many world records as well. Mary's been a great competitor."

Slaney might own a building at Nike's headquarters but for injury. And a couple bad breaks. Knight hates to see athletes lose the opportunity to compete.

"Twenty years ago, another Oregonian who didn't fit the mold, Steve Prefontaine, fought a battle with AAU, the governing body that ruled amateur athletics in those days, and Nike was at his side," Knight said in a recent defense of an athlete's Olympic team berth. "A few years after that, we were there to support the rights of women to run long-distance events when the conventional wisdom was against us. The heritage of Nike is to support the rights of individual athletes."

At Nike, anti-establishment tendencies make sense.

"We watched the establishment committees, ruling bodies over thirty, forty, fifty years, continually make decisions which basically harmed the athletes rather than helped them," Buck says. "And, it's a sad commentary, but true, that the situation has been so bad for so long.

"Essentially that's what they did with Butch Reynolds. They found him guilty, and banned him from the Olympic Games. And, lo and behold, he wasn't guilty. You can never give Butch Reynolds his medals back or his Olympic opportunity. A terrible thing.

"Tonya Harding wasn't a very popular figure, all the media was against her, but the process really alarmed us. We thought somebody should stand up and say so, so we did. I like to think that's who we are. Our support for Tonya was typical of Nike."

Typically, Nike helped pioneer professional road running. God knows it hasn't gone anywhere.

"Kinda has," Knight demurs. "Athletes are getting paid for performance, they are making a living. The money's above the table, out in front of everybody. It's open. That's certainly better than it was."

How do we re-invent track and field?

"We've tried to make our peace with TAC, with some success," Buck answers. "When you look at the position of track and field in the world today, it's tragic. Much of the problem, more than just blaming it on some U.S. officials, stems from the very top, the international level, where track and field is not managed well. That mismanagement filters down. You've got a situation where our sport is really hurting in an age when sports in general are booming.

"We try to help from time to time. We hosted 'a meeting of the minds' of some of the top people. We've encouraged televising track and field. We are as frustrated as you that we've made different efforts to improve the situation and we really haven't found a formula yet. It's more complicated than getting women's distance running into the Olympics. But we'll keep trying and we'll make some progress. I'm just not sure when.

"There is also a tradition of not looking after the sport," Knight points out. "Not benefiting the athletes. So, there's a certain mindset that doesn't even know what we're talking about.

"Ironically, when the 1996 Olympics come to Atlanta, one of the prime television shows will be track and field. Then it will just disappear for another four years."   .

His favorite athlete to watch on TV? Wouldn't be polite to mention just one, but Knight's office sits high atop, the fourth floor actually, of the John McEnroe Building.

"One of the great athletes of the sixties was Arnold Palmer, who created this enormous following, Arnies' Army. It didn't matter if Nicklaus won more tournaments, Palmer was more popular. And part of his appeal was he wore his emotions on his sleeves and he competed hard and everybody lived and died with those emotions on his sleeve. And Palmer was always just short of throwing a club. He never threw a club that I remember, but you could feel he wanted to sometimes.

"John McEnroe threw the club," Knight notes. "His emotions were out there for everybody to see. He was enormously talented, but so are a lot of them. I liked his mind. He was mentally tough and a very creative player. Rose to the occasion, better than anybody of his era. John would have the tantrums on the court, which offended people, but off the court he did a lot of decent things without much publicity."

McEnroe was an artist. So, too, is Knight. Buck Artist, sounds like a new superhero.

"I prefer to think artistically now, rather than financially," he's said. "The real test of a businessman is if he's an artist."

Grow or die, could be the man's motto. Nike is his painting.

"Part of the art is a response to media," Buck explains. "Particularly television which consistently portrays the businessman as some sort of evil money grubber. They say something like two-thirds of all the murders on television dramas are committed by businessmen. It's really too bad that's the case, because the businessmen I admire, Akio Morita of Sony, Warren Buffet and Bill Gates, G.E's Jack Welch, they are creators. They are artists in many ways. The businessman as an artist is a theme you don't hear, and I think it's an honest theme people should be aware of. So when we talk about what we're trying to do as businessmen, and busi-nesswomen, around here, I paint that picture a lot." No pun intended.

Nike is Knight's Great American Novel, the final chapter yet written.

Having finally reached the metaphorical mountain top, I ask the enlightening Knight if he has any message for the running world?

"Yeah. Keep the faith," he says, always exhorting the home team to greater heights. "The sport will transcend its difficult times to be bigger and better than ever."

Coach Phil Knight never stops competing. Never stops. The target now is to invent a new game. The end of the big race is far off. Plenty of time on the clock yet to run.

Remember one thing. At Nike, there is still no passing the Buck.

In 1979, Jack D. Welch & Dr. E.C. Frederick sold Running *magazine to Nike, where Jack became the company's second Director of Public Relations. Two weeks after a triumphant 1984 Los Angeles Olympics, Phil Knight dropped Welch from the team. Welch still wears Nike.*

Phil Knight: The Interview
February 1995

JDW: Where do you want to start, Phil?

PHK: Any old place you want.

JDW: Bowerman. Tell me about Bowerman. Then. You're 20 years old.

PHK: Obviously, I have certain biases. First of all, he was the best track coach who ever lived, which is covering a lot of territory. He really was a great teacher, in the purest sense of the word, and he was probably the biggest influence in my life, outside my family.

My family raised me. Obviously, your mother and your father, and how you grew up, really set the tone for who you are rather than any other individuals. Outside the family, there's no doubt, Bowerman was the most influential.

He taught me essentially how to compete. He used to sometimes say, "I am a professor of competitive responses, not a track coach." George Raveling picked that up, I don't think he learned it from Bowerman, but he used it later.

I think Bowerman's point was really true. He really was awesome at that. How to focus on big events, how to prepare physically, emotionally and intellectually and get the best of yourself.

JDW: How much of that have you brought to business?

PHK: As much as I could. [Laughs.] Obviously, that's one of the big lessons I try to teach around here, how to compete. I don't know if you talk to other people around the company, they'd say that about me. I think it's one of the main things.

JDW: Seems to me you always wanted to get bigger.

PHK: The goal is better, not bigger.

JDW: There is no finish line. That's always concerned me. How do you know when you've won?

PHK: You want a finish line? [Laughs.] Where is your finish line? Either fortunately or unfortunately, in business there really isn't one. Basically, companies go through cycles, but the good ones grow and improve.

JDW: JOJ saw a finish line.

PHK: You can look at it that way. He saw a finish line at Nike. I think his view was, he had made the contribution that he thought would be the most effective and his contributions in the future were going to be less effective and that he was enjoying it less. His finish line now has been transferred to coaching. He doesn't really see a finish line there. It may well be in that phase of his life. He strikes me as being totally consistent with the philosophy I just said, it just moves into different areas of life, rather than staying focused on one company or one endeavor.

JDW: And your finish line hasn't moved.

PHK: Mine hasn't moved. I am modestly, I have less interest in maturity than he does. I'm stuck. But I am enjoying being stuck. [Laughs.]

JDW: Jeff asked me to ask you a question: Why in God's name did you agree to see Jack Welch?

PHK: Donna (Gibbs) made me. [Laughs.]

Donna: Good answer.

JDW: Tell me about Prefontaine.

PHK: In a lot of ways that was the Bowerman spirit epitomized on the running track. Pre embodied everything a competitor should try to be. He was ferocious. We still raise his name around here a lot. It's the one personality statue that is built on the campus.

JDW: Reminds me of Christ and Christianity.

PHK: People have said, 'Well, that's Nike's church.' [Laughs.]

JDW: This doesn't seem like a business anymore.

PHK: I don't think it's a religion and I don't think it's a cult. But I think Nike does have a lot of emotion related to it, and I like that. People want to be emotionally involved in their jobs, and their businesses and their companies, and we do try to promote that.

JDW: Joanie Benoit?

PHK: You have obviously, the first three, you have touched on my very favorites. Her win in the 1984 is the single most moving moment in track and field for me. Right off the charts. Having watched her and, if you will, having been with her from the time when she worked in our little research lab back in Exeter.

She won that gold medal against a lot of odds. She had surgery during the course of the spring and there was some question, could she make the team? She made the team and everybody was worried could she stay with the Grete Waitz's and the Ingrid Kristiansens.

Well, she took off on her own and never looked back. When she crossed the finish line, the first winner, gold medalist, of the first Olympic women's marathon, and then she grabbed the American flag. It was enormously moving.

That doesn't define Joan Benoit, but when you say Joan Benoit, that incident stands out above all the others. Obviously, she had a lot of other great moments. But when you talk Nike and the pride it has in athletes that have worn the stripe in battle, she stands right near the top of the list. Obviously, we named 6, 7, buildings around here, and one was named after her.

Let's see. There's Bowerman Drive, but the buildings are Prefontaine, Joan Benoit, McEnroe, and Jordan, Bo Jackson, Dan Fouts, Alberto Salazar and Nolan Ryan. That's 8.

JDW: The buildings are named after 35-year-old people.

PHK: They did a lot.

JDW: Bowerman, Benoit, Pre and Knight, four names in a single paragraph. What's the common bond?

PHK: My reaction is, which one doesn't belong? Obviously... the competitive thing runs right through all four.

JDW: You lost a lot of races, watched a lot of behinds, Phil.

PHK: [Laughs.] Those were learning experiences. Absolutely.

JDW: I just did a piece on Pre. I talked to Dellinger. He had just come up with this theory of Fear. Fear. Fear is the reason these guys are running the way they are. Competitive response is a nice phrase, but where does that come from? You had it and I had it, didn't mean we were Pre. Dellinger thinks the key may be fear. The fear of losing in front of your home team, letting your fans down...

PHK: Someone once said to Jimmy Connors, "You're a ferocious competitor. And he said, "It isn't that I like to win so much, it's just that I am afraid of losing. I think they all have that.

JDW: How motivating is fear to you?

PHK: It's huge. [Laughs.] Sure, I think you touched on a big part of it. You set certain goals, but you know you really don't want to lose.

JDW: What is there to be afraid of?

PHK: I don't think it's fear in the sense I think that you're timid and shaking and afraid of challenges. I think it's a situation where you're afraid of letting yourself or your friends and acquaintances and associates down.

The most horrible moment in any business, especially this business, which revolves around a huge amount of emotion and emotional attachment to a company and its products, is when we have to lay people off. It's just, it's just awful. Just rips at you. And that's a fear thing. I don't want to go through that again.

Yet I know that I will. Because you can't be aggressive and go after it, so you just to keep it at a minimum, without overreaching sometimes.

I can remember when we went public in 1980, something like 7500 people bought stock in Nike. That original list sat right on the back of my credenza for about three years. That was the last thing I would look at when I sat down at my desk every day. "My God, I'm gonna let these people down." [Laughs heartily.] "They put all their savings into this company."

JDW: Mary Decker Tabb Slaney?

PHK: Ah, well, I think that, umm, she's worn Nike shoes and she's not worn Nike shoes. But I think she's also one we've been real proud of. She's achieved a lot. She overcame a lot to set the records she set. I like her, and I think she's been a really great competitor who has overcome a great deal to achieve the things she has done. She obviously didn't get the Olympic gold medal she wanted and so, when most people think of her, I think they think of that, that moment when she fell down at the Olympics, but she accomplished an enormous amount. She held what, every American and many world records as well.

JDW: Just for a change of subject. Tonya Harding and your support for her legal battle.

PHK: I think we watched the sort of establishment committees, ruling bodies, continually over 30, 40, 50 years make rulings which have basically harmed the athletes rather than help them. And it really is a sad commentary, that that's been true to the level that it has and for so long.

When we were watching that process evolve. Cathleen Brennan, a writer for the *Washington Post* commented on *Nightline*, she said, it was just evolving, we weren't sure of Harding's involvement, Brennan said, "The Olympic Committee is embarrassed by Tonya and doesn't want her around the Games. And this is the same body who is going to be judge and jury on the facts." Cathleen Brennan is a first-rate reporter, so I believed it to be true.

Essentially that's what they did with Butch Reynolds. They found him guilty, and banned him from the Olympic Games. And, lo and behold, he wasn't guilty. You can never give Butch Reynolds his medals back or his Olympic opportunity, combined with his career, it's just a terrible thing.

That was what we wanted to do, when sorta all the media was against Tonya, she wasn't a very popular figure, but the process really alarmed us. We thought somebody should stand up and say so, so we did.

JDW: What does that say about Nike?

PHK: I like to think that's who we are, it was sort of typical. I know that Don Katz who was right in the middle of writing the "Just Do It" book, when we announced it, he hadn't had any contact with us for about a month, he called up and said, "Of course."

JDW: I was at Jeff's house and we couldn't figure it out, and then basically we said, "Of course."

Nobody's got you entirely figured out yet.

PHK: Good. Good.

JDW: Except for me. [Laughs.] The fear, the competition, loyalty came out in my research, I start to get artist vibes out of you now.

PHK: Part of it is a response to media. Particularly television, which consistently portrays the business man as some sort of evil money grubber. They say something like two-thirds of all the murders on television dramas are committed by businessmen. It's really too bad that's the case, because the business men that I admire, Akio Morita of Sony, Warren Buffet and Bill Gates, just up the road, GE's Jack Welch, they are creators, they are artists in many ways.

The businessman as an artist is a theme you don't hear, and I think it's an honest theme people should be aware of. So when we talk about what we're trying to do as businessmen, and businesswomen, around here, I paint that picture a lot. No pun intended.

JDW: Weiden and Kennedy. What are your thoughts?

PHK: Very positive. Makes me smile. They are very creative guys who worked very very closely with us and it's been, you know, one of the most enjoyable parts of the business. Nike's artistic sense absolutely comes through in our advertising. And it's a two-way street from Weiden & Kennedy to us and from us to them.

JDW: Salazar.

PHK: Well, he's also a ferocious competitor who won't quit and who is still running a lot of miles and has high ambitions and he won the Friendship Marathon in South Africa over 53 miles. He's still running very very well and competes as good as anybody.

JDW: McEnroe was the only top athlete I ever met at Nike who I thought was a horse's ass. Was I wrong?

PHK: I think you were wrong.

JDW: Why am I wrong?

PHK: I suppose in a lot of ways. One of the great athletes of the sixties was Arnold Palmer, who created this enormous following, Arnies' Army. And it didn't matter if Nicklaus won more tournaments, Palmer was more popular.

And part of his appeal, I thought, was he wore his emotions on his sleeves and he competed really hard and everybody lived and died with those emotions on his sleeve.

And he was always just short of throwing a club. He never threw a club that I remember, but you could feel like he wanted to sometimes.

John [McEnroe] threw the club. His emotions were out there for everybody to see. A lot of people say, well, he was enormously talented which he certainly was, but so are a lot of them. The thing I liked about him was his mind. He was mentally really tough and very creative player. Rose to the occasion, almost better than anybody of his era, and then, behind all that, behind all that, off the court, he would have the tantrums on the court, which offended people, but off the court he did a lot of really very decent things without a lot of publicity.

When Stanford University was trying to build that tennis stadium, he was the leading contributor, even though he only went there one year and there was no publicity for it. And he's the leading contributor to his private school that he went to, and when he wants his own kids to go to that same private school, so he got an apartment really within four blocks from there.

I think there's a lot of decency in a person that the media chooses not to print. They'll sell more papers talking about how explosive he is and his marriage to Tatum going bad, and those sorts of things which I think really don't define the man.

JDW: *How close are you to throwing a club?*

PHK: I've thrown one a time or two. [Big laugh.] We had one bad year, 1984, I think I broke seven phones. I've gotten over that. Finally, the telephone repair man gave me a lecture. He says, "How immature."

JDW: *I was here that year.*

PHK: Right! [Laughs.] It was a tough year. I guess you weren't around to kick, so I threw the phone. [Laughs.]

JDW: *That was the year you got rid of me. Took me ten years to recover. Actually, Jeff Johnson's the one that got me over it.*

PHK: Oh, that's great.

JDW: *How do you transfer your athletic competitive essence?*

PHK: To shoes?

JDW: *Yeah, meaning your business, meaning your life, meaning how you go about your day.*

PHK: Oh, there are a lot of similarities between athletics and business. Talk to a lot of people who have done well in business, they'll tell you the best training they ever had was on the athletic field. Which is tragic, that part of the debate, the role of athletics in society, never shows through. The transference to business is logical. Obviously, it's the same kind of deal. You don't have a monopoly position, unless you own a public utility, so you're fighting for shelf space every day of your life.

JDW: *Show up on time dressed to play? Work as a team?*

PHK: Absolutely. All of that, sure.

JDW: *Nike's role in Olympic distance running?*

PHK: You remember that. Essentially, that was one of our proudest moments. We helped fund the lobbying to get women's distance running into the Games. There was no women's event longer than 800 meters. We thought it was a shame and a travesty, so we put some money behind it, and worked with *Runner's World* and other people to get them in there. Which was ultimately successful.

JDW: *And then Joanie won.*

PHK: And then Joanie won, right. [Laughs.] Which wasn't necessarily the plan but we were happy with it.

JDW: *Billy Jean King? Is she a lesbian or not?*

PHK: [Laughs.] Well, I don't know. Why don't you call her?

JDW: I remember Nike was very cool about Billie Jean. We were behind her 100%.

PHK: I still believe that. Whatever her sexual inclination is, it's in no way a drawback from her athletic accomplishments and the things she's really done for the sport of tennis beyond her athletic accomplishments.

JDW: Marrying Tatum O'Neal is not too important.

PHK: [Laughs.] It's not the significant thing. [Laughs again.] Good analogy.

JDW: Pre would have demanded it.

PHK: Right.

JDW: Heroes and heroines?

PHK: You named some of them. Pre, Bowerman, Benoit, McEnroe. Mary. And Salazar.

JDW: Any new ones?

PHK: That's one of the fun parts of this job. New ones arrive all the time. Whether it's tennis or football or basketball or running, we have heroes that perform on the athletic field every season. That keeps me real interested. Michael Jordan did it for 9 years straight. So some heroes are the same old ones, but there are new heroes all the time. Every year I am amazed and entertained.

JDW: Phil Knight as a coach. You do much of that?

PHK: Maybe. Basically, as the company goes through changes, my role and the roles, for lack of a better word, the executives around here change.

I think you saw that in the mid-1980s, when people like Jeff Johnson and some of those other really great entrepreneurs left; they really didn't want to make the transition to kind of managers as opposed to entrepreneurs. So, the company had to make that change.

When we went public in 1980, we had something like eight vice-presidents and in 1990, only one of them was left. And we had eight new ones. That really reflected that change.

My own role obviously changed during those years as well. Now, as we're getting into bigger numbers, the hands-on becomes really difficult. It becomes more of a genuine coaching values, more of a role than it ever was.

JDW: How do you share those values?

PHK: You do that in terms of staff meetings and relationships with people on this floor. There are times you get out and talk to the people.

JDW: Any message for the running world?

PHK: Yeah. Keep the faith. The sport will transcend its difficult times to be bigger and better than ever.

JDW: When you think about it, historically, you are the shoe guy in this country. Nobody else like you in our nation's athletic history. When you started Nike, the runners were Mills, Lindgren, Daws, that's only a generation ago.

PHK: That's right and it will come back. It's too good a sport.

JDW: Jimmy Valvano? John Thompson? What do you learn from these guys?

PHK: Thompson's on the board now. They had certain things in common with very different personalities. Both of them were teachers, ferocious competitors. I think we have them give talks to employees for the same reasons we've touched on, to pass on that competitive edge from the athletic field into business.

It isn't a competitiveness that means cut-throat kill-your-grandmother, it means just day in day out knowing there's a competitor out there and we have to be better in order to beat that competitor.

The nice thing about Valvano and Thompson, two extremely different personalities, it shows from different types of personalities you can get the same sort of values. Thompson has gone on to be a member of Nike's board of directors, which I think is pretty cool.

When Jim Valvano, it was really meaningful to me, for right or for wrong, on his plaque which is right down here in front of this building, there was a pot of flowers which were contributed anonymously. With a little card that says, "If heaven is a playground, they just got a great coach."

That really captures the sort of the things we're trying to do in business. We are very emotionally involved with the people and the products and the sports events that surround us.

Chapter Eight

Politics and Money

We've gone from a $100 stuffed into an amateur's spikes to corporate sponsorships and million-dollar prizes. The transition wasn't always smooth, wasn't always easy. And as the number of runners, as participation grew exponentially, those who craved power swept in to fill the vacuum. Others manned the battle stations to protect the sport. In the middle were the athletes. And I offered my opinion.

Bill Rodgers (in hand-lettered t-shirt) winning the 1975 Boston Marathon

Looking Back to the Seventies
January 1980

In 1970 Jerome Drayton, Derek Clayton and Ron Hill were the world's greatest marathoners. Joe Henderson had just left *Track & Field News* to become the editor of an obscure bi-monthly called *Runner's World.* Jim Fixx was a pudgy magazine executive and I was a basketball player.

When the last decade began, Frank Shorter had never run a marathon and the women's World Record was 3:07:26. There was no Falmouth, no Nike, nor even a New York City Marathon. There may have been a Fred Lebow but few cared. The best road racing shoe was the Onitsuka "Marathon" which sold for $9.95.

In 1970, the winner of a marathon wasn't paid $10,000, entry fees were often less than a dollar, and perhaps six races in the country gave t-shirts to the top finishers. No runner marketed his own line of clothes, and there were no running stores.

In 1970, 1,000 men – and no more than ten unofficially entered women – ran the Boston Marathon. Entry restrictions were imposed for the first time. A runner had to have fulfilled one of three obligations to participate: have previously run a marathon under four hours, have competed in a least two ten-mile races, or have gained the approval of his local AAU official. The BAA was the largest, most elite marathon in the world.

When the last decade began, Miruts Yifter was probably still 37 years old, and the Olympics were still important.

Oh, some things do remain the same. It seems there has always been a Hal Higdon, a George Sheehan, a Francie Larrieu, a Bay-to-Breakers, a Johnny Kelley. The men's marathon best is *still* Clayton's 2:08:34. And so few really care. Perhaps few really should.

What we have done is not as important as what we will do. Where we have been is not as important where we are going.

And where are we going? Beats me. Certainly not to Moscow. Some will head for Boston and New York. The superstars will head for the bank, as the obscure amateur/professional dichotomy evaporates. Television will discover us, so maybe we can anticipate celebrity-sponsored races on the tube weekly: "Hi, this is Howard Cosell speaking to you live from the Michael Douglas Open 10-Miler. Now a word from our expert commentator Ollan Cassell..."

In the next decade, more of us will care, more of us will long for the simple days of the 70s when business was business and running was running. Then again maybe we'll be playing golf. Running is just a fad, isn't it?

The State of the Union
January 1984

When my editors asked me to write a "State of the Union" message about road racing, it seemed – after some consideration – an enviable opportunity to resign as a Senior Editor. I have been reporting on this sport in these pages for 4½ years. This has not been a large part of my life, but it often seems a major portion of road racing's. So much has changed.

In my first column, Herb Lindsay was mentioned as "the newest sensation," Lasse Viren won the Philadelphia Distance Run, Patti Lyons set a half-marathon record of 1:14:04, and Joan Benoit's 2:35:41 win at the Nike/OTC Marathon was just 26 seconds slower than her own American standard. I outkicked Debbie Eide in that same race.

If only my writing had improved as much as Eide's running. She made the World Championships last year and I am still cranking out verbiage for a bunch of guys who can recite the winning times for Edwin Moses' entire undefeated streak. Maybe Eide worked harder; certainly she is more talented.

Last year was a tough one for many of us. In retrospect, 1983 seemed a particularly difficult year for road racing. Benoit's awesome 2:22:43 World Record didn't seem to generate as much publicity as did the pacing controversy which followed. The only recollection most of us have of the Pan-American Games is the drug scandal which saw a couple – or was it dozens? – of Americans flying home in alleged disgrace.

The best I can figure, if you're a woman, you can now set a World Record in four different categories, i.e., a women-only race, a mixed-sex event, a point-to-point route, and a loop course. So much for a lack of opportunity.

This sport, which would seem so elemental, appears curiouser and curiouser. I particularly like the new IAAF rule which requires an Olympic participant to designate, before the semis, the brand of shoes he or she will wear in the finals. This regulation undoubtedly serves to protect the television spectator from the onslaught of commercialism. At the same time I truly marvel at the fact not once this year, except in jest, did I hear mentioned the infamous "contamination rule." Little grief there.

In 1983 few people commented about Alvin Chriss or Ollan Cassell or Fred Lebow or Adrian Paulen. Now I believe one or more of those guys is dead or retired, but it seems positive that the general acrimony of the sport has diminished. Then again, maybe this group didn't deserve (some of) the abuse directed its way in the past.

That is probably the best news of the last year. The athletes worked hard and the politicians made their deals quietly. We all do that which we must, but a certain sense of decorum was missing. It is back.

One reason the year was great and the sport improved lies with the New York City Marathon. The colossal struggle between Geoff Smith and Rod Dixon, the pace and their own bodies, was perhaps the best drama televised. Such images go far.

So, too, did the photographs of Mary Decker with her BMW or Carl Lewis watering the lawn in front of his palatial estate. An interpretation of amateur regulations which permits such overt capitalism certainly answers the question *Track & Field News* asked in 1979: "Is TAC really a new organization or just the same old AAU with a different name?"

Such philosophical quandaries were of major import to me a few years back. Now, as I realize I could really care less about which marathon has the most entries or whether the money is above the table or under it, my enthusiasm is renewed. My fatigue was a result of too much caring about too many unimportant segments of running. I had allowed myself to forget about the dedication, the discipline, the physical genius, the guts of an Alberto Salazar or a Greg Meyer. I believe the running community was forgetting also. Certainly many fans were.

1983 was the year we all remembered; 1983 seemed a time of reaffirmation, a rebirth of the fire which warms the souls of runners and fans alike. "Let the agents and promoters fight it out," the athletes seem to be saying. "We must prepare for the Olympics."

Unfortunately, I also believe this renewal of spirit will last only until the end of the men's Olympic marathon, the final event. Then, all hell will break loose. I will watch it. I may report it but I avowedly will not let the inevitable commercialism cloud my love of the sport. There are only six things more beautiful than two great athletes giving their utmost to win a race. I shall never again forget that.

I am not resigning either. I like it here.

A Decade on the Roads: 1980-1989
May 1990

Let me begin by saying I expect you to disagree with me. In fact, I insist. This is personal stuff.

But when my masters called and said, "We want you to write about the greatest road runners of the '80's... maybe, maybe not... do whatever you want... try to capture the entire decade in a half-page... we need it Monday," I thought of Mrs. Samuelson before I hung up the phone.

And then I started to think about the rest of it, the last ten years, that is. That took longer. I remembered the belt buckle Benji Durden got for making the Olympic team that didn't go to Moscow. Benji, leading the Cascade Run Off and crashing to the ground as he slipped in a small pile of Mt. St. Helen's volcanic ash.

ARRA & Alvin Chriss. Grete. Rod Dixon on his knees in joy at winning New York; Orlando Pizzolato the next year, stopping eight times in those last few hot miles.

Sitting in the LA Coliseum as Gabriele Andersen lurched and staggered those final meters. Anne Audain's reign. Jim Fixx's death. The foreign domination of the U.S. road circus. 2:21:06. 2:06:50. Alberto Salazar.

Actually, Berto came to mind earlier than that. I wanted to credit someone else. Surely there have been faster runners, athletes with golden prizes. But there is only one Salazar.

Joan Benoit and Alberto Salazar. The Pixie and the Pit Bull. Those two meant the most to me.

I think about the great duels and I see Dick Beardsley rushing to glory, only a few hundred meters from the Prudential Center. Alberto is with him and the two fight it out like Ali and Frazier. Staggering almost, Salazar opens a door to a place he only visits in the most desperate of times and he pulls out some extra part of himself.

The Finns call it *sisu*. In Japanese, it's *konjo*. Guts. A defiance of defeat as much as a determination to win.

And so he did.

Then there was New York City, Rodolfo Gomez. Another titanic struggle. The unsinkable against the unstoppable. Side by side, they enter Central Park. A cloud of dust, momentary disorientation, and Alberto emerges with the lead. A genius move.

Nowadays, when some guy produces the race of his life, how do the sports writers describe it? "The fastest time by an American since Alberto Salazar..."

Joan Benoit Samuelson might be tougher. And she won the first Olympic marathon for women. The one race every female in the sport wanted to win. Joanie not only did it, she walked away from the world's best in the process. Walked away. In front of Peter Ueberroth and everybody. She kicked butt. She took names. With style. With grace.

But the memory that burns brightest is the expression of pain and relief etched on Benoit's face as she finished first in the U.S. Trials... 17 days after arthroscopic surgery on her right knee.

At the time I wrote, "The measure of greatness is not how well you do when things are going easy, but how well you do when the going gets tough. Joan Benoit doesn't thrive on adversity, because she is not a fool. She feeds on achievement because she has ability. She is who she is and that is an Olympian in the truest sense. She only wants to find her limits."

Ah, yes, the '80's. Let's see, I ran my marathon PR in September'79, about the time Ned & I sold our magazine to Nike. I bought a big BMW and an excellent house in the west hills of Eugene. I left my sweet wife of ten years and ran off with the PR Director for the Pepsi 10k. Two special women. Got canned from my own magazine, hung around Nike for a few years. The 80's? Oh, yeah, but that's another story. – JDW

Show Me The Money – I'll Run A 2:08
March 1997

You want to see the money? New Balance has offered to show it to you. The shoe manufacturer will pay $1,000,000.00 – that's one million dollars – to the American man or woman who, in this calendar year, surpasses the fastest U.S. marathon times on record. That's Bob Kempainen's 2:08:47 (Boston '94) and Joan Samuelson's 2:21:21 (Chicago '85).

New Balance asks only that the times be achieved on U.S. soil – 61 marathons qualify, including point-to-point, potentially aided courses such as Boston. The more egregiously downhill routes have been excluded.

New Balance has dangled the greatest financial carrot in the history of running. Is anybody chasing after it?

The last great – I mean *great* – American male marathoner was Alberto Salazar, now a Nike executive. "I don't feel the Million Dollar Challenge is going to have an effect," he says. "There's only a handful who you could imagine training any harder or going any faster. The whole concept is alarming when you think about it: that a million dollars – just the offer – could motivate an athlete to train more. I'd be disappointed to find out they've only been going at 90%."

"I can see where the money might encourage athletes to sustain their careers," Salazar adds. "Older athletes might try longer to run fast. Somebody at the end of their career might make one final heroic push."

Ranked No. 5 among U.S. marathoners last year, Steve Plasencia is in the twilight of a long and illustrious career. Twilight? More like sunset. Dark even. "I'm 40 years old. You need people who are on the rise," says Minnesota's cross-country coach. "It's a huge gamble for anybody. I'd have to quit my job and I'm not about to do that."

"You'd have a better chance to win a million bucks by buying lottery tickets," says Salazar. "Frankly, I don't see anybody but Todd Williams with a realistic shot at it. He's the only one who's even close. For the women it's even more preposterous. Lynn Jennings is untested; she might have a better shot than any man."

Ask Jennings about the Million Dollar Challenge and she laughs. Peals of laughter. Ha,ha,ha,ha. Run a marathon for the money, that's rich.

"I'm running 85 miles a week, hundreds and hundreds of miles already this year," Jennings notes, "and I haven't spent even a quarter mile thinking about that $1,000,000." Followed by more laughter.

Jennings, who as a 17-year-old ran 2:44-and-change in '78, has no marathon plans.

"Money wasn't what led Joanie to run 2:21," Lynn points out. "As for the prize money at Worlds, I won the World Cross Country Championship three times and didn't get any prize money. Performance doesn't equal money and money doesn't equal performance."

"I'd put money up that Jennings couldn't do it the first time," bets Boston legend Bill Rodgers. "Williams could do it. I think he's really a marathoner. He could've medaled in Atlanta. If Todd could win Boston or New York City – run a 2:07:54, which I think he can easily do – the kids in this country would sit up and notice. Todd shouldn't delay any longer."

Todd Williams, the athlete most often mentioned as a possible millionaire, won't be running Boston but he won't delay his marathon debut much longer. "I'll run a marathon in the fall," he says. "The money's not the reason; I was going to run one anyway. It does throw a bigger carrot out there."

Williams turns 28 this year. It's time. "I'm going after it the same way I go after everything else – 110%," he says. "I train so hard anyway; if money comes into my pocket, it's only a bonus."

The *money* has changed his race tactic, though, because the best way to get rich is to go for broke: "I am going to run that pace from the gun until my legs fall off. '1:04:30' would be nice to hear at halfway, followed by a tailwind."

Williams muses, "If someone who hasn't run fast for a few years comes out of the woodwork to beat me, I'll tell you one thing, I'll be the first person there with a piss cup."

Ranked No. 6 last year among American women, Gwyn Coogan says, "The money doesn't make a difference to me, but I'm sure it'll make a difference to a lot of people. Well, I can't say that. That sounds self-righteous.

"I think it's a great thing to have out there, that million-dollar offer," continues Coogan, who is sponsored by New Balance. "The money has brought a lot of attention to our sport. It means something more coming from a small company. I know New Balance didn't take out any insurance. They are taking a risk."

But are they? Not even worried enough to cover their butts. What kind of risk is that?

"To be honest, at first we didn't have an insurance policy," says Joyce Furman, a marketing representative at New Balance. "Then we realized it only made good business sense to protect ourselves. After all, we believe it's going to happen. We want it to happen."

Show me more money. To entice higher quality fields, the IAAF is offering $60,000 to the winners of the World Championship marathons (and $30k and $20k for the lesser medals). Yet only two women broke 2:40 at the U.S. Women's Trials, where as many as three WC berths are available. Basically, nobody showed up.

The prize money at the World Championships doesn't float Coogan's boat. "I haven't paid any attention to the prize money," she admits. "Other people will say, 'Of course, Gwyn doesn't have a snowball's chance of winning any of it.' I've always wanted to be on a World Championship team. But it's going to be Athens; it's going to be hot."

And the million bucks is reserved for races run on U.S. soil.

Coogan instead has her Athens sights on a 10k spot, but husband Mark, runner-up in the Olympic Trial 26-miler last year, does have his eyes on the marathon prize.

"I'm not going to change my plans, but I know some people who did," he says. "They were going to London, now they're going to Boston. I'm just giving it one shot in the fall, probably Chicago. I'm sure my next marathon will be a PR, weather permitting. My 2:13:05 at the Trials was worth a 2:09 at Boston."

Keith Brantly was close behind at Charlotte. "I'm a realist. From my perspective, my PR (2:12:58 at New York City in '93) is four minutes slower than the American best. I've got to get to 2:10 first," Brantly explains. "That doesn't mean I'm not thinking about the money. But I tell you what, I'd *pay* a million bucks for a four-minute improvement."

Jerry Lawson ran 2:10:04 at Chicago last year, equaling the official

American Record held by Pat Petersen. "I'm still debating with myself whether the Challenge is positive or negative for the sport," says Lawson. "The money's good for the attention it's brought marathoning, but... Chasing the time is the best aspect.

"I haven't changed my plans," Lawson continues. "I am running London. If I set the AR there and don't get the million, well, so be it. If New Balance really wanted a new American best, they wouldn't have excluded foreign courses. The best races aren't necessarily on U.S. soil."

Can Lawson run 2:08? "Probably not this year," he admits. "If everything fell into place, I'm likely still a few steps, small steps, short. I can see 2:09:15."

After London, Lawson plans to race the World Championships, skipping Pittsburgh but advancing as one of the time qualifiers. "The WC prize money means nothing to me," he says. "It sounds cheesy, but I want to run in Athens as my patriotic duty."

Don't be surprised to see Lawson start his third marathon of the year in the late fall. On U.S. soil.

"If I was running just for the money, I'd be better off getting a real job," says professional runner Keith Dowling, who does his running under the adidas banner. Dowling, ranked No. 7 in the U.S. off his 2:14:30 PR at the Trials, is "pretty cynical" about the Challenge: "I find this whole thing just a New Balance advertisement. Really, how is this going to help anybody get better?"

Dowling won't change his plans and he's not running Boston. "I have to be thinking 2:11, 2:12, first," he admits. "I've got my sights set on Chicago. The course is friendlier; it comes at a better time of the year. The weather will have more to do with a 2:08 than the money."

Ask 38-year-old Mary Slaney about the million-dollar offer. She has run 10k in 31:45; ran a 3:09:27 marathon at the age of 12. Disregard her two-dozen foot and lower leg surgeries and she would seem a likely candidate, but until this story was being written, she wasn't in the loop.

"This is the first I've heard of it." She's surprised. "Are you serious? It's news to me." She thinks for a moment. "There's no question: I would *not* risk my health for a million dollars." Slaney has no marathon plans. For now.

And ask her about prize money at the World Championships. "I didn't know anything about that until today," she says. "A notice came with the World Championships entry form. I'm entering, but I threw it in the trash without looking at it."

"If you are running for the money, you're running for the wrong reasons; you're in the wrong sport," Slaney notes. "I still run for the same reason I always have — because it's fun."

"Who knows what younger runners are looking at this and getting interested in running a marathon?" asks former ARRA head Don Kardong. "I've always contended money won't get you to run faster but it can certainly help your focus."

When Kempainen ran his targeted 2:08:47, Arturo Barrios, then a Mexican national, finished two places ahead in 2:08:28. Barrios is a U.S. citizen today and he's thinking about becoming a millionaire. "To be honest, the money didn't get me motivated. I was planning on running a marathon anyway," he says. "But then I heard about this and I thought, 'Hey, if it happens, it happens.' I always see the time first, then the money."

He sees the road paved with gold. "If I win the million, I am going to put it all in the stock market," Arturo points out, as if he's given Wall Street some thought. "If you look at the last 100 years, that's the best place to get rich. Second is real estate." The problem here is that you have to cover a lot of real estate in a short period of time.

Kempainen himself is in semi-retirement at this point as he fulfills his medical residency requirements, but there are rumors he may be "reconsidering."

The women's Trials winner, Jenny Spangler, is coming off Achilles surgery and won't be able to make a dash for cash.

The Challenge has had no impact on Cathy O'Brien, whose 2:29:38 makes her the 10th-fastest woman in U.S. history. "I was already planning to run a marathon this year," O'Brien says, "probably in the fall."

Samuelson's 2:21:21 seems more unassailable than Dr. Kempainen's 2:08:47, so the top women haven't actually decided how they'll spend the million dollars. "Not that people want to sell themselves short," O'Brien notes. "But I think we all have respect for that mark. It's tough to say it's even within reach."

"A million dollars provides me with a focus I wouldn't otherwise have," says 2:08:58 runner Mark Plaatjes, who surprised with his win in the '93 Worlds. "One of the things that really pisses me off is New Balance and everybody else thinks the money is safe, and it's not safe. I am going to go for it at Boston. I don't care who's there. If no one wants to go with me at that pace, I'll do it by myself."

We live in a country where pro football offers a million dollars for a 35-yard field goal during halftime (made), and pro basketball offers a million for a fan canning a 22-foot set shot (missed). Why shouldn't pro running offer a million for a 2:08 marathon?

Still, money may not be the answer to what's ailing running in this country.

"Money killed the sport. There's no doubt in my mind," states Salazar. "I ran Boston for nothing at a time when I could've earned $60,000 at another race. We lived five guys to a house and ate macaroni & cheese for dinner. Five nights a week. If you are running for money, you wouldn't be in this sport to begin with."

The legendary Frank Shorter offers, "Today the agents are in control rather than the coaches. It's that simple. The Challenge puts an end to all the lip service American runners have been giving themselves about training and racing at the same time. The Challenge provides the opportunity to help them work through their collective denial."

The most successful distance runner in the U.S. today is unquestionably Bob Kennedy. "He's the one guy out there who is absolutely not motivated by money," Salazar says. "I have the utmost respect for him. He does not spit without thinking how it will affect his running."

And Kennedy is not about to run a marathon. "Not even if they paid me $3 million," he told Williams.

This is the U.S. Let's face facts; when money talks, it screams. At the moment, everybody seems to be listening. New Balance has our attention.

Show me the 2:08:46. Show me the 2:21:20.

And the million dollars is all yours.

Just Go Retro: Making America Great Again
December 1998

It has come to this. Turning into Victory Lane at Disney's Wide World of Sports Complex – the site of USATF's inaugural Club National Cross-Country Championships – reminds me of nothing so much as Nike's Beaverton headquarters campus. Architecture stylized in homage to the hype in sport.

And so the circle is closed. Nike and the other shoe companies threw so much money at the runners' world they smothered the club system.

Look around. You don't see the Florida Track Club, University of Chicago TC. You'll find few, if any, of the historically famous teams. Certainly, the Jamul Toads are absent. Athletics West, too.

Look around. You don't recognize any shoe-company reps. This speaks volumes about the low-key nature of the Association Club harrier championships.

No agents. No Kenyans. No Bob Kennedy, no Lynn Jennings. No excuses. Nobody had their hand out.

Despite some profound dissatisfaction with the overall organization and conduct, this event signaled the start of something new. The rebirth, hopefully, prayerfully, of a club system which once provided the backbone of any modest success this nation formerly enjoyed in distance running. The clubs are the bridge, maybe the tightrope, between the 22-year-old college grad and the 28-year-old international competitor.

Developing even one would help.

What does it say about the club system when an old, burned-out former high school girl's coach can instantly create one of the nation's top team?

"It's pathetic," answers The Farm Team's Jeff Johnson. "And what's more startling, it was easy."

And Johnson knew it would be easy. "That's what is so sad," he adds. "The first time we got five guys together, we were the best team in the country. Anybody could do what I did."

Tragically for the sport, too few are trying. The most famous face at the event belongs to '88 Olympian Bruce Bickford, who is doing what he can as coach of Massachusetts' Lowell Striders.

"It's great just to get teams together again," Bick explains. "We don't see enough of it anymore. We should have more team championships. Team races would do really well on television. The attitude is different about everything now. Why? Not enough people pushing for clubs. Athletes racing on the roads for $300. I don't know why team competitions aren't more popular. I really don't.

"We can't get our best runners to go to the World Cross-Country Championships anymore. I hear athletes saying it conflicts with track. Bullshit. The rest of us did it all the time. Porter did it, I did it, Craig Virgin.

"Maybe coaches are getting too technical," Bick suggests. "'These are the races you have to run,' they tell the athletes. 'You gotta stay on this schedule, nothing else is going to help you.' Well, *everything* helps you to a point."

The U.S. Army team is advertising New Balance on its uniforms. The Defense Department can't swing the cost of a few singlets?

"You have to know how to run cross-country to run a great track race, and vice versa," Bickford says. "First of all, the strength you get from cross-country, mentally, physically, you can't get running the track. You just can't."

You wonder at all the athletes who aren't here today, athletes who could have competed in a U.S. national championship. "Exactly," Bickford agrees. "I think it was fantastic that Pat Porter could win nine nationals. That's something you can take with you."

Concludes Bickford, "Seems like fewer people are running for the love of the sport and that's the big problem. It's nice when you get free shoes. I like free shoes myself. But it's no reason to run for somebody."

This could possibly be the smallest crowd ever at a national championship. Athletes this age can drive themselves to the race, so they don't even bring their parents with them.

The coach has his arm around his young runner, a bundle of nerves moments before the race. "It's nothing you haven't done a hundred times, probably do again another 100 times," he comforts her in a soft voice.

"You are well prepared. You will do the best you can and the race will be what it'll be, and then it will be over and you can start getting ready for the next one. I am proud of you already."

John Goodridge of Nike Club East exults, "The whole concept is fantastic from a developmental standpoint, in terms of encouraging local clubs to participate in the sport. It's one of our biggest weaknesses. We simply do not have a legitimate post-collegiate support system."

This is not the U.S. National Championships, the same championships won by Frank Shorter and Porter and Jennings, some of the greatest ever. That race will now be held in February, supposedly the better to coordinate with the international schedule.

This event is for the local clubs, for athletes who live and train and wait tables in the same town. Never heard of most of these runners, never heard of some of their clubs. Or even some of their towns.

The results will be screwed up whether the finish line technology involves popsicle sticks or computer chips.

"Running put me through college," says Andre Williams, after leading the Reebok Enclave to victory. "I've traveled, made a lot of friends. But I was also a waiter at Planet Hollywood for three years. I make $4000 a year running for Reebok. People see the Bob Kennedys and the Todd Williamses, the top guys, but they don't understand there are a lot of us still trying to get there. Every year, I close the gap. Nobody knew who I was, but every year I kept running. I kept closing the gap.

"I just keep plugging away. I didn't live in Kenya. I didn't run to school. I'm a regular American kid," says the 27-year-old North Carolina grad, who placed 5th in the USATF track 5000 last year.

"We knew we had to go out hard," Williams says of the race. "I don't know if the first mile was accurate, but it was 4:24. Then we settled down. Around 4M, the heat started to make a difference. You could hear guys around you gasp. When you are running in a big pack like that, heat radiates from other people.

"The plan, at some point, Kenyan-style, was get to the front and start pushing, no matter how we felt. I led a mile, then somebody else led. We shared the pace. With a half mile to go, I put it down."

Listen to your body. One of the sport's cardinal rules seems to have been ignored by its leaders. Listen to your body, the tens of thousands of athletes who belong to clubs. The club system works.

There are 1100 members of the Central Massachusetts Striders, and one of them is coach Bob Sevene.

"This race teaches kids how to run up front in a very competitive situation, instead of just showing up and running way in the back until they can move up to the next level to learn to be competitive and try to win," Sevene explains. "Plus with money from the shoe companies drying up, we have to go back to the club system."

Just go retro.

Sev, like Johnson, is an amateur coach. "I have never taken a dime from an athlete in my career," Sevene notes. "I just don't believe in that. I believe you are a teacher, and teachers don't get paid by their students; they get paid by the institution they teach at."

The club system hasn't failed U.S. running, we have failed the club system. Are Johnson, Bickford, Goodridge and Sevene so special? The answer is yes, but are there more like them? Of course, just like there are more athletes like Andre Williams.

And more like Blake Phillips, the women's champion here. As a member of the New Balance elite squad, she didn't count as a scorer in the club standings, but she did win her first U.S. title.

She trains with Goodridge, but it's difficult to get five good women together. "There aren't many female running bums, so it's more difficult to put together a team," one coach surmises. "Women might be too practical to move around the country, rent a house with a dozen other guys, eat macaroni and cheese twice a day and chase a dream that may not ever come true."

Remember, gang, every place counts, so you all have to finish. Because a club is just a group of athletes chasing a dream together.

Chapter Nine

The Greatest

And the first shall be last. If there was a Mt. Rushmore of running, the four faces carved in stone would be Joan Benoit, Alberto Salazar, Mary Decker, and Steve Prefontaine.

These are personal choices, with no disrespect to many other deserving athletes, but this quartet transcended the sport and their names will live forever.

Little Joanie:
Appearances Can Be Deceiving
September 1982

Young Joanie representing the Liberty Athletic Club

A top masters runner once asked me a question about Joan Benoit. It was a question borne of frustration and admiration, a query full of wonderment and awe.

"How does she do it?", mused my friend, himself a tensely-sinewed, highly-disciplined athlete still in the hunt for that elusive sub-2:30 marathon.

"Benoit looks like some butterball cherub, without the slightest hint of muscle. Yet she can crush the opposition more often than not," he continued, admiringly confused. "2:30:16 is incredible for a little girl like that."

What adjectives must have come to mind when he learned that Benoit had run 2:26:11 at the 1982 Nike Marathon? The Boston University women's coach is suddenly very close to the World Record of 2:25:29.

"I have questioned if I could run with Grete [Waitz] and Allison [Roe]," Benoit admits. "Now I know I can." The former and current holders of the WR will have to wait to run with Benoit. She has no specific marathons planned: "We'll just have to wait and see."

The wait to reach the top has been a brief pause for Joanie: she has been there before. Among the U.S.'s very best road racers in 1978, there she was, one down from the top. Ranked No. 3 in 1980 and No. 2 again in 1981, she hit the top in 1979. That year, running in only her second 26-miler, she won the illustrious Boston classic with a time of 2:35:15, then an American Record.

Graduating from Maine's Bowdoin College – as did President Franklin Pierce, poets Nathaniel Hawthorne & Henry Wadsworth Longfellow and sex researcher Alfred Kinsey – Benoit continued to write her name in the record books with another AR in the marathon (2:31:23) and 10 miles (55:42).

In 1981, she seemed to slow not a tick. Twice she broke the half-marathon standard, ultimately to 1:11:16. She covered 25 kilometers in 1:26:21. But suddenly – or maybe not quite so for a competitor – the music stopped.

Actually, the tunes had first faltered in the Olympic year of 1980 when she underwent a pair of separate operations in less than two weeks time. She came back, but slowly, to gain her No. 3 ranking.

"I think the anesthesia gets me more than the operation itself," she says.

Lacing up a new pair of Nikes

It was time to go under the knife again last December, both Achilles needing repair. Only two days later, wearing walking casts on each leg, there was Joan Benoit on an exercise bicycle, pumping away, her thoughts already focused on a defense of her Falmouth title.

Biking nowhere for 30-45 minutes daily "against good resistance," she added arduous interval sessions to maintain her aerobic conditioning. "Actually," she notes, "my fitness level increased when I wasn't running."

So impressed was she with this part of her rehabilitation she plans to reduce her mileage greatly this winter, probably remounting her trusty two-wheeler and not going far at all.

At the beginning of the year, however, mileage was her primary concern. The first week of March, with a 40-mile total, marked her first serious quantity work since the surgery. And 40 is hardly "quantity."

By the end of the month she had doubled that. Although this gifted athlete normally averages less than 90 miles every seven days, she did exceed the century mark in each of the two weeks preceding the Nike Marathon. Joan was a tad nervous.

She was also somewhat anxious on May 8 when she lined up for her first race of the year – the Old Kent River Bank 25k. Just 131 days after the anesthesia wore off, Benoit was again a winner.

More importantly, she was still marvelously fast, finishing in 1:26:31, a time second only to her own American Record. The 25-year-old Benoit was a bit surprised: "Originally, I had thought that Falmouth might be my first good run."

It wasn't. Wasn't the first, that is. The Cape Cod Extravaganza, in which Benoit crushed not only a strong field but also Waitz's course record, was just one pearl in a strand so lustrous only unbeaten Anne Audain's year can compare.

Testing her fitness, Joan traveled to Norway this summer, recording the best American 20k ever, 1:09:11. Waitz ran 1:07:50. Not discouraged, Benoit decided to test her speed over 5000m in a track race. Now she *was* discouraged. Despite a personal record 15:40.42, she says, "The race was pretty disappointing. I got walloped."

Defeat, like surgery, seems to make Benoit stronger. Must be the scar tissue. Winning a couple more short races in decent times, she headed to Falmouth, looking for Grete. When the Norwegian great withdrew with an injury, Joanie blitzed Waitz's course record by 39 seconds, with a time that works out to a 5:10 pace for the 7.1 mile route.

Flushed with satisfaction, Benoit tried the Bobby Crim Ten-Miler. She left with the victory and another American Record (53:18). The stage was set for her big marathon.

As we all know, the script is the essence. With coach Bob Sevene as co-author, Joan fine-tuned. When the curtain went up, she got her act together in a hurry, clocking personal bests at 15k ("50-something"), 20k (1:07:40) and 25k (1:25:20). Between miles 10 and 11, she caught a fellow competitor – read, a man – and suggested that they push to catch a large pack of runners just ahead.

"I told him that would make it easier for us," she explains. "He just looked at me and asked if I knew how fast I was going. I don't run with a watch, so I said, 'No.' When he said, '2:20 pace,' I just thought 'oh-oh' and slowed down."

Between 25k and 35k, hearing no further splits, Benoit experienced a psychological low, but she came on strongly in the last 5000. "I felt so good it was like I was running a track race," she recalls. "I had too much left. I thought about sprinting but... I didn't want to showboat."

She's just not the type. "I don't know if I could've gotten the World Record but I know I could've run another 20 seconds faster," she avows.

"I was kind of surprised by the AR," she admits. "Before the race I decided I'd be disappointed if I won and didn't break 2:30. Sub-2:30 was the goal."

The goal now is a successful season for her Boston University cross country team. "They told me before Nike, 'If you make us proud of you, we'll make you proud of us,' relates Coach Benoit. "That, and those young women, are very important to me."

So, Joan Benoit is still a softie. She admits to pumping a little Nautilus now and then. And now there is a hint of definition around her biceps. But her big strength is in her head; her ability to concentrate, to focus.

It's like that old football mentor used to say: "This game is 20% guts, 40% talent and 50% mental."

Joan Benoit is more, so much more, than the sum of the parts.

The Trials and Tribulations Of An American Hero
June 1984

We have always had heroes. My dad remembers the Babe, Joltin' Joe and Ben Hogan. There was Mickey Mantle, Willie Mays and Bob Cousy when I was a kid. Today there's Dr. J, Carl Lewis and John McEnroe. There is also Joan Benoit.

Have you ever seen such courage? Not since Willis Reed dragged a leg behind him in the 1969 NBA playoffs. Not since that Japanese gymnast dismounted with a broken leg in the 1976 Olympics. Well... Benoit's 2:31:04 win at Olympia looked that brave.

It takes talent to be fast. It takes guts to be a winner. The Finns have a word, *sisu*, which means, roughly, a combination of pride, determination and guts. The Americans have a similar word - Benoit.

The measure of greatness is not how well you do when things are easy, but how well you do when the going gets tough. Joan Benoit doesn't thrive on adversity, because she is not a fool. The Maine Coaster feeds on achievement, because she has ability. She is who she is and that is an Olympian in the truest sense. She only wants to find her limits.

Joan Benoit may have approached the limits of frustration in the weeks before the Marathon Trials. She had made a comeback from double Achilles surgery to run a breakthrough 2:22:43 World Record in 1983. But that was on her timetable. This time The Athletics Congress is setting the schedule. Benoit had to run 26.2M faster than all but two other women in the United States and she had to do it on May 12, 1984.

It was March 16 when Benoit began to worry. During about the 14th mile of a scheduled 20-miler, the well-oiled machine developed a mechanical malady. Her right knee evidenced a "catch," sticking so that Benoit was unable to go through the complete running motion. A mile later the knee completely shut down. "It was the first time in my life I ever walked out of a training run," she remembers, still rather incredulous.

It was not the last time. She took the next day off, then ran 10M, finishing with a sore knee. Understandably concerned, Benoit called Dr. Robert Leach, the surgeon who had done such exemplary work on her Achilles. Leach administered a cortisone injection and Benoit took another day off. Still feeling some pain, she nonetheless managed ten good days of training. Then, after a track workout at Harvard ("One of the best of my life," she recalls) Benoit rested for three minutes, and began to jog down. She couldn't.

"I knew by that point that this was not a runner's normal complaint." A run the next day became a walk and another drive to the doctor's. Leach injected the knee with more cortisone. Benoit didn't run for five days. Then a three-mile run left her in pain and frustrated.

Justifiably concerned with MT-Day looming closer on her calendar, Benoit flew to Athletics West headquarters in Eugene, Oregon, home of Coach Bob Sevene. It is also, not coincidentally, where noted orthopedic surgeon Stan James lives. Dr. James advised an additional five days of rest and heavy doses of Butazolidin. It was April 17. "He said it was too late to do surgery," Benoit explains, "but when I first tried to run again, I had to walk after three miles. The leg would just lock up."

It was too late NOT to operate. James inserted an arthroscope into the knee and, after a delicate but thorough inspection, still didn't find much. "The pain was so darn deep," said Benoit. "It was almost impossible to treat." It was difficult to locate, but when James got there, he snipped the plica band. It was April 25; there were just 17 days until the Trials.

On April 26 Benoit was on a hand bicycle maintaining her cardiovascular fitness. The day after that, she was swimming. April 30 and Benoit ran 55 minutes without pain. The knee was tender, but the leg worked. Joanie was a runner again.

That Benoit is a competitor probably explains why she went out again that same day for 60 minutes, some of them at 10mph speed. On May 2nd, ten days before the Trials, she ran an hour and 48 minutes. The knee was fine, but Benoit was injured again.

"I overcompensated with my left leg, and that caused a strain in the hamstring," said Benoit. "Why did I run so much, so soon? Well, I like to go into a race feeling strong, feeling charged up."

On May 5, exactly a week before the event, the Number One seed could not run. Every sort of treatment was tried. Benoit did it all, including soaking in a bathtub of ice water - complete with cubes. Anything was worth a try.

Enter Jack Scott, you know the one. With the Electro-Acuscope, you probably don't know that one. It is a non-medical healing machine which supposedly supplies a low-level electrical stimulus to the body. The current produced is similar to that which naturally occurs in healthy tissue. Benoit spent a lot of time, I mean a lot, up to nine hours daily, with the machine. One way or another, she was going to be charged up.

May 8: Benoit, feeling better by the minute and wondering if she could run hard for 2 1/2 hours, covered 17 miles at a reasonable tempo. She didn't know if she could win a marathon but she was now confident she could start one.

"After that run, I knew I could go the distance. I didn't know if I could compete against a pack at 20M," Benoit said, as she remembered the emotional roller coaster she rode in the days before the Trials. "This was the worst possible way for me to go into a marathon." It may well have been a blessing in disguise.

May 12: nowhere near top form, Benoit found herself far in front at 20M, nowhere near a pack. Injured or not, she is still the Miss America of road racing. She is on her way to Los Angeles and that marathon will be different.

May 18: a week after her Trials' victory, Benoit was back home and still concerned. "The knee feels great, but the hamstring problem is lingering on," she said. "I'm doing a little running, but next week will be another easy week, before I start training hard again."

Benoit will train hard, but undoubtedly smarter. That one week of 130 miles will not be repeated. "I'm still pretty beat up from the marathon, but I'm really raring to go," she enthused. "Usually at this time of the year I'm burned out. But, because of the injuries and days off, I'm ready."

Ready but not prepared. The preparation begins now, at home, away from the media, away from the controversy. She remains perturbed at the news coverage of her victory at Olympia, which seemed to focus on the easy story - Jack Scott and the Acuscope.

"I don't doubt that the machine was responsible for some improvement, but I'm not convinced that any other therapy wouldn't have helped," Benoit said. "Remember, if Stan James had not performed the surgery, nothing would have worked. We tried a number of therapies. Rich Phaigh's massages were instrumental. Dr. Steven Roy was a big help. It was not one miracle machine."

It was a miraculous performance by a well-coached, highly dedicated, most intelligent athlete. The Joan Benoit story is not about doctors or drugs or massages , alternative exercises or hot packs or ice baths, not even electro-faith healing. No, this is a tale of strength and courage and talent and desire and discipline. It is a tale with the conclusion yet to be written.

The conclusion, of course, was the gold medal victory in the first ever Women's Olympic Marathon. - JDW

Joan Benoit: In Her Own Words
January 1985

A pensive Benoit

Joan Benoit is the kind of woman songs should be written about. Maybe several songs. "The Ballad of St. Joan." A word picture put to music.

Can you imagine what this woman was like as a youngster? Close your eyes. It's easy, isn't it? Fresh pink cheeks in the Maine snow. Going a little too fast on her skis. How about a crisp fall day with short white legs under a plaid field hockey skirt, flashing ahead of her competitors toward the goal?

Open your eyes. Close them again. Watch her now in Olympia. Boyish dark hair, incredible strength and anxiety conflicting on her face as she waits for the finish line to arrive before her body fails her heart, her will, her guts. See her incredulity as no one follows her toward the gold medal in the golden sunshine in a town this woman could only visit before going home again.

For those of you with less imagination and a library card, look on page 55 of the January 14th edition of Newsweek. *Right! Turn to "The Newsmakers," and there's our little Joanie standing next to a fifth-grader named Charity. Joan's outfit (please forgive me, J.B.) even looks a little like the schoolgirl's, Charity is honored at Studio 54 by* Ms. *magazine for "spunk," among other things. Spunk.*

Joan Benoit in a dress from "Little House on the Prairie" sandwiched between Cyndi Lauper, a rocker with orange hair, and Geraldine Ferraro, a woman who was a heartbeat away from being a footnote in history. Now that's an image. Now that's spunk.

Close your eyes. Imagine there's a whole lot more to Joan Benoit than a new clothing line, magazine covers, gold medals and world records. Because there is so much more...

JDW: I am interested in how life's been since the Olympic awards ceremony. What has been the biggest change?

JB: Well, I never have any time, that's the first thing. I guess the best statement... and I've said it before... is that until the Olympics, I scheduled my day around running. After the Olympics, I scheduled my running around my day. Before, nothing took priority over running.

JDW: What has been the greatest lesson?

JB: It is very difficult to say "No." Finally, I am learning how to say "No," and I am learning how to say it graciously. Everybody wants to touch an Olympian. There really aren't very many of us. There are even fewer med-

medalists and not many gold medalists at all. But, really, how long can you go on the banquet circuit?

JDW: You sound frazzled.

JB: If I had decided the Olympics was my last competition, the situation might be different. But I have some goals, some other things I still want to accomplish. Whenever I have time now, I find myself overtraining and courting injury.

JDW: I suspected you'd have more trouble with the acclaim than the winning.

JB: The race of my life was at the Olympic Trials. As accolades themselves, the Olympics was it. But that was a relatively easy run. But... this lack of time. It is hard for me to say "No more competitive running," because there is more to do.

JDW: Must you hibernate to continue to improve?

JB: I hope not, because I don't want to and I don't think I should. It's mostly a matter of scheduling. Scott (Samuelson) and I haven't seen much of each other since we got married. We set aside a month or so around Christmas, when he's out of school, to be together and it's worked pretty well. But something always seems to come up.

JDW: Like what?

JB: I was very honored to be a recipient of one of *Ms. Magazine*'s "Women Of The Year" awards. However, the presentation ceremony was during the month Scott and I had set aside. We wanted to stay close to home. I was the only one of the 12 women to say I couldn't make it. The magazine called and said Peter Ueberroth could make it and he had agreed to accept the award on my behalf. He had just been named "Man Of The Year" by *Time*! That changed my mind. I went and enjoyed it immensely, but it sure wasn't in the plans.

JDW: Can you ever train well again?

JB: I just don't know. Of course, I believe you can do anything you want to do... I don't think most people understand. Running is a very selfish sport. I'm lucky. It's quiet here in Maine and Scott has his own life with his own goals, so that I'm not pressured that way.

JDW: What's been the biggest hassle?

JB: Constantly being harassed. Oh, I don't want to use that word. Race directors have been very demanding. When I run a race, it is very difficult to go to ten media opportunities on Saturday and then run my best. I'm going to make a deal with them from now on. I will go to a race to promote it, or to compete in it, but I can't do both. I will answer questions after a race, of course, but it's important I have the opportunity. To do my best.

JDW: We've talked about the downside of fame. What's been good?

JB: I haven't changed! My attitude hasn't changed all that much. My friends are still my friends. I don't treat them differently and they don't treat me differently. Oh, notes from so many people. Little gifts. The awards, the invitations.

Right now I'm watching the sun go down and an American flag is flying in the breeze. Senator Mitchell of Maine had three flags flown over the Capitol. He gave one to me and the other two went to Maine's other Olympians. A former governor gave me a state flag which flies below the U.S. flag. That's pretty special.

JDW: You're pretty special yourself. Do you do any work with charities?

JB: I've "worked" with the Multiple Sclerosis Society and with the Special Olympics. You have to give something back. I've taken so much from the sport. That's one reason I coached at B.U. for two years.

JDW: How are the locals treating you? Didn't you get trapped by fans this past summer in a local supermarket?

JB: Hardly trapped! Besides, that was during tourist season. Maine people rarely go out of their way to congratulate you. They respect me for who I am, not for what I've done.

JDW: What does Joan Benoit miss most about those pre-gold days?

JB: The thing I've missed the most is not getting into a daily routine. You never know who's on the phone or who will make an 11th-hour plea.

JDW: Edwin Moses once said, "An athlete has a heavy responsibility placed on him whether he wants it or not."

JB: Society looks up to athletes. For someone to do something that's not cool, it is difficult to swallow.

JDW: Like getting arrested? Or blaming your opponent for causing your fall? Seems like so many of our heroes and heroines – at least in this sport – have fallen from their pedestals.

JB: I know how the press can distort the truth. I know it. Edwin is a marvelous man and I respect him a great deal.

JDW: Let's change the subject. What's so special about lobstering?

JB: That's just something the press got ahold of. It's something I really don't do. Not at all last year. I have friends who do lobster. It's very similar to running in some ways. Working hard, being alone.

JDW: How is your running coming along?

JB: My training is not going well at all. It's been very erratic, more bad runs than good runs. My right knee [the one operated upon before the Olympic trials] has been doing well. There were some minor problems after the Olympics, they went away with rest.

JDW: You do sound tired. You mentioned goals earlier. What are they?

JB: There are a few things I want to accomplish. I want to give it an honest effort. At least I will have tried.

JDW: Joan?!

JB: I want to improve my marathon time. I'd love to try to break 2:20. I'm not saying I will, but I think somebody will in the next two years. I'd like to run a sub-31:00 10k.

JDW: You'd "love to try"? What kind of goal is that?

JB: Well, if I'm not capable of running a sub-2:20, I'm at least capable of improving on the World Record... I once thought maybe the Olympics might have been my last race. But I think there's a lot of room for improvement. It's frustrating. I'm worn out. I can't do what I need to do.

JDW: I have heard from a fairly reliable source Fred Lebow was willing to offer you a 7-year contract to run the New York City Marathon.

JB: That's the first I've heard of it. I know Fred is anxious to have me run L'Eggs, but I haven't made a decision on that yet. I am not currently scheduled to run any marathons in '85.

JDW: What's the most money you've ever been offered to run a single race? What's the most you've ever turned down?

JB: The most I ever rejected was "a considerable sum." I never knew the actual figure because I simply decided I didn't want to run the race. I learned later – from published reports – the Chicago Marathon was willing to pay me $50,000, the same as they supposedly paid Carlos Lopes.

JDW: Before the Olympics, I predicted if Joan Benoit won and the race received sufficient television coverage – both of which happened – then we'd see an incredible upsurge in road running by women. Why do you think women haven't rushed to the streets following your victory?

JB: You were wrong! Golly, I don't know. Perhaps women are too smart, too sensible. The television coverage emphasized how difficult it was to run the marathon. Gabriele's [Andersen-Scheiss] problems finishing certainly put a damper on the race as a motivator.

JDW: You've said that the press often distorts the truth. Joan Benoit is one of America's darlings. A real sweetheart. Sugar and spice and everything. How distorted is that?

JB: You have me mixed up with Mary Lou Retton.

JDW: What do you think people's image is of Joan Benoit?

JB: I don't know. I guess they think I am someone who is a winner, someone who has overcome adversity... operations... and the odds. I was an underdog at the Olympics. I gave people hope. I showed them that you can win even when you're not the favorite.

JDW: Anything more?

JB: That people need time to recover from great feats. Some people can just keep going on and on... I can't! But sooner or later it catches up to you. I went through the knee surgery, the trials – which was by far the most difficult race of my life – then the Olympics themselves; all the hoopla. Then the biggest moment of my life, my wedding. Now, not even being able to muster up enough strength to run a simple 10k.

JDW: I was hoping you wouldn't still seem so tired.

JB: I'm still trying to do too much. I don't know where the time goes, but it's gone much sooner than it used to be.

JDW: What's your favorite sport?

JB: My favorite sport? Good question. I think I'd be wrong if I didn't say "running." Skiing is a favorite. We skied for four hours today.

JDW: Just how good were you as a field hockey player?

JB: I was a good collegiate-level player. I used a little bit of finesse with my stick but my endurance was as good (or better) as anybody else's.

JDW: Is your house finished yet?

JB: [Sighing] Jack, it will never be finished.

JDW: You got married recently. Any thoughts about starting a family?

JB: Yeah, but I think it'll be a while yet, at least until Scott's out of business school. We don't know yet. I don't know just how long I want to compete, but I wouldn't necessarily quit to start a family. Ingrid Kristiansen had a baby and came back stronger than ever.

JW: I hear childbirth is like running a hot weather marathon on a hilly course with a bad leg? Why don't you consider yourself a marathoner?

JB: I haven't run as many marathons as I have 10ks… other track races or even shorter road races. I just haven't done that many of them.

JDW: Back to the important stuff. What's your name now?

JB: I am formally and officially Joan Samuelson. It's Swedish, not Norwegian. Of course, in running, I will remain Joan Benoit. It seems dumb to sign a picture of Joan Benoit winning the Olympic gold with the name of Samuelson.

JDW: What's the nicest thing about being famous?

JB: I, uh, I can't think of anything. As I said, I can't even get into my daily routine.

JDW: Jim Fixx used to think the best thing was having someone meet you at the airport.

JB: That is good! Oh, let's see, I've been bumped into first-class a couple of times… If I call for snow tires, and tell them I'm Joan Samuelson, they'll say, "Okay, lady, bring your car in a week from this coming Thursday." If Joan Benoit calls, the tires will be on by tomorrow.

JDW: One last thing. Where's the gold medal?

JB: Why does everyone ask that question?

JDW: Because everyone doesn't have a gold medal and we all wonder where we'd put it if we did.

JB: Right. My gold medal is in a bureau drawer with candlesticks and trivets.

JDW: Of course. Right where I'd keep mine.

In the issue of Track & Field News *in which this interview appeared (February 1985), there was the following postscript.*

I did not want to interview Joan Benoit. My editors, a merciless group of polyestered pixie patrons, made me do it. The press may indeed distort things, e.g., reality, but Benoit is, it seems, a true American hero. She is also a very private person, in an introspective sport, who has become world famous for the simple task of running.

Interrogating Benoit reminds me somehow of building an 8-lane highway to a secret, special glen deep in the forest. To publicize is – at least an attempt – to change. Joan Benoit is fine just the way she is. – JDW

46 Days On The Road With Mrs. Joan Benoit Samuelson
March 1988

I am trying to imagine what it's like to be Mrs. Joan Benoit Samuelson right now.

With just a few weeks remaining before the Trials Marathon, what's this woman up to? What's she doing in her spare time?

Late at night on a Monday after she'd been outatown for a while, I finally reached her. Just that a.m. I'd caught Joanie on her way out of the house, so I asked if I could call her tonight.

"Uh, Jack, I've got three other people already calling tonight." Then she paused and said, "2 o'clock. Call at 2:00."

Damn, I didn't think and called at 2:00 my time. *My* time. No answer. No answer. I went for a run and when I got back I sharpened eight #2 pencils, popped the top off a 16-ounce Coors and called again.

Busy. The line's busy, and it finally dawns on me I should've called at 2 o'clock *her* time. Geez. And I realize she's probably got three writers on the phone asking her all the same questions – about her baby and her running and the Olympics – that she doesn't want to answer necessarily. The line's busy for over two hours and I just know she's been answering the same old questions. I just know she's not going to be in the mood to chat.

When Mrs. Joan Benoit Samuelson answered on the third ring, I stammered out an apology about my egocentrism re time zones and the lateness of the hour.

I wanted to ask about her training and what it's like to have a baby and the Olympics and can a 41-year-old guy understand what it's like to be the defending marathon gold medalist and a new mother. That's mostly what I wanted to ask. I figured Joan was about the only woman in the world who could tell me what's it's like.

She was tired. I can't really remember what I asked, but I'll never forget her answer.

"Jack, I just started running last week. I hurt my back. I took six weeks off. Just started again."

I can't really express my disappointment, the sense of loss I began to feel as I replayed that phrase on the brain... "Just started again." It was soon to be March 15.

"You had a baby. You're America's hero. The Olympics are coming up. You're somebody I care about. So, what does this mean for May 1?" I inquired.

I prayed for good news. I can't tell you how much I wanted to find Joan Benoit in the best of shape. I've kinda had this image of her as Super Mom winning that second gold in Seoul, then coming home to help Lee Iaccoca sell Jeep Eagles to the people who are sick and tired of coming around a tight bend to find not one but two Hyundais in the left lane. And you got to know she'd be a better President than George H.W. Bush.

I think Joan Benoit is special.

So, you have to believe I was, well, slightly shattered when I heard "just started again." Joanie deals with her injuries better than I do.

"Well, Jack, I believe in miracles," she offered, like another blow upside my head, "but your guess is as good as mine."

Aarrrgh! I can't believe it. Is this really necessary? Aren't Mota, Martin, Kristiansen and the Commies enough? Can't she at least please be injury-free?

"How bad is it?" I asked. And so we began to talk. I couldn't bring myself actually to interview her.

Joan Benoit is injured. "Lucky if I can run 6 miles," she said. And I could barely hold up my end of the conversation.

She sensed my disappointment, and despite her fatigue began to try to cheer me up.

"It's not so bad. The limp is almost gone." 46 days until the Olympic Trials and the limp is almost gone?! Somehow I am not consoled. So Joanie kept pumping me with positive thinking.

"Six weeks ago, I could barely walk," she said. "I'm swimming a lot. I'm staying fit. I'm seeing someone for my back every day. It's getting better every day."

"Well, that is encouraging," I conceded, without much enthusiasm.

46 days.

"You know," she went on, "it only took me a month after delivering Abigail to get back into the same shape I was before I got pregnant."

"I *was* impressed with that 34:42 10k just three months after giving birth," I said.

"Well, Jack, if I can run 15 miles by April 1, and get three 20-milers in before the Trials," she said, "I should be able to toe the line. First of all, I need to get healthy. That's the most important thing."

"Then what?" I wondered.

"If I'm coming on strong, I'd go for it."

She did cheer me up. I started to get excited. Yes, this was Joan Benoit after all. This was the woman who came back 14 days after arthroscopic surgery to win the '84 Trials, then waltzed away into the sun to win in L.A.

Sure, she could do it. No problem.

But... 46 days?

"I don't want to go to the Trials to run a marathon unless I have a reasonable chance to make the team," she explained. "It's frustrating. I'm feeling strong; I'm feeling motivated. And the U.S. times just aren't competitive and that's a little hard to swallow."

"That's true," I replied. "The last time I looked, the fastest qualifying time was 2:31 something. Can't you just go to Pittsburgh and give them The Benoit Look?"

She didn't know what I meant. "Can't you go and be Benoit and psych them into submission?"

"Jack, I don't think it's going to work that way. There are a lot of women who are working hard and have dedicated themselves to making the team. I'd have to earn it."

I didn't think to ask her if she's been doing some of her legendary workouts on the exercycle. And I saw no sense in asking about her training.

"But, you're still going to try, right?"

"Jack, that Olympic moment was so special to me that I don't believe I can ever capture it again. But I'd sure like to try."

Joan might not get to do it. She might maybe make the team in the 10k. Personally, I'm visualizing a gutsy, but not debilitating 3rd place finish

May 1. Then a summer of problem-free, painless training. At Seoul a series of surges between 18-21 miles causes Kristiansen to snap like a dry twig and Mota's stomach cramps; Dorre is caught on a bad day; only Martin is a threat. I'd settle for a silver.

But, 46 days?

I still don't know what it feels like to be a new mother and defending gold medal winner. (I'm sure Joan will tell me someday.)

One thing I *do* know about is wanting to run an important race and being injured, unable to prepare properly, wondering if you'll even be able to give it a decent shot, wondering if you should even try.

I do know something about that. And it's not fun.

46 days.

I have an inordinate affection for JBS. I have ever since I saw her being pushed down the hotel hallway – in a laundry cart – at the Houston Marathon in '82, thereabouts. Laughing and squealing. I was laughing and she was squealing. Many years later and now many years ago, I visited her at her home. She had the most completely dust-free, beat-to-crap treadmill I have ever seen, placed in front of the picture window overlooking the water. Later, I asked her how she was doing. Bent over, hands in the dirt, she responded, "My garden grows, but I have no time to weed." – JDW

Little Mary Decker - The Revival
July 1994

Little Mary : airborne, indoors and in the lead

Slaney's back.

The rumblings started late last Fall, like drums along the road circuit. Slaney's back. With her eye on the 1996 Olympic 10,000. And get this, Alberto Salazar is coaching her.

Brown ponytail streaming straight, Mary Slaney covered the rain-slickened New Times 10k in a course record 32:38. Her first competitive effort in a year. Following her Phoenix flight, Slaney chilled out at Manchester's 4.748M Thanksgiving melee. Mercury fairly froze at 18 degrees. Slaney warmed to the task, finishing in 24:31, far in front of Olympians Judi St. Hilaire and Cathy O'Brien. Slaney's back... indeed, that was all they saw of her.

Mary: older, outdoors, still airborne

A literal Marython, her career. "I never look back," Mrs. Mary Decker Tabb Slaney once said. The rest of us should.

She has seen untold thousands of athletes come and go, yet she runs on.

When asked what keeps her going, Mary Slaney says the first thing that comes to mind: "Training, long runs, racing." The actual activity. The process, not the result. The doing. Not fitness, not winning, not medals nor records, not fame. What she enjoys most about running is... running.

"It's a feeling – a feeling that's difficult to put into words," she tries to explain. "It's like being a junkie. I love to run. I crave it. I get my fix and I just want more.

"You see, running isn't hard for me. When I'm fit, I can push harder.. And the harder I push, the better the feeling becomes. So I want to go faster and faster. Eventually, I push too hard, and that's when I've run into problems.

"I don't equate running with pain. Maybe I don't feel the pain the way others do. For me, the only time running hurts is when I'm injured. I equate injuries with pain."

Is it fair to call her fragile?

"I guess it's fair," she concedes, with disarming charm. "Either that or stupid." Stupid, she's not. "I'm just a little bit stubborn."

Study the readers' surveys. One out of three is injured every year. Slaney has always done her part to keep those numbers up. Talk to her about leg problems, and she sounds like a medical specialist, tossing off one Latin term after another. She has lost count of the number of operations, surgeries, invasive medical procedures – call them what you will – she has undergone during her career.

"Fourteen to 16," she estimates. Not quite one per year.

Looking at her injuries as mandatory rest periods, perhaps she has lasted so long, in part, because of all the layoffs.

"We'll never know that," she says. "I don't think I would've retired. I don't think I'll ever retire from running. Not completely. Not ever."

Slaney has learned a couple of things from her numerous setbacks. "I've learned how to make numerous comebacks," she says. "When you're younger, you think you're bulletproof. Sooner or later you find out that's not true. I've finally learned, if the doctor says it'll be eight weeks until you heal, it'll be eight weeks. If he says 12 weeks, it'll be 12 weeks. Too many times, I tried to rush back from injury and simply prolonged my problems. I've learned my lesson."

She could teach. It's a simple sport. You've heard it before – stay to the left and get back as soon as you can.

Fifteen years ago, Slaney said she needed to be able to call someone 'Coach.' "I think everybody needs to. Particularly at this level. I could tell somebody else what to do – that's easy. But I can't be objective enough with myself. That's simply too difficult." The need remains the same.

Enter her old and true friend, Alberto Salazar – a world-class guy who has been to the top himself. "He's been a great coach. Just great," Slaney explains. "He's not manipulating, not controlling like certain coaches I could name. He cares. He cares differently. He puts my goals and my racing ahead of his own running. He doesn't feel threatened. He wants *me* to succeed, be healthy and perform well. That's his only motivation."

Listening to Mary talk, she sounds like a once lonely child who has finally found someone to play with. "Working with Alberto has been a lot of fun. I've never had a training partner whose schedule was remotely like mine. Now I have somebody to run with who actually slows me down. More important, I'm learning, finally, how to train."

For all she has accomplished, she wants to do so much more. "My motivation hasn't changed. It's the same as when I started running. I think I can do better. I think I can run faster."

Yet there's more to her life than running in circles. Sitting in her home – a traditional two-story five miles north of Eugene's Hayward Field, in a flat neighborhood full of families and good for running – Slaney sounds less like a Zen priestess of physicality and more like a young wife and mother.

"Having a family puts the rest of your life in perspective. The world does not revolve around my running the way it used to," she says. "The way I thought it used to."

There's more to life. "I'd probably be a neurotic mess if I didn't have Richard and Ashley," Mary admits. "They certainly make dealing with injuries and other setbacks much easier."

She has been happily married for more than nine years to Richard Slaney, who's currently in the business of buying, selling and restoring old aircraft. "I'm happy for him," Mary says. "He's making a living doing something he loves."

Then there's Ashley Lynn, an animated third-grader who turned eight last spring. "I have to set an example now," proud Mary relates. "Such a good child. Absolutely no disciplinary problems ever."

Ashley is not a runner. "She's very academically oriented," says Slaney. "She wants to be an actress."

Gifted with a certain fluid flair for the dramatic herself, Ashley's mother has always been more than an athlete. Mary Slaney is a performer.

"I'm simply inspired to get better. I'm aiming at the 5,000m and the 10,000m, and I don't consider myself experienced at either distance. I've only run one 10k on the track – *ever* – and three 5ks – *ever*. I have to believe there's a great deal of room for improvement."

She hasn't given much thought lately to running a marathon. "Secretly, I think Alberto would like to see me run one, if there was some way to guarantee I wouldn't get injured. And, of course, there's not. Richard is dead set against it. After all, he's the one who has to live with me when I'm hurt. We all know it's not the smartest idea we've heard.

"I really don't know what my best racing distance is," Slaney concedes. "Depends on the most recent injury and the latest training, I guess. Honestly, I think the 5k could be."

And does she think she can still win an Olympic gold medal? "Of course." And she knows how'll she'll do it. "I can out-kick anybody."

A runner's career ends when her legs are exhausted, when the heart gives out and the drive dries up, when the mind says 'no'.

Mary Slaney isn't even tired yet.

Little Mary Decker

"I never look back," Mary Slaney once said. The rest of us should.

At age 11, very little Mary Theresa Decker sees a notice for a park department cross country race. She doesn't have the faintest idea what 'cross country' is, but she enters the 3/4ths of a mile competition and wins. A natural, she spends her first track season as a sprinter.

The next year is 1971. The soundtrack from Jesus Christ, Superstar is the country's top album. Old Johnny Kelley is only 63. Cheryl Bridges becomes the first American woman to break the 2:50 barrier for the marathon. Doris Brown sets the American record for one mile (4:39.6). Derartu Tulu is born.

Decker turns 12 and becomes a middle-distance racer. She runs a 5:04.8 mile and finishes the Palos Verde Peninsula marathon in 3:09:27. Competes in track meets next two days. Two days later, she undergoes an emergency appendectomy. The doctor says her condition is brought on by too much running. A prophetic diagnosis.

1972. Five burglars are caught creeping inside Democratic Party offices at the Watergate complex. Dave Wottle wins Olympic gold at 800m. Blue Ribbon Sports, a distributor of Tiger shoes, becomes Nike. Richard Chelimo and Maria Mutola are born. Decker, age 13, runs 4:55 for the mile.

1973. 4031 runners toe the starting line of Bay-To-Breakers, the largest road race in U.S. history. Twelve-year-old long jumper Carl Lewis wins his age-group at a local Jesse Owens meet. Craig Virgin sets the national high school record for two miles.

Decker competes in her last open quarter. Her time? 53.8, a time which would have made her the fifth fastest prep 20 years later. At 14, she runs 23.7 for 220 yards. On a dirt track. From a standing start.

The next year, Suzy Favor starts school... elementary school. Doug Kurtis enters his first marathon. Margaret Groos runs 5:12 to win the RRCA 14-15 age-group national mile championship. Miki Gorman clocks 2:47:11 to win the Boston Marathon.

No wonder they call her "Little Mary", she's 5'3" and 90 lbs. But she earns a berth on her first national team and ranks 4th in world, number one – with a bullet – in the U.S. at 800, which she covers in 2:02.4. She runs 4:40.1 indoors for the mile.

At the age of 15, Decker sets three world records indoors. "People just expect too much," she said then. "Just because you break a record or two, people expect you to do it every time you step on the track. You can't run records to order... So I just try to do my best in every race and satisfy myself."

In the good old days, as national champion and leading half-miler in the U.S.A., Decker wins the 800 in a dual meet against the USSR. Body-checked off the track during a relay, Mary gets up and throws her baton at the muscular Russian offender. She misses. She throws the baton again. Remember the Cold War?

A stress fracture in her right foot requires Mary to spend six weeks in a cast.

1975. The Vietnam "Conflict" ends. Steve Prefontaine dies. Joan Benoit, who clips and saves articles about Decker, runs 5:29 to win Maine's state high school mile championship. Jackie Hansen sets world marathon record with a time of 2:38:19. Just a junior, Rudy Chapa is nation's top prep 6-miler. Edwin Moses enters his first intermediate hurdles race. A young man by the name of Bill Rodgers bursts upon the world scene with his first win at the Boston Marathon.

Meanwhile, Mary Decker, age 16, grows three inches and is sidelined for most of the year with shin pains. In fact, she is virtually crippled by these pains. It hurts so bad.

1976. Alberto Salazar is prepdom's top 3-miler. Lynn Jennings runs 4:55.3 indoors to become the first Massachusetts schoolgirl to break the 5-minute barrier. Decker leaves high school and heads to the University of Colorado "to escape the pressure of Southern California." Hampered by constant pain, she guts out one race indoors and misses the remainder of the year. Dominant when injury-free, she is unable to compete for a spot on Montreal Olympic squad.

1977. First issue of Running Times appears. Renaldo Nehemiah graduates from high school. Reggie Jackson belts three home runs as Yankees capture World Series.

At 19, Decker's career looks to be over. "I cried a lot," she admits, "but I don't think I gave up at any point." Dick Quax visits Boulder, points to the scars on his own calves and recognizes Mary's problem as Compartment Syndrome, where the tissues surrounding the calf muscles fail to expand with the muscles' growth. In July, Decker has first of two operations to correct problem. In August, the second.

1978. Valerie Brisco sets high school standard for 220 yards. Lynn Jennings, at seventeen too young to run officially, injures a knee completing the Boston Marathon in 2:46, the third woman to finish. Grete Waitz wins her first NYC marathon with a world record time of 2:32:30.

By January, however, Decker's comeback becomes official. Running in a series of outdoor meets in New Zealand, she lopes to personal bests of 2:01.8 and 4:08.9. Back in the U.S.A. she covers 1000 yards in an indoor world record of 2:23.6. Practically as an afterthought, Decker establishes an indoor 1500m collegiate record of 4:13.4.

Unfortunately followed by Achilles tendinitis and another bout of the dreaded Compartment Syndrome.

For which there is no national telethon. An operation in August is successful and Decker celebrates by winning the collegiate women's cross-country championship that fall.

1979. Carl Lewis sets high school long jump record. Jim Fixx's The Complete Book of Running is still atop best sellers' list. Decker becomes first female member of Athletics West.

A sciatic nerve problem springs up, so Decker is unable to train for three and a half months early in the year. She moves to Eugene, never to compete again collegiately. About those missed years Decker said, "Your body just doesn't burn itself out by the time you're 20."

But now it's summer. Decker sets mile AR of 4:23.5. She wins Pan-Am Games 1500m gold medal, runs a personal best 4:05 1500m and is ranked #2 in U.S. at that distance.

1980. Gore-Tex invented. Bill Reifsnyder outkicks Steve Spence to win Pennsylvania State High School Invitational mile crown. Salazar's marathon debut is a 2:09:41 win in New York. Joetta Clark leads prep half milers.

Do you believe in miracles? While the American ice hockey team is upsetting the Soviets at the Winter Olympics, not-so-little-any-more Mary Decker runs 1:59.7 for 880y, breaking her own indoor world record, set on the same track a half dozen years earlier.

Decker becomes the only American woman ever to hold the world mile record with a basically solo effort of 4:21.7. In fact, she's the first U.S. woman to hold any world record at a distance longer than 200m.

"But it really wasn't a race, was it?" she said. "I have to learn to run with people and not just against myself."

Working as a sales clerk in a Nike store, Decker lowers the world mile standard to 4:17.6 indoors. Covers 1500m in 4:00.8, another indoor world record.

"To me the bad things in my career were my injuries. I don't think about those things now because I'm looking ahead," the 21-year-old confides. "I'm not living in the past, not living for what 'Little' Mary Decker has done. I want to achieve more... and I'm a whole different person."

Decker wins Olympic Trials 1500 in 4:04.91, second fastest time ever outdoors by U.S. woman. But athletes lose, as the U.S. leads boycott of Moscow Games. "I would love to win an Olympic gold medal," Decker says, "but if it isn't possible, it isn't possible. Maybe I can prove I'm the best in other ways."

Some other ways. July 11, she runs an AR 4:01.17. July 15, her first 3000m on the track results in a 8:38.73 AR. July 17, 4:00.87, another AR. Three national records in a week. August 11, after missing the Olympics, a 4:00.04 AR. On August 13, Decker becomes the first American woman under four minutes for the metric mile – 3:59.43. She finishes in a distant second as Tatyana Kazankina sets an astonishing world record of 3:52.47.

"I was psychologically beaten before the race started," Decker conceded then. "I looked at the Soviet women and literally could not believe it. They didn't look like any women I had seen before. Their muscle definition is so pronounced! I don't doubt they are women biologically speaking, but, shall we say, chemically, I'm not so sure." In September, Decker undergoes Achilles tendon surgery to repair a partial tear.

1981. Prize money and above-the-table professionalism come to road racing as Nike and the Cascade Run Off pay cash for performance. Bill Rodgers collects $30,000 in appearance fees at Tokyo Marathon.

Decker injured. Does not compete. Gets married to marathoner Ron Tabb instead.

1982. Pat Porter wins his first national cross-country championship. Salazar sets national 10k record of 27:25.61.

Decker Tabb goes undefeated. Wins national championship at 1500m. Lowers world indoor mile mark three times, leaving it at 4:20.5. WR 3000 8:47.3. Sets three world marks outdoors 4:18.08, 5000 – 15:08.26, 10k – 31:35.3. AR 3000 8:29.71. Top ranked American at five different distances. Number one in world at three. Sports Illustrated names Decker Tabb Sportswoman of the Year.

1983. Ronald Reagan likes to take the credit. George Bush, too. Track historians trace the fall of the Soviet empire to Decker Tabb's double gold performance at 1500 and 3000 in Helsinki against two of the best women's fields ever assembled. Two. Gold. Medals. Count'em. Assay them.

Undefeated, she ranks #1 in world at both distances. Not to forget #2 in U.S. at 800m with PR 1:57.60. Lowers American 1500m record to 3:57.12. Divorces Tabb. Media pressure is intense. "I don't know why," she says at the time, "but interviews seem to be more draining than anything else I do."

So, she seeks a more private life and thus finds herself assailed by critics. "I don't think I'm spoiled," she says in her own defense. "I don't think I'm a brat."

By year's end, Decker has run the fastest dozen 1500m races in U.S. history, the thirteen fastest miles, the eight fastest at 3000 meters.

1984. Junior Ed Eyestone wins collegiate national 10k championship. Lisa Weidenbach places fourth in marathon trials. Benoit wins first Olympic women's marathon. Slaney sets road AR for 10k with 31:38.

Everybody remembers The Fall. It's the stuff People magazine is made of. Zola Budd cuts in front of Decker, who crashes to the track, injured and screaming. Maricica Puica goes on to glory. The rivalry with Budd, by the way, never existed except in the minds of certain untutored scribes and television broadcasters concerned about ratings.

1985. Cathy Schiro is top high school 3000m runner. Decker celebrates New Year's by marrying big Richard Slaney, British discus thrower – a very solid guy.

Too few remember the next time Budd and Mary Slaney step onto the same track. Slaney exacts her revenge with a 8:32.91 victory, more than 3 seconds faster than Puica's gold winning time. Budd is a very distant 4th.

Slaney is unbeaten in 14 races outdoors. She sets five new national marks including 5000m in 15:06.53. And a world best mile in 4:16.71. Wins Grand Prix easily, defeating both Puica and Budd. She once said this was her best year.

With the year's fastest times, Decker is ranked #1 in world at 1500m and 3000m. Puica is second-best at both distances.

1986. Suzy Favor completes her reign as country's top high school miler.

After nine hours of labor, Slaney gives birth to Ashley Lynn on May 30th. Six days later – don't try this at home, girls – Ma Slaney goes for a run, admitting later she tried to come back too fast. Fourteen weeks after giving birth, Mary runs her first road mile in 4:32.01, finishing 6th at NYC's Mercedes mile. November, she undergoes arthroscopic surgery on her right Achilles.

1987. Toshihiko Seko wins Boston Marathon. The country's top high school sprinter is Quincy Watts. Slaney continues to be plagued by Achilles problems. Does not compete.

1988. Lisa Weidenbach places fourth in marathon trials. Slaney runs her first track race in 19 months, a 4:09.14 1500m victory. "I feel really confident that all the problems are over," she says after the race. Her 3:58.92 win at the Olympic Trials gets her to Seoul where she places 8th. Ranks 8th in world, tops in U.S. Decker doubles, also winning the Trials' 3000m with a time of 8:34.69. Finishes 10th at the Olympics. Ranks #8 in world, #2 in U.S. at 3000m.

1989. Berlin Wall comes tumbling down. Pattisue Plumer takes away Decker's 5000m AR with a 15:00.00 clocking. Mary ranks 7th in U.S. at 1500m with her 4:23.9 indoor mile.

1990. John Campbell, 41, runs 2:11:04 marathon. Plumer becomes only the second American woman ever ranked #1 in World at 3000m. Slaney, the first U.S. female so honored, can't even recall why she didn't compete that year. "Probably injured," she suggests. "Probably Achilles tendonitis."

1991. John Kelley runs his 60th Boston Marathon. Steve Spence wins a bronze – not a gold – with a 3rd in the World Championships marathon and becomes the first U.S. male long distance runner to claim a major medal since Frank Shorter's Olympic silver in 1976. There is much hype about how this bronze – not a gold – signals a resurgence in American distance running fortunes.

Francie Larrieu Smith, ironically the woman Decker replaced as this country's greatest middle distance runner, breaks Mary's 9-year-old 10k record.

Slaney runs 2:01.28 for 800m and a 4:23.35 mile. Her 8:43.19 3000m mark earns a number four ranking among Americans.

1992. Lisa Weidenbach places fourth in marathon trials. Craig Virgin runs – and loses – a race for seat in the Illinois State Senate.

Fourteen weeks before U.S. Olympic Trials, Slaney has surgery to correct plantar fascia injury. "Your body heals in a certain way," she says. "You can't speed it up." After building a sizable lead in the first two laps of the 3000, Slaney fades to a distant, non-qualifying 6th. "If I had gone out slower, I probably would have run a better race, but that's just not me." In the 1500 meter race, Suzy Favor Hamilton, now grown up, out-kicks Slaney for final berth on U.S. team.

Just for fun, Slaney runs a 5k in 15:52.5, earning a #10 ranking in U.S.

1993. Thirty minutes after a 10k, the Chinese women are ready to race again. Meanwhile, Slaney is again injured. Again, surgery - this time to remove nearly an inch of heel bone. Mary does not compete until rising again in Phoenix.

1994. Slaney starts the year at the inaugural Walt Disney Marathon, where she runs the first 11 miles at 5:20 pace for a workout. By May, she has had surgery. By June, she's running again. It should be an interesting fall.

Mary psyching up for another shot at an Olympic gold medal

In the history of running, Slaney stands alone. Nobody even remotely like her, before or since. How do we measure this Marython?

At last count, Slaney had set 36 American records (23 outdoor, 11 indoor, 2 on the road) and 17 world records (6 outdoor, 11 indoor). Not so long ago, she owned all 8 middle and long distance American records on the track. 800 –1:56.90(85), 1000 – 2:34.8, 1500 – 3:57.12, 1M –

4:16.71 (85), 2000 – 5:32.7, 3000 – 8:25.83, 5000 – 15:06.53, 10000 – 31:35.3.

No other American woman has broken four minutes for the metric mile.

Crunching the numbers over three decades. Slaney has been world ranked in five different events, 17 times among the planet's top ten. Eighteen times she's been ranked #1 in the U.S., 27 occasions among the top five. Named four times – more than any other woman – U.S. Athlete of the Year. She's bounced back from more knockdowns than Sylvester Stallone. She's done everything possible except win an Olympic medal.

Now she's aimed at Atlanta. Stay tuned for the next Mary-go-round.

Other than my reaction to seeing her fall in Los Angeles at the 1984 Olympics, my most distinct memory of Mary is running with her one day when we were both staying with John & Nancy Gregorio. I was in fairly good shape and she was either coming off a knee replacement or about to give birth. Maybe both. I busted my ass to stay close enough to talk, listening to her chatter, me unable to respond. Luckily, it was a short, easy day for her. – JDW

Salazar's Future of Days Past
February 1989

Alberto jogging, Jack approaching oxygen debt

Rumblings are beginning to come out of Eugene. Sightings have been reported as if a UFO had been seen hovering over Hayward Field or the Amazon Trail. Credible sources have testified. "The Rookie" lives!

Now 30, Alberto Salazar is healthy at last. It has been too long.

Salazar's maladies – consistent knee and hamstring problems – began in 1983. Legendary for his near-maniacal work ethic and staring at an Olympic showdown, Alberto trained through the pain. After a disappointing 15th-place performance in the L.A.'s Olympic marathon, he says, "I was never the same again."

The surgeries – the left knee and the right hamstring – began in January '85. Spring came, and with it the discovery of nerve damage to, you guessed it, the right hamstring. Thus continued an odyssey that ended an Olympiad later. Last autumn, the strength in Alberto's right leg had reached something on the order of 97%.

"I knew then that I was completely healthy, that I could come back," he now says confidently. The knee was fine, the hamstring finally worked properly... oh yeah, there were back problems.

The former Oregon star tried a variety of potential solutions. Oddly enough, one of the most esoteric – deep muscular massage – proved successful.

"I went to a rolfer last October," he recounts, "and it hasn't hurt again."

Anyone who ever watched Salazar run remembers his unique style: legs barely lifting, swinging low like a metronome, his back cocked as if a hungry pit bull was locked on his butt. Salazar's form was one of a kind.

When Alberto was the world's greatest marathoner, most observers decided this peculiar style must be effective. After all, the man ran 2:08 that way. He ran a 27:25 10k and a 13:11 5k on the track. He won the big races, he beat many of the best. He was one of the best.

And then one day he wasn't.

"I knew my injuries were the result of the way I ran," he explains. "I knew I had to correct my running form." At Seoul, where he watched the last 2M of the marathon on a small monitor in a sandbagged bunker along the DMZ, Salazar had a conversation with one of the sport's most knowledgeable technicians, Tom Tellez.

"We talked and he said that I had an inefficient stride and that it was becoming more inefficient," says Salazar. "I knew that was true. He says there's one right way to run and he eventually convinced me."

So, last November, Alberto headed for Houston and he finally learned how to run correctly from the man who guides Carl Lewis.

"I had always used my hamstrings to push myself, where I needed to be using my quadriceps to pull me," he notes. "Coach Tellez basically taught me to run completely differently. He had me change my stride within a couple of days."

Back in Eugene, the results were immediately apparent. "I was able to keep up with guys I hadn't been able to stay with before," Berto says, sounding like a man who thinks he has found the winning lottery ticket in his pocket.

"We had been running 5 halves at 2:20 pace with an easy half interval (3:00); within a week I was able to cut it down to 2:12. Since I've been rolfed and changed my stride, I don't even get sore. My form is so correct. Compared to the old way, there's so much less pounding."

Give a man a fish, you feed him for a day. Change Salazar's running style so he can train without pain, you nourish him forever.

"The other day, we ran 20 x 200 in 30.5," he said in early February. "A year ago the most I could do was 10, and now I do 20 like it's walking. The progress has been slow but consistent. A month ago, I did ten miles at 5:05 pace. Now I can do that for 15 miles."

Doesn't sound so slow. The main problem now is conditioning and strength. Call it "muscle memory." He can't maintain his new style at faster speeds; his body wants to run in the same manner it has since those early days in Massachusetts. "If I try to maintain the new style at 4:40 pace, I can't do it yet," he explains.

"Like Wednesday, Don Clary, Kevin Ryan and I were doing 5 x 800 with a 300 interval. We ran 2:24, 2:20, 2:16, 2:11. I was feeling good and wanted to push the last one. We went out in 62... I came back in 70. I wasn't ready to do a 62."

Salazar is getting ready. He has been putting in 60 miles weekly for the last two months: "I get everything I can out of every level. I'm going as fast as I can. When I can run that last half-mile repeat easy in 2:06, then I'll move up. I'm just taking it a day at a time."

The man doesn't have plans per se, but he definitely has a comeback philosophy that doesn't include an immediate return to the 26-miler:

"When I feel I can run a 14-minute 5k, I'll jump in a race where that time is competitive.

"I want an entire track season where I can run as fast as I did before, then I'll look toward a marathon... not until then."

This is a new Alberto Salazar. Older, wiser, with a new form that gives him hope of new greatness, a future of days past. Now a successful restaurateur, Salazar seems, well, comfortable... with running, with life.

"Running isn't so complicated as it was before," he says quietly, perhaps remembering foibles of the past. "I know I don't have to be as serious, as intense. As," he pauses, "obsessive. I think I can enjoy it more."

That in itself would be a great victory.

Salazar. You Know Who I Mean

July 1994

Alberto getting it done

Ask Alberto Salazar what in God's Name he was thinking when he won South Africa's famed Comrades Ultra Marathon, you get a long story.

"That's like asking, 'What's your philosophy of life?' There's no quick answer. Obviously, I haven't run well in 10 or 12 years. I've had a lot of physical ailments, injuries and health problems. All those years, I worked with different doctors to get better, doing everything possible in my power to find an answer.

"I always felt God was trying to teach me a lesson. Finally, I was able to appreciate the rest of life and put things in proper priority. Just because I wasn't running well again, I had no reason to be bitter or to feel like I'd been cheated or gotten a raw deal. *Finally, I saw how thankful I should in fact be.*"

The italics are Alberto's, the italicized words emphasizing the veteran athlete's new optimism. Instead of focusing upon the few bad things in your world, count your many blessings.

"If a really insignificant aspect of my life, like running, was the only thing not going exactly like I would want," Salazar pauses, searching for the right words. Don't sweat the small stuff. "Once I came to that point, I began to enjoy life, enjoy my family, more.

"With that came a second thought. If I ever was to run well again, if God wanted me to, then next time around, rather than let running be an end in itself, it would be a thing I could use to share my faith, my new-found perspective on life.

"God does exist, things happen to us for a purpose, we must have faith and we should try to live the way God wants us to." Amen.

"Although I was semi-retired," continues Salazar, a devout Roman Catholic, "I thought perhaps it wasn't in God's plans for me to run well again. Whenever I was ready to completely lay my shoes down, totally allow myself to get out of shape, run only a few miles per day, I'd meet someone with a novel suggestion about how I could reverse some of my physical problems. And so I would train hard again for a while. The end re-sult was always frustration.

"In the last year, all the loose ends started to come back together again. Number one thing medically was my running. It wasn't just about running fast, it was about running tired all the time.

"I was always sick, always run down. Every time I would get a cold, it'd turn into a sinus infection. I'd run 5 miles and that felt like a marathon. We're not talking about five-minute pace, we're talking seven-minute pace. I felt terrible.

"I met a sports doctor who said I might feel better again about running and my overall general health if I tried a new medication called Prozac, an anti-depressant drug.

"Prozac *immediately* turned things around for me. Energy levels shot back *immediately*. I continued to feel better and better."

Salazar's health improved dramatically. In February, in workouts, he began to surprise himself. "I went out to run repeat 200s on the road. I run for 30-35 seconds as hard as I can, then I rest for 45 seconds, so every minute-and-a-half I'm into a new one. I planned to do twenty, I did forty of them. I was psyched."

Salazar started to train seriously for the 53.75-mile run from Durban to Pietermaritzburg. "Six months before Comrades, I thought maybe that's the sort of race I could run well in. My strength was really good. I could do long runs and I wouldn't feel tired. My mileage started creeping up until finally I was doing 120 a week. Still, I felt like I was recovering. The Prozac just seemed to get my system back to normal.

"I believe God engineered all of this. He works in ways through other people. It's not always just a miracle, where there's a flash of lightning and a voice says, 'you're healed.' We have to have faith in order to see His Hand behind it. I believe that's what happened in my case. All these little things finally came together in His good time."

Alberto designed his training specifically for Comrades, emphasizing long runs and hill work. "Rather than do what I'd done in the past, becoming really fast for the 10k, then moving up to the marathon, feeling very efficient and easy at that pace. In a way, I had the same philosophy, but I backed off. After all, I only had to do 6-minute pace for Comrades.

"As a result, I was able to put in this steady distance work. I would run a 30-40 miler at 6:15 pace. Three days later, I'd come back with an interval workout, 10 halves in the low 2:20s. All of a sudden, the good medium quality, with the high mileage, started to add up. I started getting really strong, and the ability to run 6-minute pace was very much enhanced.

"I did a lot of work on the treadmill, which was another key for me. I have a new Precor treadmill, fixed so it can do 4-minute pace. I can go up- or down hill. I probably did two-thirds of my mileage per week on the treadmill."

Comrades surprised Salazar. "A lot different than I imagined. One limiting factor in a race like that is your ability to resist fatigue and the amount of glycogen depletion you undergo, how much energy your body uses up.

"I used to think a guy in 2:08 [marathon] shape would kill everybody in a ultramarathon. After this race, I no longer believe that to be true." Salazar's winning time of 5:38:39, by the way, works out to 6:18 pace.

"You go out thinking this is going to be pretty easy, then you get to 30-35 miles, The Wall hits you." He chuckles at the memory. "I mean, it just *hits* you. You go from feeling easy until suddenly you feel like they forgot to put the cap back on at the gas station, and all the gas slopped out 30 miles down the road. The tank's empty and you still have a long way to go. At that point it's really a struggle - a war - to keep going.

"Unlike other races, where you can feel you're dying and stuff, and still it's not that hard to finish. You can slow down. You can say, 'yeah, I'm going to lose two minutes over the last 20k in this marathon,' but you can still finish. You've still done your running.

"In this race, you don't know literally if you'll still be running in five minutes. There's nothing left. I mean, you feel like you could collapse any second. It's not even a matter of picking it up or not slowing down. It's a matter of, 'Am I even going to be able to finish this thing?' Muscularly, you're wasted; mentally, you become very disoriented. Willpower diminishes rapidly as well. You have to push yourself to hang in there.

"My overall mentality is completely different than before. Before, I used to think, 'well, I'm tougher than everybody else, I can beat them.' Frankly, I said a lot of prayers during this race. It was really a miracle I was able to finish, because I wanted to drop out with 20 miles to go. Still hard to believe I was able to run another two hours after I felt completely exhausted.

"I thought, 'I'm probably going to collapse. At any time. Faint dead.' I thought, 'I'm not going to drop out. I'd rather collapse than quit.' I said I was running for God. To go out there and quit the first time I started hurting, people might've thought, 'he's not too serious about his faith.'

"The old me probably would've dropped out," Salazar, age 35, admits.

The Comrades Marathon starts at sea level with an 800m elevation gain mostly in the first half. The rest roller-coasters up and down big hills. "The hills were brutal. A series of hills, about five or six of them, one-and-a-half to two-and-a-half miles long. Six percent grade. It's the hardest thing in the world to get to the top of the last one without walking."

Not even any prize money.

Salazar's next excellent adventure remains a mystery. "I am going to take it easy. I'm not going to run any fall marathons. If I continue to progress to the point where I can be competitive in a marathon, then I'd certainly give it a shot. For the time being, for once, I am just going to enjoy the moment. Not be so worried always about the future, not about the races or the times I want to run.

"Whatever happens, I figure that'll be God's plan. I'll do my best. I'll definitely, the next few months, not go back and do 120 miles a week. I'll do 90 to 100 miles, running speed a couple times weekly, nothing real intense or ambitious in terms of improving consistently. Take it a day at a time."

Counting his blessings. Still taking Prozac.

"Comrades underscored for me the fact you can have a long dry spell, a drought, which turns around quickly when you get everything working right. Comrades makes me very optimistic."

Alberto Salazar is healthy again, living proof good things happen to those who believe they can.

It's a miracle.

Pre lives! S'pose Pre had lived? What if?

May 1995

Pre with his eyes on the prize

A book could be written based on a single question: what if Pre hadn't had too much to drink that night at Geoff Hollister's house and got back to his own bed safely? Think about it. Or simply gotten hurt, better yet, and came back stronger than ever. Think about it.

If I am any judge of creativity, and I am, this is a good idea, one somebody could run with. Whoever owns Pre's future controls the franchise.

S'pose Pre had lived.

S'pose a couple of strong buddies, Mac Wilkins comes to mind, followed Pre down the hill from the party at Hollister's. Maybe Phil Knight is driving the car and they come around the corner and there's Pre's little MGB turned over, a tire still spinning. Everybody piles out of the car and rushes to Pre.

"Can you breathe?" Mac asks his friend.

"Barely." Comes the whispered response. Those superhuman lungs.

"Can you move?" Knight wonders. Pre wiggles his hands, lifts his legs, those incredible legs. "Yes."

"Should we try to move him or wait for help?"

Knight doesn't know what to do next. Help isn't coming. Nobody wants to leave to seek aid. And nobody wants to stand there and watch helplessly as the car presses down on Pre. Too crushing.

"We can lift the car," Wilkins offers, moving toward the car. "You pull him clear."

Knight isn't so sure. Pre coughs weakly, a death rattle perhaps caught in his throat. He lifts his free arm, reaches a hand out, like that guy on the ceiling of the Sistine Chapel.

"Just do it," Pre says.

Anybody else would've died, doctors said, but Pre, he was so strong, so gutsy, so not-ready-yet-to-die, Pre lived. Imagine that comeback.

He's hurt so bad he can't compete until the Bob Woodell Meet the next spring. An entire year lost, in his prime. Hayward Field is alive, full to the rafters, where the rubber snakes hang. The weather is typical Bluegene, Oregun, gray, overcast, rain, dark for days.

Suddenly, a hush. Like E.F. Hutton was talking and everybody in the stadium had stopped talking to overhear a stock tip. So quiet, you could hear Tom Ragsdale, one of the meet officials, fart. A brave ray of sunlight, like hope, pokes through the cloud.

Slowly, like background noise, a murmur begins to grow. The ray blossoms into a bright beam. The noise begins to wash across the infield, waves washing from the East stands to the West stands. And back again.

It's him. Pre. The beam of light shone on Steven Roland Prefontaine, followed him like a personal spotlight as he jogged onto the Stevenson Track. Everybody stood. They cheered, they applauded, they stomped their feet and shook the stands. Hadn't been this much noise here since his last race. No. This was the most noise ever.

The finish line. All they can see is Pre's back.

Pre lives! Again!!

Consider two POVs [points of view]. Third person omniscient, supposedly the easiest to do, and first person Pre.

S'pose Pre lived? He would've been a changed man. Stopped drinking and driving. Started wearing his seatbelt. The accident was like a slap across Pre's face, not something he could run away from. He had looked at Death's Door and he was determined to do better if given a second chance.

I imagine Pre and Little Mary Decker getting married, making it work right the first time. She comes to Eugene out of high school, see, and enjoys this storied collegiate career. Actually earns her degree. Pre keeps Mary from over-training, so she doesn't get injured. Pre teaches Mary how to run in a pack, so she doesn't fall at the Olympics. He'd keep her out of trouble. Probably become like the Sonny & Cher of running.

S'pose Pre had lived. I see him going public in his fight against the boycott of the '80 Olympic Games. It was Pre's comments before Congress re the virtue of individualism in sports which lifted the hearts of America's athletes and seized the competitive spirits of the entire nation. I see Pre's People beating Carter's. Mary gets her gold medal in Moscow, while Pre gets outkicked defending his 5k crown. Pre won't make excuses, says he just got outrun, but many point to the price paid in politics.

S'pose Pre had lived. He'd have won a couple gold medals. Set a world record or two. Might've won the AAU/TAC/USATF national cross-country about 15 years in a row. He'd have won the Boston Marathon. New York, too. Captained a Nike team to a course record victory at the Hood-To-Coast Relay.

S'pose Pre had lived. He'd be 45-years-old now, a legendary baby-boomer (target market.) Probably already retired from his job as Senior Vice-President of World-wide Athletics. Pre, like Jeff Johnson, is too entrepreneurial by nature to remain with Nike. After a year at the new campus, "felt like I died and went to heaven," Pre said after moving into his fourth floor suite in the, what else, Steve Prefontaine Building. Phil's Place, Pre always called it. Still humble.

Anyway, Pre retired and he and Mary built a dream house along the Mackenzie River.

Maybe he'd be coaching. With the money he got from his Nike stock and all the celebrity from his gold medals won in '76, '80 and that gutsy silver in the '84 Los Angeles marathon when he was 34 and injured, well, he's a man who can do whatever he wants. Still pulls down a pretty penny for store openings and motivational speeches to tired middle-managers. He's a man who can do whatever he wants and he wants to coach.

And who would he coach? Some version of The Karate Kid, for sure. And Pre would teach him everything he knows. And that would be the story. The wins, the losses, the training, the guts, the pain and the partying, cross-country and cross-training, dealing with doubt and defeat as well as Pre's code. He lived by the Code and he teaches the Code.

"To give anything less than your best is to sacrifice the gift."

Pre's Code, that would be the message.

And at the end The Kid dies.

There is no finish line.

Pre Goes to Hollywood

Steve Prefontaine: The Movie is coming soon to a theater near you.

At press time, announcements imminent. Rumors abound. Tom Cruise as Pre. Imagine The Fonz running 10k. Tommy Lee Jones as Dellinger. Brando as Bowerman. Julia Roberts as the beautiful surgeon who falls in love with Pre when she sews his legs back on after a particularly brutal set of intervals. Just once I wish they'd find a runner and teach him how to act instead of trying to teach an actor how to run. Why assume a 3:55 mile is easier than crying on cue?

Papers remain unsigned, thirty hours of tape unedited. Producers haven't decided on a title. (Flash! "Fire on The Track.") But CBS is tentatively scheduled to air an hour-long documentary on Sunday, June 4th. Check your local listings. Quintessential Oregonian Ken "Never Give An Inch" Kesey, author of *One Flew Over The Cuckoo's Nest*, narrates the tale, which features the "gunslingers" of Pre's era. Dave Wottle, Dick Buerkle, Dave Bedford, Ian Stewart, Lasse Viren and Jeff Galloway, among others, offer testimony.

CBS plans a memorable afternoon of track & field. The NCAA Championships (tape-delayed) precedes the Pre bio, which will be followed by coverage of the 1995 Prefontaine Memorial Classic, live from Eugene's Hayward Field. The House that Pre built.

Then there's Tinsel Town. Last year, two flicks about Wyatt Earp. A man who died of natural causes, by the way. Now, twenty years post Pre's passing, not one but two major studios have Prefontaine biopics planned.

Walt Disney Studios hopes to hit the big screen in the summer of '96, a month before the Atlanta Olympic Games. The Mickey Mouse outfit has the full cooperation of Prefontaine's family.

Where's the book, Kenneth? Prefontaine contemporary Kenny Moore, in conjunction with Robert Towne of "Personal Best" fame, is said to be working with Warner Brothers on an unauthorized version of the young runner's life.

"There's a great deal of similarity between Eugene and Hollywood. Both small towns, very competitive. Everybody knows what everybody else is doing," says Geoff Hollister, a confidante of Pre's on a leave of absence from Nike to produce the documentary and assist Disney's effort. "I'll be glad when I can get back to the shoe business."

Pre loved competition, sure, but he appreciated teamwork, too. He was also the kind of guy who could appreciate "unauthorized." See you at the movies.

Remembering Pre

Pre... an antecedent... to be in front of... to come before... superior.

What he really wanted to do was play football.

In 1964, Steven Roland Prefontaine, an eighth-grade bench warmer, weighed one hundred pounds and stood five feet tall. Any bigger, he would have made a great middle linebacker. He had the heart of a giant.

"He was too small for football and he got tired of sitting on the bench all the time," says his father Ray, a barrel-chested French-Canadian woodworker. "He wanted to find something he could do, something he could enjoy."

Determined to be a winner, Pre lost his first race.

He was motivated. As a sophomore, he didn't get to the state meet. That district qualifier the only poor performance of his career.

"In high school, he was laying in the front room on the floor, and we were watching TV, and he said, "Mom, I am going to the Olympics," recalls Elfreide, a petite German war bride and seamstress. "I said, 'Steve, how can you?'" Focused.

He went undefeated the remainder of his high school years, running 8:41.5 for two miles, a national record which lasted over two decades. Pre competed internationally while still a boy, already faster than the legendary Zatopek. Gifted.

Hard working. He always had a job. "Steve worked three jobs, so he could have a car," Ray remembers. "We picked out a Ford Fairlane, with an engine smaller than he wanted. I told him, that car will stay parked in front of the house forever if your grades suffer." Steve maintained his B average.

"He was not stubborn," his mother says.

"He never caused us any trouble," says his father.

He always had his goals set, written down and taped on his bureau in his tiny bedroom in a little blue house at 921 Elrod Street.

"If you want to come to Oregon," legendary Coach Bill Bowerman wrote in a note to the pride of the Marshfield Pirates, "There is no doubt in my mind you'll be the greatest distance runner in the world." Coachable.

Pre drove to college in a pastel blue '56 Chevy, back end jacked up, mag wheels brightly gleaming, fluffy faux fur tastefully accenting the interior, dice dangling from the rear view mirror.

"What I want," he admitted at an early age, "is to be Number One." Driven.

Steve Prefontaine entered the University of Oregon in 1969, considering a career in insurance or interior decorating. He was quickly nicknamed "The Rube." Eugene is something of a backwater burg even today, which gives you an idea what Pre was like coming out of Coos Bay, a seaport town of loggers and fishermen and housewives and shade-tree mechanics. He ended up majoring in Broadcast Communications.

Communicating came naturally to him. Pre wrote letters and talked on the phone simultaneously. He could curse a blue streak. Outspoken.

As a freshman, Pre won the NCAA cross-country championship. The following spring, a dozen stitches in his foot, he won the NCAA national 3-mile title. He captured both crowns every year of his collegiate career. Dominant.

Pre was always a celebrity. His first year at the University of Oregon, he appeared on the cover of *Sports Illustrated*. The headline under Pre's photo read "America's distance prodigy." Magnetic.

He had charisma, before he could spell it. He was more candid than tactful. Simple and true. Pre was as good as his word. Beneath his early cockiness and arrogance, there was a defensive streak, wide but shallow, which eventually faded away like a seasonal stream.

During his sophomore year, he would get up at six a.m. for a half-hour run before preparing his fraternity's breakfast. Easy runs, he never went over a six-minute pace. He believed anything slower had no benefit.

Pre preferred city streets to country trails. The hubbub of commerce more interesting than a rural setting. He didn't like to run beyond ten miles, twelve was about as far as he would go. He avoided hills when he could.

He had to be top dog even in workouts. The rare occasions when a talented teammate finished ahead of Pre were cause for reflection and revenge. He took names and kicked butt the next time.

Pre trained to race. He didn't leave his race in a hard workout. He was persistent and he was patient. Most young runners want to be good too soon. Want to run all those miles so they can get there early. In the long run, that's a mistake. Good things come slow. Particularly in distance running. Pre was only on the edge of where he was going to start running well.

Bill Dellinger

He rarely lifted weights. His exceptional upper body strength was clearly the result of his father's genes, although Pre included chin-ups in his daily routine. He was always doing sit-ups.

As a junior, Pre won the Pac-8 cross-country championship. Typically penurious, Oregon offered to send him to the NCAAs, but was unwilling to send the entire team, which had placed second in the league. Pre said he would not defend his national title unless the team went with him. The team went and, like its captain, won the championship. Loyal.

He hated the idea of being perceived as a super jock, everybody treating him like he was unapproachable. By now his nickname was "World," as in world famous. He wasn't famous to himself.

Pre did what he felt like doing. He seemed constantly in motion. Never satisfied. Yet always calm in the heat of battle. His flame burned brighter, but Pre was cool.

Warm. Never afraid to hug a friend or throw an arm over a buddy's shoulder. Kind to old women and considerate with little children.

I was only 14 and Pre sort of adopted me as a project. He was concerned with the number of races I ran and the kind and amount of training I was doing. Too much at a young age, and I think he felt protective. Pre was afraid I'd fall into the burn-out syndrome. In some ways, Pre was just like all the rest of us, do as I say, not as I do. Pre was the kind of person, if you wanted to run competitively, he would do everything he could, and use everything he knew, to help you be as good as you could be.

Mary Decker Slaney

Pre lived in a short single-wide mobile home at the River Bank Trailer Park along the Willamette River. A railroad track bordered the property, so his home shook every two hours all day long. His scholarship paid $101 a month for room and board. For extra money, he delivered cars to dealers in California.

Meticulous. Pre ate quickly and he'd always wash the dishes first before leaving his house. A green salad eater, he watched his weight, which could climb at times. He liked to put peanut butter on his pancakes. Liked pastries. Liked sugar. Liked bowls of ice cream before he'd go to bed. He was often in bed before 10 o'clock.

"I never saw him moody," remembers his roommate Pat Tyson. "He was a real kind person." Considerate.

Around town Pre wore blue jeans, t-shirts, mementos of track meets gone by, and suitably scuffed training shoes. Otherwise, he dressed fashionably. He wore double-breasted suits and ties on road trips. "He was a stud," remembers one teammate. "The rest of us dressed the best we could, but you just looked at him and went, 'Wow, he's a good dresser.'" Style.

Pre had stinky feet. He didn't wear socks when he ran, so he had to keep his shoes outside, particularly in the spring and summer, when they became especially rude.

Tremendously energetic. Never slowed down. Fast in everything he did. Impatient. Hyperactive. Involved. Pre lived more in twenty-five years than many men do in a normal lifetime.

He loved dogs. Lobo, a good-sized German Shepherd mongrel Pre rescued from the pound, was his best friend and a favorite training companion. Pre enjoyed gardening and carpentry, building things with his hands. He built a darkroom. Photography was his main hobby, taking pictures, mostly of nature.

Steve liked girls. He loved beer.

He drove fast. He enjoyed driving with the top down, wind in his face, radio blasting. He enjoyed basic AM rock and roll. He never seemed to learn the lyrics, so he'd make up his own words to the songs, off-color and off-key. Elton John's "Rocket Man" was a particular favorite.

Pre was – an understatement – highly competitive. "I love to compete against people," Pre said, "and not just track & field, but almost anything." He never ran a road race.

He never missed a meet or a workout in college due to illness. Rarely injured, he suffered periodically from sciatica, a painful inflammation of nerves in his back and down the back of his legs.

When I think of Pre, I think first about his consistency and his work ethic. Pre was all business. When it was time to train, he trained, when it was time to race, he raced. Pre didn't make excuses. He was self-motivated and self-disciplined. He was always striving to get to that next level.

Todd Williams

Pre almost always expressed doubts before a race. "I'm not really up to this today," he'd say. He was worried about going bald.

Superhuman. Pre used oxygen better than any other runner ever tested. His ability to deal with fatigue, his threshold for pain, was simply greater than normal. He could push himself harder. Never ducked an opponent. Pre would run sub-four minute miles in training, he would run them alone. He worked tirelessly to be the best prepared athlete to toe the starting line. Tough.

You couldn't be just a little better than Pre and expect to beat him. A little better wouldn't be good enough. Pre wanted to win more. He gave every race everything he had and he always thought he could have run faster. He simply refused to believe there was a better runner in the country. There wasn't.

He ran a 1:54.3 half mile in high school, he was the third fastest miler in U.S. history, and many so-called experts said Pre didn't have a finishing kick. And perhaps he didn't.

Pre was blue-collar kind of guy with a workingman's ethic. He was a front runner, because it was his nature. He had little patience with sit-and-kick tactics. He won some races maybe he shouldn't have.

To race, you call upon a flow of energy you can't get in practice. What causes this flow of energy? Fear. Fighting for survival brings that flow out in an individual more than anything else. When a situation is life-threatening, people get a flow of energy they don't normally have. You read all kinds of stories, the little woman lifting a car, for example. In terms of competing, it's the ability to call upon an extra reserve of energy.

The fear of losing can be great. A few individuals feel the fear of not winning, of not doing what the fans expect, and they are able to get this

flow of energy most athletes can't reach, the ability to go beyond what is
normal. Pre had that flow of energy.

Bill Dellinger

Courage. "He had so many of those races he should have lost and
didn't; he always had that little thing hidden away in a sack somewhere,"
says Olympic marathoner Don Kardong, a contemporary who, in ten attempts, never beat Pre. "You knew this time he wasn't going to do it, then
he did."

Like the 1500 meters in a dual meet against Oregon State in 1972.
Fresh from an American Record 5K the previous week, ragged from too
many beers the night before, Pre unexpectedly found himself facing Hailu
Ebba, a 800m specialist with a world-class kick. Pre moved into the lead
at 400 meters and pressed the pace, while Hailu hung on his shoulder. Pre
pushed hard; Hailu hung tough. On the final backstretch, Hailu made his
move to pass. Pre fought him off. The last turn, the Ethiopian speedster
tried again to take the lead. Pre moved him out into lane three and dug
deeper. Ebba's form fell apart in the final straightaway, while Pre won
with a personal record. Some say this was Pre's greatest race.

Others point to the 1973 NCAA cross-country championships in Spokane, Washington. It was Pre's final collegiate season. His back was hurting again and his confidence was low. Halfway through the race, Nick
Rose, a marvelous British runner from Western Kentucky, enjoyed a fifty-
meter margin. Pre had second place locked up and a good excuse. He
could have quit, could have lost; instead he charged. Two miles later, Pre
took the lead, the champion again.

"Pre, God, he just gutted it out somehow," Kardong, a Spokane resi-
dent, recalls. "People here still talk about that. They all go to that golf
course when we have the district high-school meet. Every year somebody
brings it up, 'Hey, remember when Pre...?' Pre never seemed surprised
when he beat people, it was the rest of us who were surprised."

Steve Prefontaine's best race may have been a three-mile in Eugene,
the Hayward Restoration Meet in June, 1974. Pre and Frank Shorter were
determined to break 13 minutes and agreed to share pace-making duties.
The plan worked fine for nine laps, then Pre led for the next three. He was
not pleased. Shorter jumped Pre on the final lap and shot into a 10-meter

lead, which he held into the final turn. The crowd came completely un-glued.

Kardong was running third. "I was maybe fifty yards back. It wasn't what it looked like as much as what it felt like. The fans were pounding those wooden stands and shouting. Beyond exciting, so loud it was un-nerving. The noise actually rattled my stride down the final straightaway."

Shorter was going as hard as he could; his lead looked dangerously in-surmountable. But there was no escaping Pre.

"I almost let him win," Pre admitted after the race. "Then, something inside of me said, 'I want to beat him.'"

And he did, in an American Record 12:51.4. Inevitable.

Pre was about flat out going for it. He hated losing. Every race his op-ponents knew they were gonna hurt. Forget about sit-and-kick, Pre's races were grueling from start to finish. He raised his game to another level. He had guts. That's what Pre meant to me.

Todd Williams

As Pre moved through his life, he had the impact of a large weather mass affecting the climate all around him. Myth now, fact then. Rain would fall all dreary day, drench gray the competition until he stepped onto Hayward Field, then blue skies opened and the sun would follow him like a spotlight as he warmed up. A performer.

Pre's People, they called themselves, the fans who filled the stands at Hayward Field. The noise would start to build from the moment he stepped onto the track. "There he is!" And the clamor grew. "It's Pre!" The sound would follow him. "Pre!"

The crowd loved him for his unbridled energy, his raw determination, his relentless desire. And he loved them back. You could see it in his eyes as he ran. Pre's People could see it, too, so they cheered louder, and he ran faster, so they cheered louder still.

"Pre!" Still louder. "Pre!" Still faster. "Pre!" As the race went on, faster and faster, lap after lap, "Pre!," louder and louder, "Pre!," washing to and fro, his name would echo and ricochet from east to west and back again. "Pre! Pre!" Towards the finish, every man, woman and child on their feet propelling the hometown hero toward the finish and victory. "Pre!" The race over, he'd take a victory lap, nearly full speed. "Pre!" Waving at fans and friends.

"He said, if it wasn't for them," his father Ray recalls, "he couldn't have done what he did."

Pre seemed invincible at home. He competed thirty-six times at Hayward Field. Lost to three specialists at their best distances. Set two personal records and tied another in those defeats.

He was an icon and a iconoclast. Irreverent. Went looking for trouble, like a knight on a crusade. He was a pioneer in the battle for athletes' rights. He was fighting – successfully – Ollan Cassell before many of today's top competitors were born. Pre was the Anti-Nixon.

Pre was Nike's original endorsement athlete, receiving $5,000 his first year under contract. The swooshes, hand-glued to the side of Pre's first pair of Nike spikes, fell off and littered the track on Pre's maiden run in his new shoes.

He was incredibly focused. When the starter's gun fired, he was in a different world; not many people ever get there. He raced like he was a prize fighter, throwing everything he had against anybody who climbed into the ring with him. His contests weren't necessarily about speed, but about who was left standing.

Take your best shot. "A lot of people run a race to see who's the fastest," Pre said. "I run to see who has the most guts."

The way Steve Prefontaine approached running, his aggressiveness, the tenacity, the desire to win every single race he ran, no matter what it took, that's what I hope people get from thinking of Pre.

There's been a lack of will among U.S. athletes to put everything on the line. Americans were basically satisfied competing against other Americans and running 13:30, 13:40 in the national championships, being first, second or third. "Great, I made the team." Then, boom!, they go to a major championship and get destroyed. Steve Prefontaine would've never settled for that. Never.

Bob Kennedy

Pre lost that 5000m at the '72 Olympics, got outkicked for a medal but he made the race great. He forced the pace. He gave everything he had. Because he gave everything, he had a tendency to fade slightly in the final yards. He finished fourth. He was young, there was still time.

"He wanted the gold medal so bad," Elfreide explains. "It was the biggest disappointment in his life."

Some say Pre was not the same after Munich, he was more human. He didn't lose often, but when he did lose, he bounced back. He grew from his defeats. Resilient.

He was always talking about his future, the life he'd lead after he retired from running. He never slowed down, he was getting faster, his best running still ahead. But, for all of us, there is a finish line.

Pre drank. Pre drove. Pre didn't wear his seatbelt.

Steve Prefontaine, age 24, died May 30th, 1975, on a road he knew every inch of, the metal of his gold MGB convertible pressing on his chest, powerful lungs unable to expand. And in a way, the future of track & field in this country died with him.

Transcending the sport, he was by far the most popular runner of his era. Like James Dean, ahead of his time, never replaced. Singular.

Pre died believing he would win an Olympic gold medal. Pre's People will die believing it, too.

We miss him still.

Go Pre!

At the time of his death Steve Prefontaine held every national long distance record from 2000m to 10k.

Pre's racing career began March 25, 1967 and ended May 29, 1975. During those eight years, he competed in 151 races, excluding indoor or cross-country events.

He dropped out of one race with a pulled stomach muscle. His victories totaled 118, a winning percentage of 76.5.

He set fourteen American Records, seven while still a collegiate athlete. He was the first track athlete in NCAA history to win the same event four consecutive years.

Faster runners have come along in the past twenty years, none so unforgettable.

Gone, sure, but not forgotten. Never forgotten.

Pre's "Memorial" at the scene of the accident